THE GREAT EXPANSION

The Ultimate Risk that Changed the NHL Forever

THE GREAT EXPANSION

The Ultimate Risk that Changed the NHL Forever

ALAN BASS

iUniverse, Inc.
Bloomington

The Great Expansion
The Ultimate Risk that Changed the NHL Forever

iUniverse books may be ordered through booksellers or by contacting:

iUniverse
1663 Liberty Drive
Bloomington, IN 47403
www.iuniverse.com
1-800-Authors (1-800-288-4677)

ISBN: 978-1-4502-8605-3 (pbk)
ISBN: 978-1-4502-8606-0 (cloth)
ISBN: 978-1-4502-8607-7 (ebk)

Library of Congress Control Number: 2011901159

Printed in the United States of America

iUniverse rev. date: 1/19/2011

Contents

Acknowledgements

Writing a book, specifically your first ever book, is a very tedious task, as I found out quickly. It requires the help of numerous other people, including those who give you information, those who give you writing and publishing tips, those whom you bounce ideas off of and even those who simply keep you sane while you sit and type away on the computer.

Although hundreds of hours of research, writing and editing went into this book, there are numerous people I need to reach out to and acknowledge for helping me with *The Great Expansion: The Ultimate Risk That Changed the NHL Forever.*

From a purely motivational standpoint, I must thank Bryan Thiel for convincing me and challenging me to write a book. His book on the Chicago Blackhawks is an incredible read that all hockey fans should own.

Greg Caggiano, a close friend of mine, also helped keep me sane throughout my initial research and later work in the book. He was a person that I could bounce ideas off of, in addition to ranting and babbling incessantly to until I realized he wasn't even listening. But I thank him a great amount for being there to help me out and lift me up when I hit rough patches.

I also must thank Bruce "Scoop" Cooper, an NHL historian, for helping lead me through the process of writing a book. Beyond the original interview I conducted with him simply to obtain some information from a man that covered that era of hockey, Scoop took me under his wing and walked me through the process of writing a book. During the 2010 Stanley Cup final and afterward, he would continuously ask me how everything was going with the writing and offer any help he could provide. His research and experiences rubbed off on me, giving me an opportunity to feel as if I lived through that era.

Thanks to Ed Fraser and Dustin Pollack from *The Hockey News* for helping me with some preliminary research and going through

THN's archives for me. Thanks to Brad Kurtzberg for his book on the California Golden Seals and for taking the time to speak with me regarding the franchise.

I also have to acknowledge John McGourty of NHL.com for helping me out with all of my writing, before my book was even a thought in my mind. Thank you to John for also helping me out with information in the '60s.

Jiggs McDonald, the former play-by-play man for the Los Angeles Kings, helped me a great deal with my knowledge on the LA franchise, and I thank him wholeheartedly for that. His rapport and experience with Jack Kent Cooke helped give me a better understanding of the franchise at that time.

Thank you to Adam Raider for helping me out with my Minnesota North Stars chapter and to both him and Brad Kurtzberg for giving me tips on getting my book published.

I also must give a big shout out to Ike Richman, who works in the Philadelphia Flyers' PR department. Ike was a huge help in showing me the NHL Network's production of *A Day That Changed the Game* and the HBO special on the Broad Street Bullies, in addition to giving me access to the archives of the Philadelphia Flyers. Ike also helped me get in contact with Mr. Snider, the chairman and founder of the Philadelphia Flyers. Mr. Snider's contributions to this book were extremely helpful and his words were an inspiration in my work.

That leads me to give special thanks to Mr. Ed Snider, who was a huge help for me throughout my research. I truly appreciate the time he took out of his busy schedule to speak with me and give me a better understanding of the founding of his franchise, from start to finish.

Thanks to Barry van Gerbig of the Oakland Seals, Jack McGregor, founder of the Penguins and Jack Riley, the inaugural GM of the Penguins, all for taking the time to speak with me. More thanks go out to Don Waddell of the Atlanta Thrashers, Ed Lang of the Nashville Predators, in addition to the entire Atlanta Thrashers and Nashville Predators PR department.

A quick, but hearty thanks goes out to Dylan Wade, member of NHL Alumni, for helping me get in contact with numerous former NHLers.

Others that I must give quick thanks to include Stan Fischler, Bert

Olmstead, Bill Torrey, Vic Hadfield, Rod Seiling, Paul Henderson, Orland Kurtenbach and every other person that took the time to speak with me and give me information on 1967 expansion. Thanks to Google News Archive for helping me locate articles from the mid-sixties on NHL expansion. I also must thank HockeyDB and Hockey-reference for the stats that I took from them for this book.

Lastly, I must give thanks to my dad, who helped critique my work and challenged me to make this project as successful as possible. Thanks also to all of my close friends and family for giving me support in my work and continuing to support me through everything I do. I hope that everyone close to me has as much fun reading this as I did writing it.

Introduction: Looking Back

It is May 19, 1974. The Philadelphia Flyers have just defeated their archrival Boston Bruins by a score of 1-0 in Game 6 of the Stanley Cup Final. The fans are ecstatic. Philadelphia is going crazy. Not only is this the first Stanley Cup for their beloved Flyers; This is the city's first major sports championship since the Philadelphia Eagles won the National Football League championship in 1960. And even bigger: this is an *expansion* team doing it. In just seven years.

As future Hall of Famer Bernie Parent – the Conn Smythe Trophy winner as the playoff MVP – and future Hall of Famer Bobby Clarke grasp the famous silver trophy from National Hockey League President Clarence Campbell, there are grins on the faces of every player, coach, fan, and inhabitant in Philadelphia. But they are not the only ones to be grinning over this Stanley Cup victory. Deep in the hallways of the Spectrum, the old building that the Philadelphia Flyers called home when they entered the league in 1967, Campbell is walking away from the ice surface where he just awarded the Stanley Cup to a team that was not part of the Original Six. He is grinning like the Cheshire Cat as well. He knows it. The rest of the league's owners know it, too.

They made the right move.

Choosing to add six new teams to the league in the late 1960s was a huge risk by Campbell and the NHL owners. Bill Jennings, the then-owner of the New York Rangers, was one of the few members of the league in favor of expansion, in addition to Stafford Smythe, the president of the Toronto Maple Leafs. In fact, Jennings even headed a committee to determine which six cities would be granted major league hockey teams.

Looking back, expanding the league seemed sacrilegious. The Original Six was a term known to every hockey fan and many other sports fans: the Montreal Canadiens, Detroit Red Wings, Toronto Maple Leafs, Boston Bruins, New York Rangers and Chicago Blackhawks. These six teams made up the NHL since the 1942-43 season. There were random teams granted access to the league ever since the NHL came to be in 1917. But none of them ever stuck.

The Montreal Wanderers literally became wanderers when their arena burned down on January 2, 1918, causing the team to shut down. The Toronto Arenas, Ottawa Senators and Quebec Bulldogs, all teams when the NHL formed in 1917 – in addition to the Montreal Canadiens and Wanderers – became scarce before 1934. The Bulldogs were sold and deactivated for a season before finally being moved to Hamilton for the 1920-21 season. The Arenas became the St. Patricks. The Ottawa Senators moved to St. Louis before the 1934-35 season, then subsequently folded.

From 1925 to 1942, teams were placed all over the map. Montreal was granted another team, the Maroons, before they folded on March 17, 1938. Hamilton lost their team in 1925 and subsequently became the New York Americans. Pittsburgh was granted a franchise in 1925. The next year, the Detroit Cougars came to be. The year after, the St. Patricks became the Maple Leafs that are so beloved in Southern Ontario. The Cougars became the Falcons, then the Red Wings. Pittsburgh's team moved to Philadelphia, then the Philadelphia Quakers folded. The St. Louis Eagles that became of the Senators folded in 1935. The Americans "withdrew" prior to the 1942-43 season (see Chapter 1).

Six of the teams granted entry into the NHL remained, of course: the Original Six. The Montreal Canadiens were founded in 1909, while the franchise that eventually became the Maple Leafs was born in 1917. The Boston Bruins joined in 1924, while the Chicago Blackhawks, New York Rangers and Detroit Cougars (eventually the Red Wings) expanded the league in 1926.

Each of these teams paid between $12,000 and $14,000 to join the National Hockey League. But that is nothing compared to the $2 million price which the teams in 1967 had to pay to be a part of the greatest hockey league on Earth. That sum is even less than the $80 million that the last four NHL franchises paid to enter the league (the Nashville Predators in 1998, Atlanta Thrashers in 1999 and the Columbus Blue Jackets and Minnesota Wild in 2000).

In 1965, Clarence Campbell announced that the NHL would double in size and allow six new teams into the league for the start of the 1967-68 season. Fans were furious. Owners were irate. From a hockey standpoint, why change the NHL? As the saying goes, "If it ain't broke, don't fix it." But from a business standpoint, of course it made sense. More teams most likely means more exposure of the game in North America.

Exposure was something the NHL had little experience with in the 1960s. The United States television contract with CBS had recently run out and the only networks broadcasting the games were regional networks in the Original Six cities. Those living in cities outside of Montreal, Toronto, Chicago, Boston, New York and Detroit knew very little of the game. In fact, many had never even heard of the National Hockey League.

"As far as the papers here, the NHL didn't even exist," said Philadelphia Flyers' founder Ed Snider. "There was nothing in the Philadelphia papers about the NHL's plans for expansion." [1]

Hockey was just another sport to American cities like Philadelphia. Even Los Angeles, one of the most populous cities in the United States, knew almost nothing about hockey and the NHL.

But for six cities, that was all about to change. In fact, for the entire continent of North America, in addition to the Original Six cities, the word "hockey" and the National Hockey League would never be the same after what transpired on June 6, 1967.

1943 – **Detroit Red Wings**, defeated Boston Bruins 4-0

1944 – **Montreal Canadiens**, defeated Chicago Blackhawks 4-0

1945 – **Toronto Maple Leafs**, defeated Detroit Red Wings 4-3

1946 – **Montreal Canadiens**, defeated Boston Bruins 4-1

1947 – **Toronto Maple Leafs**, defeated Montreal Canadiens 4-2

1948 – **Toronto Maple Leafs**, defeated Detroit Red Wings 4-0

1949 – **Toronto Maple Leafs**, defeated Detroit Red Wings 4-0

1950 – **Detroit Red Wings**, defeated New York Rangers 4-3

1951 – **Toronto Maple Leafs**, defeated Montreal Canadiens 4-1

1952 – **Detroit Red Wings**, defeated Montreal Canadiens 4-0

1953 – **Montreal Canadiens**, defeated Boston Bruins 4-1

1954 – **Detroit Red Wings**, defeated Montreal Canadiens 4-3

1955 – **Detroit Red Wings**, defeated Montreal Canadiens 4-3

1956 - **Montreal Canadiens**, defeated Detroit Red Wings 4-1

1957 - **Montreal Canadiens**, defeated Boston Bruins 4-1

1958 - **Montreal Canadiens**, defeated Boston Bruins 4-2

1959 - **Montreal Canadiens**, defeated Toronto Maple Leafs 4-1

1960 - **Montreal Canadiens**, defeated Toronto Maple Leafs 4-0

1961 – **Chicago Black Hawks**, defeated Detroit Red Wings 4-2

1962 – **Toronto Maple Leafs**, defeated Chicago Black Hawks 4-2

1963 – **Toronto Maple Leafs**, defeated Detroit Red Wings 4-1

1964 – **Toronto Maple Leafs**, defeated Detroit Red Wings 4-3

1965 – Montreal Canadiens, defeated Chicago Black Hawks 4-3

1966 – **Montreal Canadiens**, defeated Detroit Red Wings 4-2

1967 – **Toronto Maple Leafs**, defeated Montreal Canadiens 4-2

CHAPTER 1

Pre-Expansion Hockey

IN ORDER TO FULLY understand expansion in 1967, it is important to understand what hockey was like in the years before. The league was filled with just the Original Six teams from the start of the 1942-43 season until the Great Expansion in '67. As the 1930s came to a close, World War II was beginning and quickly reaching its heights. Citizens of the United States and Canada were being sent to Europe every day. Players in the National Hockey League were disappearing, having to fulfill their civic duties before even thinking about a Stanley Cup Championship.

When the 1942-43 season began, it marked the first time that the only teams competing were the members of the Original Six. The Montreal Canadiens had won four Stanley Cups up to that point, including one in 1916, when the National Hockey League was the National Hockey Association. The Toronto Maple Leafs franchise held claim to five Stanley Cups (only two as the Maple Leafs). The Boston Bruins won three: 1929, 1939 and 1941. The New York Rangers won the Cup in 1928 and 1933. The Chicago Blackhawks won two as well, in 1934 and 1938. The Detroit Red Wings won two consecutive in 1936 and 1937.

As the decade turned, though, teams were losing players by the bunch. The war was going strong and players needed to serve for their country, many of them never returning to play the game they love.

Teams had trouble staying competitive. But the 1940s, '50s and early '60s brought new challenges, new faces, new leadership and even new rules to the NHL. A few teams were able to stay competitive throughout the decade, while other teams set new standards for mediocrity and failure.

In 1942, the NHL was ready to begin its 26th season with seven teams: the Boston Bruins, Chicago Blackhawks, Detroit Red Wings, Montreal Canadiens, New York Rangers, Toronto Maple Leafs and the Brooklyn Americans. The Americans' day-to-day operations were run by Mervyn "Red" Dutton, who also served at the helm of their front office. Dutton was tall and lanky, but like any former hockey player, was built. He had short, styled dark hair and, as an executive, was always dressed top notch.

He was a former NHL player who had played for both the Montreal Maroons and the [then-named] New York Americans. His NHL career lasted 10 seasons and 448 games, but the defender was never a dominant player. Moving into an executive role in the league proved to give him the same success – or lack thereof. In four seasons running the Americans, Dutton's team missed the playoffs twice and never made it past the first round of the playoffs. This was in the Americans' repertoire, having only made the playoffs in five of their 17 seasons.

But with the United States becoming more involved in World War II, more and more American players were leaving the NHL to serve their country. The Brooklyn Americans were made up mainly of American players, so the other owners in the league had questions about the team's competitive capabilities. After all, with players like Lynn Patrick, Toe Blake, Elmer Lach and more, how could a few true NHLers keep up with the likes of the legendary Montreal Canadiens and the Jack Adams-coached Detroit Red Wings?

Dutton tried to quell the owners' concerns by explaining that other teams were also losing players to the war, but the league would have none of it. After a long meeting before the regular season began, the league decided to suspend the Americans from operation, with the intention of allowing Dutton to bring his team back when the war ended. Dutton left the meeting dejected, but with hope for the future of his franchise.

Dutton's team was not the only organization to be crippled by the war. The Philadelphia Quakers and St. Louis Eagles both folded in the 1930s, as the war became imminent. The Montreal Maroons suspended their operations in 1938. Many aren't aware that the famous Montreal Canadiens almost relocated to Cleveland, Ohio, but were ultimately bought by three local owners who kept the team in Canada.

Numerous famous NHLers had to leave for the war, many of them unable to return to hockey. Some stars were, indeed, able to make a comeback into the league after serving for Canada. Hall of Famer Woody Dumart, a mediocre left wing for the Boston Bruins in the 1930s, missed more than three seasons in the early '40s, but returned to post career numbers in 1946-47 – just his second year back in the NHL.

Sid Abel, the Red Wings left-winger from Melville, Saskatchewan, missed two-and-a-half NHL season in the mid-1940s. When he returned to game action, though, he posted career numbers as well, including 69 points in 1949-50 and 61 points in 1950-51. Abel was inducted into the Hockey Hall of Fame in 1969.

Toronto Maple Leafs center Syl Apps won the Calder Trophy as the NHL's rookie of the year in 1936-37, but just over six years into his career, he left to serve for the Canadian Armed Forces. When he returned to the Leafs in 1945, he posted 40, 49 and 53 points in what would ultimately be the final three seasons of his Hall of Fame career.

Boston Bruins center Milt Schmidt would miss three-plus seasons while playing for the Boston Bruins. His career high before the war was 52 points – but he surpassed that total twice after returning from the war. He even won the Hart Trophy as the league MVP eleven seasons apart. He was inducted into the Hockey Hall of Fame in 1961.

Contrary to common belief the war actually helped the careers of many NHL players. Not everyone who left the league returned after the war, and certainly the majority of players who returned did not pull Hall of Fame careers out of the air. However, many were successful in the league.

But as the Brooklyn Americans left the NHL, the league was cut down to six teams – thus the Original Six era of the NHL began.

The NHL entered the second year of the Original Six era during the height of World War II. Though former players were losing their lives and current players were leaving their NHL posts to serve their countries, the league was ready for a new era of high offensive numbers.

Therefore, the Montreal Canadiens went out to solve their problems between the pipes. After intense contract negotiations, GM Tommy Gorman and coach Dick Irvin were able to agree to terms with Bill Durnan, a promising goalie. Durnan was a big guy – built like a typical professional hockey player – yet had the face of a teenager. He looked much younger than he was, but was mature beyond his years. Constantly focused during the game, Durnan was always motivated to be the best he could.

But the mental aspects of his game were far from his specialties. Durnan was ambidextrous and wore two gloves that allowed him to both hold his stick and catch the puck with each hand. With this unique goaltending style, Durnan dominated the league and led the Canadiens to a 38-5-7 season, winning the league's regular season title by 25 points (in a 50-game season). Durnan went on to win the Vezina Trophy in 1944. Durnan was almost 30 years old when he was signed, but having already had success in Canada's senior league, the Canadiens clearly knew what they were getting themselves into.

But the next couple seasons proved to have many ends. The end of World War II allowed numerous former NHLers to attempt comebacks into the game they loved. However, most of them were unable to get into the same shape they were in before serving and were forced to "retire" from the league.

There were also some stormy ends to relationships and business. After Red Dutton's Brooklyn Americans were suspended from play before the 1942-43 season, the league promised him that when the war was complete, he could bring his team back to competition. Dutton resigned from the presidency of the NHL front office, giving his role to assistant Clarence Campbell. He did this on the assumption that his Brooklyn Americans would be allowed back in the league and that he would be allowed to manage the team.

At the annual preseason NHL meetings, though, Dutton had this conversation with Conn Smythe, a member of the board of governors:

"There's this other matter; the franchise in Brooklyn."
Well, there's this stony silence.

Finally, Connie Smythe says, "Yes, Red, we've talked about that."

"So?"

"There are complications."

"Like what?"

"Well, for one thing, Madison Square Garden wants two franchises."

"What?" I say. "But I've talked to people in Brooklyn. They've got a site and they're ready to put up a $7 million dollar building as soon as I get the word from here."

"Yes. Well, the Garden wants two."

I look around the room and nobody's looking at me...I get the message.

"Gentlemen," I said to the governors, "You can stick your franchise up your ass."[2]

After Dutton left the NHL office for the last time, a new era headed by Clarence Campbell was beginning. Hockey's popularity would skyrocket as a result of Campbell's actions in the front office. Attendance would max out, while the quality of the on-ice product would become better than it had ever been.

Changes were still to be made, though, before expansion was even a serious thought. In 1964, it was announced that Frank Selke, the Canadiens' GM, would resign and that a man named Sam Pollock would run the team. Pollock had success with the Canadiens' farm system and the owners believed he would succeed in the front office.

And success he had, as he would eventually go on to win ten Stanley Cups in his Hall of Fame career.

The 1964-65 season proved to be the first of those ten championships for Pollock, as the Canadiens beat out the Toronto Maple Leafs in six games to advance to the Stanley Cup Final. Playing the Blackhawks, who had upset number one seed Detroit in the first round, Montreal was able to squeeze out a seven game series win, bringing the Cup back to Montreal for the first time since 1960.

Pollock's new regime and his instant success metaphorically brought in another end of an era for the NHL, as the 1964-65 campaign was the last season with the intention of keeping just six teams in the league. The Great Expansion was announced at the beginning of the 1965-66 season, with six teams being added to the league, doubling its size. The announcement of the news was so big in the hockey world that most people don't even remember which teams succeeded in those final two years. The Canadiens would win the Stanley Cup for the second straight year in 1966, while the Toronto Maple Leafs would go on to win the championship in 1966-67, the final time Toronto would win the coveted trophy.

But the big news was not who won the championship or who was the league's best player. The big news was what would happen to the league when it became a league of 12. Hockey was incredible before expansion – fast paced, exciting games with rivalries all around.

In fact, the rivalries are what made NHL games so thrilling before 1967 – and would subsequently keep the game exciting in the 21st century. Any fan of modern hockey understands how exhilarating and exciting rivalries can be. Division foes played each other six times in the 2010-11 NHL season. Conference opponents played each other four times. This, in itself, creates heated, passionate rivalries – some of which result in vandalizing (see Philadelphia Flyers, 2010 Stanley Cup Final).

Prior to 1967 expansion, though, teams would face off 14 times each year – more than twice the amount division rivals see each other today. In a season that was a month shorter than it is today, teams would often meet numerous times per month, allowing new chapters of each rivalry to be written every week, sometimes twice per week. Fans would hate each other, in addition to the visiting teams. Toronto Maple Leafs fans hated the Montreal Canadiens. Detroit Red Wings fans hated the Chicago Blackhawks. Boston Bruins fans hated the Maple Leafs. Everyone hated the New York Rangers. These intense rivalries led to some of the best hockey in the game's history.

During these rivalries, though, only three teams consistently shared the Stanley Cup – the Canadiens, Maple Leafs and Red Wings. With famous players such as Maurice "Rocket" Richard, Bernie "Boom Boom" Geoffrion, Toe Blake, Elmer Lach and Doug Harvey, the Canadiens would win ten Stanley Cups in the Original Six era. Hall of Famers Gordie Howe, Ted Lindsay and Terry Sawchuk would lead the Red Wings to five Stanley Cup championships in that time period. The Maple Leafs, with iconic players like Ted Kennedy, Johnny Bower, "Red" Kelly, Frank Mahovlich and Dave Keon, would be victorious in ten Stanley Cup finals, just like the Canadiens. Though the Chicago Blackhawks won one Stanley Cup in the Original Six era, Montreal, Toronto and Detroit would be the only three teams to consistently hold claim to the silver mug. These three teams seemed to hold a monopoly over the league, along with the league's best talent pools for developing new, young players.

This lack of parity, along with the fact that just six markets had NHL teams – three of which were not even in the United States – led the league's profit margins to fall short of expectations. Many Americans had not even heard of hockey, and if they had, they sure didn't know much about it. The only way to increase the league's popularity and get more national attention seemed to be to add teams.

But expansion was a new idea that hadn't quite come up since the '40s. How would the league change? How would the business be different? Would new teams be able to challenge with the dominating forces of the Original Six? More importantly, would the game's excitement and popularity decrease as a result of this "travesty" to the league?

NHL Franchises, 1917-1966

1917 – Montreal Canadiens (original team), still active

1917 – Montreal Wanderers (original team), defunct in 1918

1917 – Ottawa Senators (original team), relocated in 1934

1917 – Quebec Bulldogs (original team), relocated in 1920

1917 – Toronto Arenas (original team), still active as Toronto Maple Leafs

1920 – Hamilton Tigers (relocated from Quebec), defunct in 1925

1924 – Boston Bruins (expansion), still active

1924 – Montreal Maroons (expansion), defunct in 1938

1925 – New York Americans (expansion), defunct in 1942

1925 – Pittsburgh Pirates (expansion), relocated in 1930

1926 – Chicago Black Hawks (expansion), still active as Blackhawks

1926 – Detroit Cougars (expansion), still active as Detroit Red Wings

1926 – New York Rangers (expansion), still active

1930 – Philadelphia Quakers (relocated from Pittsburgh), defunct in 1931

1934 – St. Louis Eagles (relocated from Ottawa), defunct in 1935

CHAPTER 2

Preliminary Expansion Ideas

THE GENERAL CONSENSUS OF sportswriters was that prior to 1967, the National Hockey League had little to no interest in expanding, despite the fact that the majority of the Original Six teams only came to exist because of expansion in the early century. Expansion actually started in 1924 when the Boston Bruins were granted entry into the league. A middle-aged man by the name of Charles Francis Adams, a Boston resident, founded the Bruins. Adams' career began when he worked as a chore boy in a grocery store as a child. He rose up to eventually own a chain of grocery stores, which gave him his fortune. In 1924, he paid $15,000 to buy the rights to an NHL franchise in Boston. The Bruins were born and played their first NHL game on December 1, 1924.

When the Western Canada League folded and became the Prairie League in 1926, losing many of its players, Adams was quick to pick up the pieces. For $50,000, Adams acquired players like Eddie Shore, Duke Keats, Harry Oliver, Perc Galbraith and Harry Meeking – all of whom played integral roles on the Bruins' first Stanley Cup team.

The Bruins continued to grow their franchise through the 'twenties and 'thirties as they picked up goaltender Cecil Thompson, also known as "Tiny Thompson." Thompson would help lead the Bruins to their first Stanley Cup in 1929 and their second in 1939. The Bruins continued to perform well, as they won their third Stanley Cup in 1941 – the final championship before The Great Expansion in 1967.

In addition to the Bruins, the Montreal Maroons were brought into the league via expansion in the same year. They enjoyed moderate success, including Stanley Cups in 1926 and 1935. However, the team ended up dropping from the league before the 1938-39 season.

The Detroit Red Wings were technically admitted to the NHL via expansion when the Victoria Cougars were purchased for $100,000 and moved to the Motor city. Financially, the Cougars struggled greatly in their years in Victoria. Jack Adams, who had just recently retired as a player, explained that the Cougars were lucky if they had 80,000 fans come to their games in a full season. In fact, most of those in attendance didn't even pay for their tickets.

"One night in 1930, we played an exhibition game for some charity run by Frank Murphy, the Detroit mayor," Adams recalled. "It was a cash collection, pay what you could. Just before the game started we heard there was a guy driving up and down Woodward Avenue outside the Olympia. He had five bags of potatoes and wanted in. We took his spuds and gave him standing room."[3]

The club was moved to Detroit, renamed the Falcons and run by Charles Hughes of the Detroit Athletic Club. Hughes, who held the position of "President" in the Detroit organization, brought in numerous high-end players, including Clem Laughlin, Frank Sheppard and Art Duncan. For his money, he also received future Hall of Famers Jack Walker, Frank Foyston and Frank Fredrickson.

But the Falcons' financial woes were becoming insurmountable. "If Howie Morenz had been available for $1.98, we couldn't have afforded him," Adams said at the time.[4]

In 1935, though, James Norris, a millionaire who made his fortune in the grain business, called the Falcons organization with a demand for Adams. "Adams?" Norris said firmly, "I'll be in Detroit this afternoon. Meet me with the bankers when I take over that lousy club."

So as it was, James Norris became the new owner of the Detroit franchise and renamed them the Red Wings. Norris was a firm man; he knew what he wanted, and he got it. "We'll call this team the Wings. In fact, we'll call it Red Wings," Norris exclaimed matter-of-factly. "Our emblem will be a winged wheel, which ought to sit good with Henry Ford and the Detroit car people."[5]

Gazing over at Adams, he issued a stern statement.

"I'll give you a year on your job – on probation."

The new-look (and newly named) Red Wings became immediately more successful on and off the ice, eventually winning their first Stanley Cup in 1936 – the very next year.

With funds now readily available, Norris and Adams together were able to build a strong squad that went on to repeat their championship performance in 1937, winning their second consecutive Stanley Cup. The Wings had a bit of a dry spell for some time, but went on to win five more Stanley Cups before The Great Expansion.

In 1924, a man named Bill MacBeth had an idea to buy a hockey team and move them to the hot spot of New York City. His partner, "Big Bill" Dwyer, made millions from his bootlegging liquor business. The two of them brought in George "Tex" Rickard, who was brilliant with promotions and marketing. Together, the three of them went out and purchased the Hamilton Tigers. In January 1925, they began the construction of Madison Square Garden. Although the arena was originally built as a boxing facility, Rickard realized that he could put hockey in the same building and make more money. The trio moved the Tigers to New York and named their new team the New York Americans.

At the same time, though, the New York Rangers were expanded into the NHL by Rickard – who owned the Garden – and played in the same building as the Americans. This not only created a rivalry on the ice, but also turned into a financial battle between the two clubs in the Garden. Garden officials hated the feud between the two clubs and when it became clear that the Rangers were drawing more fans, the Americans suffered and eventually folded in the 1940s. The Rangers commenced play in the 1926-27 season, and in just one year, they were Stanley Cup champions.

"On their first appearance, the Rangers made a distinctly favorable impression," *New York Times* writer Seabury Lawrence said. "Bunny and

Bill Cook playing the wings and [Frank] Boucher at center, distinguished themselves by particularly skillful stick work and clever skating."[6]

"The 1927-28 squad won New York's first Stanley Cup," Boucher explained. "It had two very strong lines, a remarkably effective defense and good goalkeeping."[7]

The Rangers won again in 1933, seemingly en route to a dominant NHL existence. But as many Rangers fans know, it did not turn out that way. They went on to win their third Stanley Cup in the 1939-40 season, but were Cup-less after that until the 1990s – well after The Great Expansion.

One of the last expansion teams to join the NHL before 1967 was the Chicago Blackhawks. In 1926, they were brought into the league by Frederic McLaughlin. McLaughlin served the United States during World War I and later made his money selling coffee. The name "Blackhawks" came from his division in the military. His division, the "Blackhawk Division," was headed by Chief Black Hawk, a famous Illinois commander. Originally, the name was two separate words: The Black Hawks. The name continued like this until 1986 when the franchise finally decided that the correct team name would become one simple word: Blackhawks.

McLaughlin, having very little knowledge of hockey, started his team by buying the Portland Rosebuds of the Western Canada Hockey League. In addition to the minor league team, McLaughlin bought more American players, including Alex Levinsky, Cully Dahlstrom, Taffy Abel and more. In fact, he was so intent on promoting the game in America, his Blackhawks were the first and only team in NHL history to play with an all-American-born lineup.

After an unsuccessful first season, McLaughlin – serving as his own GM – fired coach Pete Muldoon. McLaughlin believed that his team was capable of finishing in first place. Muldoon disagreed and when he was fired, according to *Toronto Globe and Mail* writer Jim Coleman, Muldoon put a curse on the team.

Becoming known as the "Curse of Muldoon," the Blackhawks won three Stanley Cups in their first 39 years in the league, including championships in 1934, 1938 and 1961. Ironically, Coleman later admitted that he made up the entire dialogue because it made for an interesting story:

> The Hawks are victims of a hex Pete Muldoon put on them many years ago, after he was fired as coach. He had a stormy session with Major Frederic McLaughlin, the strange eccentric who owned the Hawks when they were admitted to the NHL in 1926.
>
> Muldoon coached the Hawks to a third-place finish in their first year, but McLaughlin was not impressed. "This team was good enough to be first," he said.
>
> Muldoon was amazed at McLaughlin's criticism, but not to the point of shutting up. "You're crazy!" he fumed.
>
> McLaughlin was outraged by such heresy. "You're fired!" he roared.
>
> Muldoon flared back in a black Irish snit. "Fire me, Major, and you'll never finish first! I'll put a curse on this team that will hoodoo it till the end of time!"
>
> And so, kiddies, that's why the Hawks always fail to grab the flag in the NHL. They cannot beat the Curse of the Muldoon.[8]

Even more ironic, though, is that the Blackhawks never did finish in first place until 1967, regardless of their success in the playoffs. Although the Curse of Muldoon was a fabrication, it indeed had some truth to it which continued to haunt the minds of Blackhawks players for decades.

During World War II, as mentioned in Chapter 1, teams began dropping from the league due to a lack of players and a lack of finances. This is how the Original Six era started. After the war ended, though, there was a postwar boom. Money was available, jobs were plentiful and sports shared abundantly in the finances of the entertainment industry.

The first possibility of expansion occurred in 1951, 16 years before The Great Expansion. "Jim Hendy thought he had Cleveland into the league as the seventh team," said hockey historian Stan Fischler, "Then Conn Smythe pulled the rug on him at the last second."

The Barons were an American League hockey team that was attempting to join the NHL as their seventh team. After six months of filling out forms, pleading their case to the league and dishing out the required money, the Barons were ready to be accepted into the league. "Our city has been awarded a franchise in the NHL," wrote a Cleveland sports columnist. "This is the most pleasurable news of the year."

But in reality, the NHL governors were only pretending to be interested to avoid charges of monopolistic practices. The reality was that the owners hoped Hendy would just give up and go away.

When Hendy pushed for his franchise to be brought into the league, the NHL had no choice but to deny the application two months later. After asking what the NHL wanted, Hendy was told the following: $425,000 to cover the league reserve fund, the franchise and working capital. In addition, 60 percent of the team's stock had to be owned by Cleveland residents. Hendy followed each of these requirements and his backers even had the support of the Original Six. Clarence Campbell even came out and said that he believed the Barons' acceptance into the league would be a boon to the hockey interest in the United States.

"Behind closed doors, Jimmy Norris queered the deal by claiming that 'gambling money' was behind the Cleveland bid," wrote the authors of *Net Worth*, "a laughable assertion considering his own mob connections and the fact that he and Conn Smythe regularly laid bets together on hockey games and horse racing."[9]

At the last second, the NHL nixed it and "shot a 'no' from a curved stick," according to Stan Fischler in his book, *Hockey! The Story of the World's Fastest Sport*. They denied the application because in the money that Hendy raised, there was a substantial advance against radio and TV earnings and concessions. These earnings would extend through two seasons. The NHL Board of Governors did not believe that this money was considered working capital and denied the franchise entrance into the league.

But in the mid-'fifties, the NHL's business was booming and a new television contract was to be had. The Columbia Broadcasting System (CBS) had negotiated a new contract with the league and was going to begin broadcasting NHL games on Saturday afternoon from the four

American cities: Chicago, New York, Boston and Detroit. Just north of the border, the Canadian Broadcasting Company (CBC), which had tremendous success with their "Hockey Night in Canada" radio broadcasts every Saturday night, decided to add a television broadcast to complement the weekly radio games.

The NHL was indeed a bit nervous about using the newly invented TV to broadcast games, as they felt it may take away from their attendance. After all, if people can watch the game for free at home, why would they pay to attend the game in person? This brought out numerous meetings among the Board of Governors to determine their business plan for the future, specifically if league attendance dropped significantly.

However, the television broadcasts did not drop attendance. On the contrary, it boosted attendance greatly in markets outside of their six cities. In fact, even though the New York Rangers finished in last place in the 1965-66 season, their broadcasting of the games on TV increased their viewership and made a ticket to Madison Square Garden one of the hottest items on the East Coast.

The NHL was doing well financially. Six cities existed, which included six strong fan bases. NHL arenas were consistently sold out, regardless of the team's position in the standings. But the game was growing faster than anyone had anticipated. Other large cities had desires to get into the league, while the fans had a hidden desire to get in the game as well.

CHAPTER 3

Expansion Gets Serious

"THE NATIONAL HOCKEY LEAGUE makes a mockery of its title by restricting its franchises to six teams, waging a kind of private little tournament of 70 games just to eliminate two teams," wrote columnist Jim Murray of the *Los Angeles Times*. "Other big money sports are expanding, but hockey likes it there in the back of the cave. Any businessman will tell you that in a dynamic economy you either grow or perish. Baseball had to be dragged kicking and screaming out of its rut. Football groped its way on the end of a short rope. Hockey just can't sit there in the dark forever, braiding buggy whips."[10]

To an extent, the league agreed with Murray's statement. Of course, they did not believe they would have to be dragged towards expansion kicking and screaming, as did baseball. But with the NHL playing to 94.5 percent capacity in the 1963-64 season, they could tell hockey was growing beyond their beliefs. In order to increase their revenue and perhaps their television contract, the NHL was going to have to expand itself throughout the United States. After all, what interest would a 19-year-old man in San Diego have in the National Hockey League if it were not quite *National*. Honestly, it was more like the *Regional* Hockey League.

"The league...is not actively promoting or encouraging expansion of the number of its members at this time," league president Clarence

Campbell explained, "But it is prepared to consider each individual application on its own merits."

"Right now we're a pretty successful operation," said Campbell at another time. "When you come right down to it, nobody can match it. We'd only be buying a headache and what for?"

"Increasing the league doesn't increase your revenue five cents per club," Campbell told the press during a news conference in the '60s. "You'd simply have more hockey and all diluted. If you expanded by only two clubs, each NHL team would have to provide six players. You just tell me what the result would be if you took six players off any team in the NHL. Any team! And what the hell do you think it's gonna do to the spectacle? It has to dilute it. These six players at the bottom echelon couldn't sell tickets, they couldn't sell a show, you couldn't put them on the ice by themselves. They are the fillers."[11]

Campbell continued by explaining the scheduling problem that would occur if the league expanded. "You can't schedule Montreal or Toronto at home on Saturday and then on the Coast on Sunday," he explained. "Who the hell would run the risk? You could get snowed in...and in order to go to the Coast, Toronto would have to give up three or four of its Canadian television dates and *that's revenue*."[12]

"[Maple Leafs President] Stafford [Smythe] and [Leafs owner Harold] Ballard were as vehemently opposed to expansion as [former Leafs president] Conn Smythe had been," say David Cruise and Alison Griffiths, authors of *Net Worth: Exploding the Myths of NHL Hockey*. "Bill Jennings...spent many fruitless hours trying to convince both men that the NHL should add at least two new teams to thwart the creation of a rival league, protect themselves from anti-trust action and lure network television. At least seven times between 1962 and 1964, Jennings tried to persuade the other governors to put expansion on the agenda at annual and semi-annual owners' meetings."[13]

But some of the owners disagreed with Stafford and Smythe. Even Ballard admitted that he was willing to expand for the right price.

"If the right kind of people come to us with $5 million and the right kind of plans, we'll listen," said Toronto Maple Leafs owner Harold Ballard. "We'd be crazy not to."

But Smythe and Ballard still did not like the idea of expansion. "Great idea," suggested Smythe sarcastically. "You figure out a way to put the franchise fee in my pocket and I'll go along. But a bunch of guys in San Francisco who have never seen hockey aren't getting any of my players." His partner, Harold Ballard, was more direct with his view: "Fuck 'em!"[14]

Though expansion seemed to be imminent, regardless of the owners' opinions, the NHL was known as a conservative league. In fact, hockey historian Stan Fischler claims that it was simply a cultural issue, contrary to popular belief. "Hockey was always conservative. Canadians are conservative-thinking people," Fischler explained. "They like the status quo. They liked the fact that they were selling out in every arena. It was a nice, comfortable situation. So why disturb it?"

The league had numerous reasons why it did not make sense to expand at that time. For one, expansion would cause the league's expenses to drastically increase, but it did not guarantee that revenues would go up as well. Travel was one of the biggest expenses at that time and adding teams would further increase this cost.

In Major League Baseball, a visiting team travels to one city and stays there for three or four days to play a full series. In the NHL, teams are traveling for upwards of 35 games per year – and that does not include any playoff games.

New teams being brought into the league would also suffer from a lack of talent. With dominant players on NHL rosters in the '60s, including Bobby Hull, Frank Mahovlich and Jean Beliveau, new teams would simply not be able to match up. If six new teams began their NHL careers, they would be starting with players of minor league caliber. This would cause a drastic imbalance of competition in the league that could last more than a decade.

Lastly, the NHL did not want what Clarence Campbell referred to as numerous "clown clubs." Citing the New York Mets' experience in joining MLB, to be discussed in Chapter 14, he believed that there were not enough dominant players in the league to create two more teams, let alone an entirely new six-team division. But the league was becoming more popular than ever, and many media members believed it was time to extend their game across the continent.

"Hockey never has pretended to be the national sport, except in Canada," said Shirley Povice of the St. Petersburg Times in 1966, "But its major league franchises are dearly coveted. There is no fan more incorrigible than the hockey buff. It is in Boston that best proof of this is offered, in the complaints of the Boston Celtics basketball owners. The Celtics have won the last seven NBA pennants yet are consistently out-drawn in their own home town by the Boston Bruins hockey team that hasn't won the NHL title in 25 years."[15]

Even the Celtics' legendary coach, Red Auerbach, could see the difference in popularity between the sports. "The Bruins open the door and the Boston Garden fills up every night they play," said Auerbach. "We keep winning titles and have to hustle and scratch to draw a sellout crowd."

Contributing to hockey's increase in popularity was that, as previously mentioned, NHL arenas were filling to almost 95 percent capacity in the mid-sixties. "Television is the new box office for every sport," said Campbell. "In the NHL we are in a tighter straightjacket than most sports because we can't sell more tickets. Last year we played to 93 percent of capacity in the league's six cities. Selling tickets is not likely to be a problem for a while.

"That leaves us with a problem of where to get additional revenue. The only answer is television. Expansion is not going to sell more tickets because we do not have more tickets to sell."

Television had become a huge moneymaker in professional sports in the 1960s. ABC paid Major League Baseball $12.35 million for the rights to broadcast MLB games of the week on Saturday afternoons. CBS paid the National Football League $28 million for the broadcast rights for the 1964 and '65 seasons – seasons filled with just 14 teams at the time. Even more outrageous was that NBC paid the American Football League – the NFL's biggest competitor – $35 million over five years to broadcast the eight-team league's games.

Bruce Norris, then president of the Detroit Red Wings, agreed with Campbell. "[Red Wings] games should be shown over one of the big U.S. networks," he said. "The chief obstacle in the way is that down there [the TV networks are] inclined to think of hockey as strictly a Canadian game. We've got to get them thinking differently about it. We've got to change the game's image."

"The way the by-laws were structured, each team could keep their local television revenues," said former NHL President John Ziegler in an interview with the author. "The Canadian teams, along with CBC, had developed a substantial revenue source from their 'local television,' which was basically national – Hockey Night in Canada. That revenue stayed with them. So the U.S. teams decided that they should pursue a liked effort in developing a national broadcast – a television presence. In order to do that, it turned out, they needed to expand in the United States. The arrangement became that the Canadian teams would vote for expansion, but they would keep exclusivity for Canada's television; and the American teams could have exclusivity for the television rights for the United States."

A group of NHL big shots even held a secret meeting with numerous television executives and showed them tapes filled with highlights of NHL games. The executives watched the video politely, then explained to call them when the league decided to expand. One TV executive even mentioned that the lesser-known Western Hockey League had just as good a shot of getting a national TV deal as the NHL did.

Even before the World Hockey Association was a thought, the NHL had another competitor. The Western Hockey League, from which many NHL teams were getting their talent, were increasing salaries and luring players to their league in an attempt to become the premier hockey league in North America.

Other sports leagues had great success expanding when competitive leagues attempted to take over their game. For example, the National Football League had a competitor in the American Football League. By adding teams, or in other words, expanding, the NFL was able to increase the popularity of their game and crush the hopes of the AFL – eventually resulting in a merger between the two.

"I haven't met with any NHL people lately, but there are other ways of presenting our case forcefully," said James Piggott, owner of the Western League franchise in Los Angeles. "And we do want in. And I can tell you it's not very far off, either."

So with other leagues pursuing expansion and succeeding, the NHL seemed to have no choice. "I agree…that expansion is inevitable," Campbell said. "With a show as good as ours, economics may someday either induce or force expansion."

"The main argument was that other sports were doing it and

succeeding," said Stan Fischler. "The Dodgers went into Los Angeles and were a huge success. Even back in the '40s, after World War II, Los Angeles was being eyed as a potential market. The only thing was, it didn't have the arena. Same thing with Philadelphia. They needed an arena. The whole point was to do it at an appropriate time. At that time, it was very difficult to get seats for games in the '60s, before expansion. They felt the time was right and they felt they could do well television-wise. A lot of the pieces just fell into place."

"The league was, for 25 years, just six teams," said hockey historian Bruce "Scoop" Cooper. "It was located in a small geographical area in North America. So I think another reason for expansion was that they wanted it to become a national sport. The *National* Hockey League. They didn't feel like it would be a major sport if their footprint was so small.

"But I guess the owners had a little beef of their own," Cooper continued. "In fact, the Norris family controlled four of the six teams. A lot of people called it the Norris Hockey League, because they either controlled the teams or controlled the buildings in which they were playing. Those were basically three teams in the United States." Because of this, Cooper explained, the Norris family, in addition to other owners, was very hesitant to add teams into the league.

"The expansion talk began after Chicago won the Stanley Cup in 1961, when Bobby Hull was the glamour boy of the league," Stan Fischler continued. "The Blackhawks were a very flamboyant, attractive team. What happened was, as the '60s unfolded and the prospect of Bobby Orr coming into the NHL began to materialize – the serious talk wasn't until 1966 and he had already made his debut in '66-67 – it was apparent that there were some lucrative markets out there and a decent return for the expansion fees.

"The real catalyst was the Rangers' president Bill Jennings. Jennings was a very successful attorney and as president of the Rangers, he was getting paid an annual sum of $1 a year, so he really didn't give a [damn] about anything or anyone else in the league. He saw that expansion would be very beneficial, and he helped push it through."

From a business standpoint, it made perfect sense to some for the league to add teams to the circuit.

"I think they just figured that was the time," Cooper said. "It made sense to them. Up until that time, these [Original Six teams] were basically small businesses. The owners of these teams were making a nice profit and they didn't want to play the gamble card. They were big fish in a small pond and I think a lot of them were afraid that by bringing in new people, by expanding, that they would become smaller fish in a larger pond."

These worries were quelled, however, by the time Clarence Campbell made the announcement in 1965 that the league was planning on doubling to twelve teams. Six new teams were going to be added to the pond that was the National Hockey League.

Initially, some of the Original Six teams and their fans were irate when the league became serious about expanding the league. After all, they had been comfortable and successful with their six teams since the 1940s. What use was there in changing the format?

Media members saw that even Campbell was not entirely confident in his decision to expand the league. When he held a press conference announcing the decision, he answered simple questions with terms such as "I presume" and "I suppose" – unusual for a man who normally spoke precisely, matter-of-factly and confidently. "No definite time limit has been set for the expansion program but it would be highly unlikely it could be implemented by next season," Campbell said.[16]

When the NHL and the Original Six owners finally agreed to expand the league by six, there were rules and regulations that needed to be agreed to by the Board of Governors. The first agreement made was that each expansion team that was accepted into the league would have to pay a $2 million fee that would be divided up among the existing six. This would equal an extra $2 million for each team, which at the time was a substantial amount of money.

"That was $12 million, which the other teams split," said Bruce "Scoop" Cooper. "Players' salaries in those days were blue-collar salaries. Ten or fifteen thousand dollars for a player was a big salary in those days. That was basically a windfall for those owners."

In addition to the $2 million fee, there was another major requirement to be an expansion team in the NHL. Any new team admitted into the league had to have a building that could seat at least 12,500 people.

"While St. Louis (*St. Louis Arena*, 1929), Pittsburgh (*Civic Arena*, 1961), and Oakland (*Oakland/Alameda County Coliseum*, 1966) had existing buildings, Philadelphia, Minnesota, and Los Angeles needed to build new facilities for their NHL expansion clubs," said Cooper. "The three new arenas – Philadelphia's *Spectrum*, Minnesota's *Metropolitan Sports Center*, and LA's *Forum* – all opened in 1967."

Regardless of the status of their arenas or lack thereof, each group that applied filled out an application and made a presentation to the league explaining why they thought their cities would be more successful than the other applicants.

Most (but not all) of the cities that applied had long histories of successful minor league teams. "Because the difference in the level of play between the NHL and the 'minor' leagues such as the AHL and WHL was relatively small prior to expansion, and there was so little turnover on the rosters of NHL's six clubs, many excellent players spent their entire careers in the minor leagues. A veteran minor league player could actually make as much (or even a little more) money in the minors than at the major league level because the differential in overall salaries was so slight," Cooper continued. "That being the case, veteran minor league players and their families often just didn't want to move."

When all the dust settled, though, the NHL received 14 applications from cities across North America – including four from various potential owners in Los Angeles. Other cities that applied included Philadelphia, Minnesota, Buffalo, Baltimore, Vancouver, Oakland and Pittsburgh. The applicants met with the NHL in various cities, including Montreal and Toronto, while they pleaded their cases and tried to sell the idea of hockey in their respective cities.

"Long ago, one evening in 1966, I was in a suite at the Royal York Hotel in Toronto with some folks from the National Hockey League," said Frank Deford of National Public Radio. "They were all feeling pretty heady. The league was about to double in size, an incursion into the United States that would take Canada's game as far south as Los Angeles. Since the NHL was a huge success in all its six franchise cities in Canada and the northern U.S., everybody was certain that great times must lie ahead in the expansion outpost."

Before those great times could occur, the NHL had to determine which cities would be the lucky six to be granted NHL teams. Much of the decision of which teams would be granted access to the league was political and business related. As Stan Fischler explains, most of it was self-serving. "St. Louis would never have gotten into the league if Mr. Wirtz didn't have a major interest in the St. Louis arena," Fischler explained. "Jennings had a buddy in Oakland named Barry van Gerbig. That's why Oakland got a franchise. In Los Angeles, you had Jack Cooke, who was a Canadian." (More information on how the six teams were granted access into the league can be found in the individual chapters on each expansion team).

When the dust cleared, the NHL announced in February 1966 that Los Angeles, San Francisco/Oakland, St. Louis, Pittsburgh, Philadelphia and Minneapolis-St. Paul would be the six cities welcomed into the NHL. Cities such as Buffalo and Baltimore were rejected due to the arena requirements. Vancouver was rejected as well, as the league had more of an interest in expanding throughout the United States.

The members of Vancouver were extremely disappointed at being rejected by the NHL. They believed they were one of the premier cities of those applying. "We've been robbed," said Jim Kearney, who was a sports writer for the *Vancouver Sun* in the 1960s. Kearney also said that during his press conference before the league meeting, Campbell "inadvertently revealed" that Vancouver submitting an application to the league was a "waste of time and effort right from the beginning."

But according to Dink Carroll of the *Montreal Gazette* in 1966, the league's screening committee (the committee that listened to each group's presentations) believed that Vancouver had a very weak presentation. Vancouver's proposed team would also involve no one person owning more than 10 percent of the team. In the league's opinion, this would make it extremely difficult for an owner to make decisions, since too many people would be involved.

"It was not a good situation out there," Campbell explained. "There was no real head to the Vancouver organization. The operation was, financially, controlled by a group of five percenters. How was the league to deal with a group of that size and variety of ideas?"[17]

San Francisco was granted a franchise because CBS maintained that if the TV contract were to be renewed with the NHL, a team in the Bay Area would have to exist. Los Angeles was granted a franchise because there was a large Canadian population in the area, so the NHL assumed that they would have no problem filling an arena. Pittsburgh's franchise was created with the help of a Pennsylvania state senator, Jack McGregor. His political affiliation helped convince the NHL to move into western PA.

Minnesota had a brand new arena built for over $6 million that was adjacent to the Minnesota Twins' ballpark. The idea of a sports complex in Minnesota spelled "money" to the NHL. St. Louis did not even apply for a franchise. However, James Norris of the Chicago Blackhawks owned the existing arena in St. Louis and had a strong desire to get rid of it. By putting a franchise in St. Louis, the NHL could ensure that one of their richest owners was satisfied. Philadelphia, the last team accepted, was granted a franchise over Baltimore at the last minute because their proposed arena was going to have more seating than Baltimore's existing arena.

The idea of expansion was moved along by Bill Jennings of the New York Rangers and David Molson of the Montreal Canadiens. Both of them were extremely interested in growing the business aspect of the game, making expansion a lucrative option. But to ensure the success of the expansion teams in early years against dominant squads like the Canadians, Red Wings and Maple Leafs, it was crucial that the Board of Governors devised a plan to determine how the expansion teams would obtain players without being too unfair to the existing teams.

The discussions regarding the rules for an expansion draft took up the duration of a half-week meeting. The general managers balked at every option, not wanting to give up any of their property. The media became nervous of the talks and rumors were started that the league was not going to agree to a plan by the summer of 1967. Clarence Campbell, on the other hand, explained the delays by saying, "I never met a generous general manager."[18]

"The new teams will be weaker and they ought to be," said then Detroit GM Sid Abel. "Why should the Red Wings spend millions to build up a franchise and then let these new guys move in on the same level?"

Sam Pollock believed the process would actually be a "forced sale rather than an expansion draft" and that "property rights of the six present owners" needed to be protected. The owners and GMs did not like the preliminary idea that each team would protect only five or six players. "We have our own interests and fans to consider," he snorted. "What is desirable, for the first few years, is that the new teams have an equality among themselves. Why should we give up a good kid to a new team when we haven't had a chance to look at him in the NHL ourselves?"[19]

Stafford Smythe, on the other hand, had a different view of the matter. "What we really need are rules to protect us from our own selfishness," explained Smythe. "I want the new teams to be competitive because they've got to be an attraction when they play in our buildings."

When the general managers came out of the boardroom, they had finally agreed, albeit reluctantly, to a plan – one which excited the new owners. The design called for each Original Six team to protect one goalie and 11 skaters. After the first, second, sixth, and any subsequent rounds, any Original Six team that lost a player was allowed to place an undrafted, unprotected player on their protected list. This expansion draft would go on until each new team had 20 players – two goalies and 18 skaters.

Campbell was not happy with the new design, though. He created a backup plan in which Original Six teams would be able to protect two goalies and 14 skaters. He believed that the newly instituted amateur drafts that would occur in 1968 and 1969 would help balance the competition within a couple years.

"The old teams won't have trouble picking out which 14 to protect," Campbell explained, "But the newer teams, they're going to have problems." Campbell was extremely optimistic, though, regarding the expansion teams' chances within a few years. "I visualize definite improvement in the new teams by 1968-69 because of the back-up plan. By 1970, they should have a glorious field day and I hope they do."[20]

When the decision was released to the media and the rest of the world, other major sports leagues in the United States responded. "I think it was probably a yawn," said Bruce "Scoop" Cooper. "Compared to the other three sports, the NHL was just considered to be a small, regional sport that was only popular in very limited markets – Boston, Detroit, New York and Chicago. So there was a little support for it there. But the buildings weren't big, the tickets weren't expensive, and it was nothing compared to Major League Baseball. Football was not as big as it is now, because the television contracts were not nearly what they are now. But those other leagues had a much larger footprint – especially baseball – and a much longer history in major league sports in North America."

But the NHL was about to make history of its own.

CHAPTER 4

Media Response to Expansion

As MANY KNOW FROM living in the new millennium, the media has a huge influence on our lives, specifically in the sports industry. Although the luxuries of the Internet and other technological creations did not exist in the 1960s, newspapers were widespread and had just as big an effect on what was going on with the NHL's expansion plans. Journalists consistently threw in their two cents on any situation, in addition to attempting to uncover inside information from the Board of Governors meetings.

Below are analyses, summaries and excerpts of various articles that appeared in newspapers throughout North America in 1965 and 1966, around the time that expansion was announced and the six new cities were approved. These articles include editorials, Associated Press releases, and general breaking news bulletins. They are both pre-expansion and post-expansion articles.

On May 1, 1965, *Ottawa Citizen* writer Andy O'Brien wrote an article entitled, "Here's How NHL Expansion Could Work." With the announcement going through the sports world that the league would add teams, media members all over the country began attempting to determine how the process would work. O'Brien begins by inviting his readers to join him with some brain teasing that is the NHL's decisions.

He questions the league's decision, though not because it is a bad one. (O'Brien actually admits that it is a great decision, but, like his readers, he questions where the league is planning to get the extra 120 players from). This, according to O'Brien, "must have put a hole through the collective heads of the Board of Governors."[21]

Explaining the plan arranged by the NHL, in which an expansion draft would take place and the old teams would make numerous players available to the new teams, O'Brien finds it odd that the plan could work. As he shows, two of the Original Six squads are already the so-called "weak sisters" of the league. The New York Rangers had not experienced playoff hockey for six of their previous seven seasons, while the Boston Bruins were in the midst of a six-year playoff drought. So, he argued, if two Original Six teams were unable to find the necessary talent to succeed when only six teams are in the league, how would six expansion teams find suitable NHL-caliber players when the league was comprised of twelve teams?

With the plan at the time being to have each of the Original Six teams protect 10 players, O'Brien brought up a couple questions: how in the world would each of the existing teams determine which 10 players to protect? Why should these Original Six clubs be forced to do this in order to help what will eventually become the competition? "After all," O'Brien writes, "clubs have grown so financially fat in recent years that trading, not price, has been the sole basis for deals." The writer continued by explaining the likely format of this so-called expansion draft (the rules had not yet been officially announced by the NHL at that point). He believed that the draft order would snake for each round (the team with the last pick in the round will pick first in the next round, continuing until the end). This would be the fairest way to conduct the expansion draft, he predicted.

O'Brien personally believed that the 10 players each new team drafted would serve as building blocks for to make numerous moves in order to improve the team. These clubs would have their own minor league teams and farm systems to develop players and help give their NHL team the best chance of succeeding at the major professional level. He even suggested that nearby cities should provide suitable arenas in order to house these minor league teams in a close enough place that players could commute back and forth between the NHL and AHL clubs if needed. For example, he explained, wouldn't it be more efficient if the Montreal Canadiens' farm team was in Ottawa instead of Omaha, Nebraska?

With these new minor league teams, division realignment would be in order. But regardless of how the two leagues would realign their conferences and teams, there would be a huge increase in jobs and an increase in the popularity of the sport. In fact, O'Brien specifically recalled a writer telling him that there were numerous "excellent lads in and around Toronto who abandoned hockey careers simply because the Leafs remained jammed with old men who seemed unlikely ever to fade away." But, of course, it was pointless to talk about realignment and a chance in the sport before the six new cities were even chosen.

Vancouver was one of the top choices, the writer believed, as he stated that a new NHL rink was almost a sure thing in the British Columbian city. The Vancouver mayor even believed his city was a top contender: "NHL expansion…would have an even greater impact on our enthusiastic sports community…a city which has no trouble getting 35,000 fans out for football certainly will have no trouble getting 16,000 out for Canada's own national sport."

Los Angeles and San Francisco were both certain they would receive teams, according to O'Brien, but San Francisco had been criticized due to their arena – even if it was unfair in the writer's opinion. "If San Francisco fans like [the Cow Palace], why should NHL critics care?" O'Brien wrote. St. Louis was believed to be given a franchise from the start, because the owners of the Chicago Blackhawks, Arthur Wirtz and James Norris, owned their arena. When all was said and done, O'Brien stated that San Francisco, Los Angeles and St. Louis were the best choices for NHL expansion and the most deserving U.S. cities.

Other choices for expansion, O'Brien concluded, were Quebec city, whose Premier was certain the team would be considered (despite being geographically close to the Montreal Canadiens); Pittsburgh, due to their NHL history and proven minor league operations; Cleveland and Baltimore, because of their success supporting other major professional sports leagues; and Seattle and Portland, simply because they were large West Coast cities that could possibly bring a television contract to the league.

New York Rangers owner Bill Jennings and Montreal Canadiens

owner David Molson both gave expansion proposals, but because the two had such similar ideas, they simply wound up merging the plans together so that they could be in agreement. The Board of Governors argued for hours over how many teams the new division should have, with the number six ultimately becoming the unanimous number.

O'Brien concluded the editorial portion of his article by arguing with himself over whether or not expanding the league by six could be a good idea. The schedule would become much longer, he explained, which would not be good for the image of the sport. However, six new "pretty uniforms" were extremely attractive for the league. Regardless of how badly they lost in the interleague games in the regular season, the Stanley Cup final would most likely be an Original Six versus an expansion squad. This new team would absolutely have a chance, regardless of the talent on the roster.

O'Brien also drove home his most important point of the entire article. For a number of years, fans had been complaining that it was the same old NHL, with no new faces, teams or players. So why were fans and media alike complaining that the product would be watered down with 120 new players joining the league? "The new deal will certainly provide new faces," O'Brien wrote. "What's more, the hungry new crop of players will stimulate the whole organization." As long as the new division and the old division were balanced within each other, it was assumed the fans would not notice.

The next portion of O'Brien's article copied a quote from NHL President Clarence Campbell regarding the master plan for the league's expansion: "The National Hockey League proposes to expand its operations through the formation of a second six-team division. Applications will be accepted from responsible groups representing major-league cities in the United States and Canada and when six new teams are accepted the new division will be incorporated into the league.

"The six cities which will make up the new division must be of major-league status and have arenas with permanent seating capacities and ice surfaces meeting current NHL standards. The new franchise owners must either own the arenas or have long-term leases thereof.

"The new division will play a partially interlocking schedule with the present six teams of the NHL. Sufficient players will be made available by the present teams for purchase by the new division so as to make the new division competitive from the beginning of its operations."

Lastly, O'Brien provided a chart with the demographic information for each current and potential NHL city, offering readers a chance to judge for themselves based on the intangibles of each applicant.

Current Cities

City	Metropolitan Population	Rink Seating
New York	10,694,633	15,284
Chicago	6,220,913	16,666
Detroit	3,762,360	13,000
Boston	2,589,301	13,909
Montreal	2,109,509	13,500
Toronto	1,824,481	13,793

(Potential New cities)

City	Metropolitan Population	Rink Seating
Los Angeles	6,038,771	12,371
San Francisco	2,648,762	12,414
Pittsburgh	2,405,435	9,280
St. Louis	2,104,669	13,000
Cleveland	1,909,483	10,000
Baltimore	1,727,023	11,264
Seattle	1,107,213	9,000
Portland	821,897	9,000
Vancouver	790,165	(To build)
Quebec City	357,568	10,500

22

When the prospect of Pittsburgh obtaining a franchise came to the forefront, *Pittsburgh Press* writer Bill Heufelder wanted to be the first to break the story. On January 18, 1966, Heufelder was one of the first journalists to announce that Pittsburgh may be granted an NHL squad when the Board of Governors make their final decision in February. "A rink renaissance may be coming to Pittsburgh," Heufelder wrote. With four cities already chosen (Los Angeles, San Francisco-Oakland, St. Louis and Minnesota), there were just two spots left – but it seemed Pittsburgh was about to win the competition.

According to Heufelder, two bids existed: the one from Jack McGregor and one from Chicago banker John S. Gleason Jr. (which never came to fruition). But because of the history of minor league hockey succeeding in the city, along with the possibility of having a well-known politician running an NHL team, Pittsburgh was expected to be one of the front-runners.

As January turned to February, the Associated Press was preparing to report which six cities would be granted franchises. On February 7, 1966, the AP wrote that two of the six new cities would be announced, after four sites were pre-approved for expansion in October 1965. (Those four sites were Los Angeles, San Francisco-Oakland, St. Louis and Vancouver). "The question of what cities will be the first to crack the tightly knit National Hockey League in 34 years should be answered within the next three days," they wrote.

There would be 15 franchise bidders, representing nine different cities in the United States, while Vancouver would be the only city outside the country to officially apply for a franchise. Although only two cities would be officially awarded franchises, according to the Associated Press, four more would be designated as eventual sites for NHL expansion. According to Clarence Campbell, the remaining four franchises would be granted in June. Each of the cities would be given a half hour to make their case in front of the Board of Governors, while the sessions would occur over three days.

"Five of the U.S. groups are from Los Angeles," said the article. "Two from Pittsburgh: one each from San Francisco-Oakland, Minneapolis-St. Paul, St. Louis, Baltimore, Buffalo, Cleveland and Philadelphia."[23]

One of the largest Canadian newspapers of the time, the *Montreal Gazette*, consistently wrote articles about tentative NHL expansion. Pat Curran was one of the most popular hockey writers of his era and was known for his high-quality editorials. One of his articles, written on February 8, 1966, discussed the NHL expansion that would be announced by the league in the upcoming days. The article, "Maybe We're Wrong", suggests that the fans and media are perhaps being a bit too critical of the league's decision.

> NEW YORK – Ever since pro hockey moguls
> started talking expansion it's been a standing joke
> that New York and Boston should be the first cities
> considered for major league status. This stems from

the continued plight of the Rangers and Bruins whose only consistency in recent years has been in beating themselves.

Canadian sports writers and unattached observers who know the finger points of hockey feel that expansion will drastically hurt the caliber of play. Since New York and Boston have been unable to find five or six players to become contenders in the present circuit, few of the 120 needed for six new clubs will be true major leaguers.

And President Clarence Campbell readily admitted as much when he opposed expansion only a few years ago. He said at the time the NHL was playing to 95 percent capacity and formation of new clubs at that time would only "dilute the hockey product."

Go Along with Crowd

Campbell may still feel the same way personally. However, as a paid employee of the new generation of NHL governors he has to go along with the crowd to stake out claims across the United States.

When you came right down to it, maybe the joke is on Campbell and hockey-minded Canadians. We have studied the science of the sport so long that we may have failed to appreciate its great entertainment value.

Take Boston and New York for instance. It's a long time since either of these clubs has had a hand in the improvement of the hockey breed yet they continually pack their rinks and at pretty good prices too.

Note this observation from Monday's New York Journal American:

"Franchise applicants were given a perfect example last night of the gold mine prospects of big league hockey. The absolutely miserable Rangers with absolutely no chance for a playoff berth, had an SRO 15,925 crowd."

It has been obvious from at least 15 applications for clubs in the expansion set-up, at $2,000,000 per bid, that the new young men at the top such as J. David Molson, Stafford Smythe, Bill Jennings and Bruce Norris can't be far wrong in seeking new fields to conquer.

Big TV Contract

There's a multi-million dollar television contract in line when the NHL becomes nation-wide across the U.S. and while the indoor aspect of hockey prevents it from outdrawing baseball and football it may still rival these sports in popularity.

How do players feel about expansion?

They are all for it in more ways than one and an after game quote by Canadiens' John Ferguson last season pretty well sums up their attitude.

Fergy had thrown a mean elbow at the Rangers Swedish hope Ulf Sterher and someone asked him why?

"There are only 120 jobs in this league. It's tough enough getting one without having to beat off the Europeans."

In a couple of years there will be double as many jobs and even if a few overseas stars get into the league there'll be work for everybody.

They won't be signing any $600,000 bonus babies but Bobby Hull should at least pick up that $100,000 salary.

Now if there were only some way to expand things for the hockey writers.

California here we come.[24]

Another *Montreal Gazette* writer, Dink Carroll, wrote a regular column entitled "Playing the Field," where he wrote editorial comments on a topic occurring in the sports world. On February 10, 1966, Carroll discussed the NHL expansion that had recently been approved by the Board of Governors.

New NHL Cities Named

The six cities that will make up a second section of the National Hockey League have been approved, and you can read about them in the stories from New York. They will be ready in time for the 1967-68 season.

Whenever the question of league expansion has come up in the past, another question has always been asked: Where will the players come from?

President Clarence Campbell has answered it by saying that a pool of players from the six established clubs has been proposed that will give the new teams a personnel boost. The new teams can recruit from the pool, which should help the new section to be competitive from the beginning. Twenty players from the organizations of each of the established teams would contribute to the 120-player pool.

What about Boston and New York, the two clubs that wind up fifth and sixth in the NHL year after year? It has been said that concessions will be made to them in the player pool.

The caliber of play in the NHL will undoubtedly suffer for a time, but with twice as many jobs available more youngsters may decide to make hockey a career. Some of them are sure to develop into what is known in the trade as National Leaguers and, even if the caliber of play isn't up to the present standard for a while, it will still be the best there is.

Each team in the expanded league will play a partial

interlocking schedule of 74 regular season games. The present NHL schedule is 70 regular season games. Each of the present NHL clubs will play two home and two away games with each team in the new division. Teams in each division will be included in the playoffs, which will be inter-divisional.

Some Familiar Names

Some of the names associated with the new teams are familiar to readers of the sports pages.

Prominent among them is Jack Kent Cooke, who once owned the Toronto Baseball Club in the International League. Since moving to the United States several years ago, he has become part owner of the Washington Redskins of the National Football League and sole owner of the Los Angeles Lakers in the NBA. He is reported to have shelled out $5 million for the Lakers.

He is imaginative, energetic, and obviously very wealthy. One of the things about his presentation that impressed the screening committee was his promise to build an arena with his own money that will accommodate 16,000. When a man does that you know he is in the business to stay.

Bing Crosby, the entertainer, and George Flaherty, president of the Shasta Corporation, which owns the Ice Follies, are behind the new team in San Francisco-Oakland. Crosby's interest in the sport is well known. He sponsors the golf tournament that bears his name, is a shareholder in the Pittsburgh Pirates, and along with Max Bell, the Canadian publisher, owns Meadow Court, the Irish Derby winner. George Flaherty is part owner of the San Francisco Seals in the Western Hockey League, who are outdrawing the Warriors of the NBA.

Art Rooney, a member of the family that owns the Pittsburgh Steelers of the NHL, is one of the group interested in the Pittsburgh franchise while Jerry Wolman, owner of the Philadelphia Eagles, is one of the group in that city.

TV The New Box Office

President Clarence Campbell was asked last June when expansion was discussed if it meant that a U.S. TV network contract was the goal of the league.

"Of course," he replied. "Television is the new box office for every sport. In the NHL we are in a tighter straightjacket than most sports because we can't sell more tickets. Last year we played to 93 percent of capacity in the league's six cities. Selling tickets is not likely to be a problem for a while.

"That leaves us with a problem of where to get additional revenue. The only answer is television. Expansion is not going to sell more tickets because we do not have more tickets to sell."

Hockey's Canadian image was a handicap some years back when Saturday matinee games were put on a national network in the United States. The network soon dropped it. Bruce Norris, president of the Detroit Red Wings, has given a lot of thought to the network problem and didn't hesitate to discuss it during the playoffs last spring.

"Their games should be shown over one of the big U.S. networks," he said. "The chief obstacle in the way is that down there they're inclined to think of hockey as strictly a Canadian game. We've got to get them thinking differently about it. We've got to change the game's image."

Transfer of the league's head office to New York may be the next move.[25]

After the league approved six cities, the Vancouver media was up in arms regarding being passed over for an NHL franchise. The *Montreal Gazette* staff immediately published a news article, entitled "Vancouver Remains Minor Hockey City", discussing the anger of the Western Hockey League's Vancouver Canucks, in addition to the fans, media and heads of the city.

Cooked Up Deal

Cyrus McLean, president of the Western Hockey League Vancouver Canucks, who headed the city's delegation to New York, described the rejection as "a cooked up deal." He said in a telephone interview that "the question of new franchises was settled long before the meetings with Campbell and the NHL governors."

The choices were based partly on obtaining maximum benefits from television coverage of NHL games, he said.

Capt. H. J. C. Terry, president of the Pacific National Exhibition where a new 15,000-seat arena is to be built, said the city of Vancouver and the provincial government should re-apply for a league franchise. He said plans for the building – to be used also as a trade and exhibition center – will go ahead.

Capt. Terry said building plans were approved by Campbell and that the structure would be completed in time for the 1967-68 season.

Members of Vancouver City Council expressed shock at the rejection and said it would result in re-evaluation of the proposed PNE arena.

Aldermen Ernest Broome, Earle Adams and Hugh Bird said there may no longer be a need for a 15,000-seat coliseum. Aldermen Bob Williams and Orson Banfield felt the plans should proceed.

Aldermen Broome and Bird wanted to know how much Stafford Smythe, Toronto Maple Leafs president, had to do with the rejection. Smythe in 1964 offered to build a coliseum in downtown Vancouver provided he were given the land, but Vancouver ratepayers rejected the proposition in a plebiscite.

Smythe had said Tuesday that the Vancouver group has "too many 10 percenters – 10 guys with little bits of the action instead of one or two who could make decisions."

The future of the Los Angeles Blades of the Western Hockey League appeared indefinite Wednesday following the award of an NHL franchise for Los Angeles to another interest.

The Blades' ownership lost out in its bid for the major league franchise to Jack Kent Cooke, a former Canadian who owns the Los Angeles Lakers in the NBA.

Executive director Jack Geyer of the Blades, calling from New York where the NHL officials met, issued this statement through his office here:

"We are severely disappointed by the award of a National Hockey League franchise in Los Angeles to another applicant.

"This decision has grave consequences to the ownership of the Los Angeles Blades hockey club as the established professional hockey club now operating in Los Angeles as a member of the Western Hockey League.[26]

Another article written by *Montreal Gazette* writer Pat Curran was regarding J. David Molson, the owner of the Montreal Canadiens. His piece, "Great Boost Says Molson", discusses Molson's consistent support of NHL expansion from the first time the idea was brought to the league and seriously considered in 1965.

> NEW YORK – J. David Molson, progressive president of Montreal Canadiens who has been one of the leading figures in NHL expansion, said Wednesday's decision of the governors to admit six new cities is "a tremendous boost for the game."
>
> He was commenting upon approval of the applications for the 1967-68 season from Los Angeles, San Francisco, Minnesota, St. Louis, Philadelphia and Pittsburgh in big-time hockey's first expansion move in 40 years.
>
> Molson had said before the meetings at the St. Regis hotel that he would be very disappointed if at least two new franchises were not awarded.
>
> "Now I'm very happy, this is a tremendous move in the right direction for professional hockey," said the youthful Montrealer.
>
> "We could have delayed acceptance of some applications but I'm satisfied that we have found very suitable partners in some of the best major sports cities."
>
> Molson said all represented governors were not initially unanimous in going forward with expansion until yesterday when the final votes were taken.
>
> "But eventually, everyone agreed that we cannot remain a tight little island."
>
> Commenting upon the surprise approval of St. Louis, Molson explained that this was one of four main cities in last year's original expansion plan along with San Francisco, Los Angeles and Vancouver.
>
> "St. Louis is still a main site for geographic and schedule reasons," added Molson.
>
> "It is unfortunate there has been some delay in getting

the right application but there are 60 days to get that
one in order."

The Canadiens president said he was disappointed
that Vancouver did not become another Canadian city
on the major hockey front. He said that applicants
from B.C. "made a poor presentation."

Cyrus McLean, president of the Vancouver Canucks
of the Western Hockey League and broadcaster Foster
Hewitt represented the group from Vancouver.

The Minnesota interests were delighted on being
accepted by the NHL and spokesman Harold
McNeely Jr. said the area was the greatest producer of
hockey talent in the United States.

The Buffalo and Baltimore applicants were greatly
disturbed at the inclusion of St. Louis, when they
themselves had made such a great pitch to obtain
franchises.

"I just can't believe it," said Seymour Knox III, who
along with his brother Northrupp, is worth something
like $300,000,000. Buffalo's bid was blocked
mainly by Maple Leafs president Stafford Smythe,
considering the proximity of that city to Toronto.

Two Accepted

Pennsylvania State Senator Jack MacGregor, who
represented Pittsburgh said hockey has a great
potential future in the United States and was
especially pleased that two cities from his state were
admitted.[27]

But hockey cities like Vancouver, Montreal and Pittsburgh were
not the only cities whose journalists were concerned about the NHL.
Florida's *St. Petersburg Times* wrote a story on February 12 regarding
the emergence of hockey in the United States. "Move Over – Here
Comes Hockey!" the headline read. Journalist Shirley Povich wrote a

breaking news article mixed with some editorial based on the league's new advancement in expanding and growing the game.

Despite the uproar, there was most likely going to be a better result from the expansion. "In expanding from six to 12 teams," Povich wrote, "the original club owners in the NHL found themselves with instant, overnight riches that dwarf even the windfalls of the baseball and football club owners." Because each owner received $2 million from expansion fees, Povich, among others believed it was one of the main reasons for doubling the size of the league.

Two million was not a large number to pay for a new club, as Povich explains, because just before 1967 NHL expansion, the NFL added Atlanta to their circuit for a fee of $8.5 million. However, because of the difference in the number of teams in each league, each NFL owner received just $800,000. In 1960, when MLB added two teams to the American League, each paid $3 million, which is even more than NHL expansion teams were required to pay six years later. Basketball? The Los Angeles Lakers paid $5.5 million for a franchise around the same time period – an unheard of price at the time. In the NFL, the Washington Redskins' owners were offered $8 million to sell the team and they laughed at the price. The New York Yankees? They were bought in 1964 for over $14 million. Basically, a National Hockey League franchise, according to Povich, was worth much less than other professional sports teams, but was still undervalued.

But Povich believed that the real money would be in the television contract the NHL would garner after expanding the league. Major League Baseball had a huge television contract, but that was dwarfed by the NFL's contract, despite that, as the writer pointed out, in one season, an MLB team played more games than the entire NFL combined. The NFL has a contract with CBS that would give each of their 15 teams $1.2 million per season. Baseball has about $300,000 in store for each team from their TV contract. NHL teams? Nothing.[28]

The next day, the Associated Press came out with their article describing the NHL's official expansion announcement as a "big surprise." The writer claims that the fans and other knowledgeable members of the hockey world believed the league would only allow two, maybe three franchises into the league. "Yet, with the devastating effect of Bobby Hull's slap shot," the article states, "The NHL dropped a sports bombshell" when they announced which six cities would be welcomed into the league.

But it was not the first time the league considered expansion in the Original Six era, explains the article. A quote from Clarence Campbell reminds fans of the bid from Jim Hendy for Cleveland to become the league's seventh team in the 1940s. As Campbell reminisces, he explains that the league asked Hendy for $450,000 in equity money, which they claimed he failed to raise. "Oh, we have had several other queries through the years," Campbell said in the article. "Tony Owens applied for Los Angeles in 1950, but the owners didn't take it seriously."

But one reason Campbell believed expansion was important was because of the effect it would have on U.S. hockey players. At the time of the article in 1966, there was just one American hockey player in the NHL – Tom Williams of the Boston Bruins. "Expansion will make a tremendous difference to U.S. players," Campbell would explain. "You will see more American players in our league. It won't happen all of a sudden. But there will be more of a genuine incentive now for young hockey players to go into minor professional leagues."[29]

On February 14, Dink Carroll of the *Montreal Gazette* decided to spread some love on Valentine's Day and asked his readers why everyone was so uptight about the league expanding. In his "Playing the Field" column, he pled with his readers to understand the decision from another perspective.

Why the big uproar?

At the risk of being charged with stupidity or, what's the worse, with being "on the owners' side," we can't understand the big uproar over the National Hockey League's announced plan for expansion.

It's not illegal, immoral, or illogical. So why the shouts of disapproval and protest, in the taverns and in the House of Commons, and the picket line outside Toronto's Maple Leaf Gardens?

Most of the squawks seem to be over the screening committee approving St. Louis as the site for a new franchise, though no group came forward from that city to make a presentation, while Vancouver, which did make a presentation, was turned down. Why? We haven't talked to any league officials or club owners about it, but we did hear Stafford Smythe of the Toronto Maple Leafs answer the question between periods of the game in Toronto on Saturday. He didn't say anything that we didn't already know.

Jim Norris and Arthur Wirtz, who own the Chicago Blackhawks, also own the arena in St. Louis and because there is a rule against the same people owning more than one club in the league, they want to sell it to a group that will operate a team in that city. What Smythe said was that Jim Norris thought the expansion meeting wouldn't take place until three months later than it did.

The next meeting is scheduled for April 5, which means that Norris and Wirtz will be given until then to find buyers for the arena. If they can't come up with them, then St. Louis is out and Baltimore is in. The screening committee said that Vancouver made a weak presentation and added that no one would own more than 10 percent of the operation, which would make it difficult for any one person to speak authoritatively for the team.

It's Strictly Business

It should be pointed out immediately that a professional sport is a business and that the owners are in it to make money. The club owners in the NHL are, in effect, partners in a private enterprise. Good businessmen try to avoid unnecessary risks. If they prefer to have as their new partners – the owners of the franchises in the new cities – men who also own the arenas, that's their business.

There was a solemn discussion last night on the CBC radio network on the subject: Is Canada losing its national sport? The question itself is for the birds.

The game of golf has always been associated with Scotland, though some claim it originated in Holland. It was brought to an early peak of perfection in Scotland and spread from there to England. The big breakthrough on the North American continent came with the visit of Harry Vardon and Ted Ray in the summer of 1914.

After World War I, a good many Scottish and English pros came out to the United States and Canada to take club jobs. We never heard that there was any great protest about it. Golf is a great game and it was bound to become popular in other countries. The pros came out to this continent because the money was good and there was a demand for their services.

If a sport is good enough, inevitably it will overflow the boundaries of the originating country. That's what happened to hockey. Amateur hockey has been played in the United States and Europe for a good many years, though the NHL did not include a city in the U.S. until 1924.

They follow the money

Expansion of the NHL was inevitable and we don't know why it should surprise anyone that they'd go where the money is. That doesn't come within any definition of treason that we've ever read, though you'd think it did if you listened to some of the debates on the league's expansion move.

Even in the United States some sports commentators

have alleged that the price the NHL is asking for a franchise and 20 players is a steal. But a lot of people wanted in and nobody stuck a gun in their backs. They want in because they think they see a chance to make a buck, which is certainly what motivates most businessmen.

The league has been saying for years that it wants more exposure on television in the United States. The club owners knew that if they didn't expand in that country, they wouldn't have a hope of getting it. Stafford Smythe also said they were aware that if they didn't expand into those cities, somebody else might. They have preempted the field temporarily, but they may have to face the challenge from another league later on. There isn't space to discuss it now.

There will be twice as many jobs for players and officials after expansion and if they're paid in American dollars, they're going to get a dividend. They can bring the money back to Canada, if they aren't prevented by guidelines from taking it out of the United States.

It's often been said that no player is bigger than the game, and it seems that no country is, either.[30]

A few weeks later, after everyone had a bit of time to think through the expansion decision and debate the pros and cons, Arthur Daley of the *Milwaukee Journal* wanted to explain his opinion to his readers. In his article, "Hockey's Expansion Step Was Late, but Momentous," he tried to discuss why the decision should have been made years earlier.

Daley quoted a famous saying, "Nothing hinders progress like prosperity." The NHL had been prosperous for years, he pointed out, as the league's teams had played to almost 95% capacity in the last few years. Toronto and Montreal each had season ticket waiting lists of at least ten years, while the other four Original Six teams sold out on a regular basis. Clearly, the NHL was doing well.

But Daley pointed out that other professional sports leagues were expanding and succeeding at it, too. The only major league that had not done so was the NHL. "The eager beavers resented the fact that their narrow territorial confinement made them a second class major sport while pro football, for instance, had rocketed to fantastic heights," Daley said. "They were convinced that hockey had the same innate violence and appeal of pro football and thus the same potential."

Daley believed that hockey's expansion movement got its catalyst from two places: the "desire to enhance the image of the game" by becoming even with other professional sports; and the "ladling off some of the gravy from that bottomless television supply bin." As he explained, color television had also quadrupled the amount of television popularity the NHL received.

Each of the potential new owners wanted a crack at the popularity that the NHL had at the time. In fact, one owner, when told his arena was not big enough for league standards, announced that he would build a new one, without even blinking an eye. But the train truly came to a halt when the league was still unable to find a potential owner for the St. Louis franchise that was conditionally granted, due to the arena being owned by Jim Norris and Arthur Wirtz. As Daley wrote, "If big Jim can't find a tenant or buyer in time...the franchise will go to eager and ready Baltimore."

Regardless of which cities would ultimately have NHL teams when the 1967-68 season began, Daley knew that although the decision came very late, it was indeed a brilliant one that would help explode the popularity of the game in the United States. "Expansion from coast to coast is a historic breakthrough," Daley concluded, "Freeing the sport from its ice bound isolation in one narrow corner of the continent."[31]

Immediately after announcing expansion in February 1966, the NHL received major interest from television networks regarding a contract to broadcast their games, starting as soon as possible. But around March of the same year, the deal the league signed with NBC to broadcast the 1966 playoffs was already in danger of falling through. *Montreal Gazette* writer Pat Curran had the scoop with his March 14 story, "U.S. Playoff TV Deal in Jeopardy.

NEW YORK – That big network television plan to show Stanley Cup playoffs across the United States appears to be fading out. The National Hockey League has encountered too many problems with previous TV commitments to close the deal on short notice.

When announced expansion gave hockey a boost in the United States last month, the National Broadcasting Company was interested in televising three to five playoff games in color. The fee was reported at $200,000 to the NHL with prime television time to be sold at $12,000 a minute.

One of the main hurdles at the time was the switching of games from Saturday or Sunday night to Sunday afternoon, the best available time with the U.S. Network. At least two semi-final games and possibly three final games were to be televised if either series went the seven game limit.

In early negotiations by the NHL's television committee, the plan seemed feasible, providing there was no infringement on previous radio TV rights. However, it was learned over the weekend that three of the four playoff clubs have problems to this effect, which cannot be solved this season.

Chicago is the big stumbling block in the United States. Radio and television rights to all Blackhawks' schedule and playoff games belong to station WGN Chicago, an independent station blocking NBC. In addition Chicago has already started closed circuit theater showings of its remaining games and stands to increase these gate receipts greatly in the playoffs.

Switching to Sunday afternoon games for Montreal and Toronto would force a change in the Hockey Night In Canada program, which has been in vogue for some 40 seasons. The Canadian clubs have commitments to the CBC and CTV networks, which have been carrying their games.

Bill Jennings, president of the New York Rangers and a main cog in the league's television committee refused comment on the network deal yesterday.

However, J. David Molson, the Canadiens president, said in Montreal Saturday that negotiations are still going on.

"It's not on and it's not off," claims Molson.

"We are having problems but there is still hope of having some playoff games on the American network.

"One American club has already committed its playoffs television rights," added Molson. "The Canadian clubs have to honor certain rights to the networks which have been carrying their games and these rights do not fit into the NBC deal."

Molson pointed out that color presentation is another problem.

"All buildings must be equipped with special lighting and there's great expense involved."[32]

Months after the announcement of The Great Expansion, *Pittsburgh Press* writer Bill Heufelder published a feature on Los Angeles Kings owner Jack Kent Cooke. Cooke was an incredible, passionate man who gave a different meaning to the phrase "owner of a sports team" (See Chapter 7).

Heufelder began his piece by explaining who this "Jack Cooke" is. He was not some ordinary millionaire who wants to own a sports team to play with in his spare time. Not Cooke. This man owned the Los Angeles Lakers, 25% of the Washington Redskins and now owned one of the NHL's newest franchises, the Los Angeles Kings. Cooke was an avid collector of baseball cards – at age 53. To him, sports were more than a bunch of games. They were his entire life. "I've been quoted that

I want to own enough teams so that I can watch one of them play 365 days a year and that's true," Cooke said to Heufelder. "The only guilty feeling is that you feel like you're never working."

The writer reported that Cooke was enjoying his time at the NHL meetings, where they were finishing up the expansion process and finalizing the rules and regulations for the 1967 offseason and the 1967-68 season.

But outside of hockey, Cooke had been successful with almost everything he touched. He first became an owner when he bought the Toronto Maple Leafs baseball team in 1952. Since purchasing the Los Angeles Lakers for just over $5 million, he had been offered more than $7.5 million for the team – and refused to sell.

Many Los Angeles fans were skeptical of Cooke, especially since at the time of the article, he was the only of the six owners not to have hired a general manager. In fact, Cooke was, at the time, having problems paying his indemnification fee to the Western Hockey League's Los Angeles Blades for usurping their territory. In addition, he had also been having trouble with the new arena plans.

But nonetheless, as Heufelder concluded, Cooke was not worried at all. Sports teams are his specialty. "Meanwhile," Heufelder said, "He is trying to organize a world soccer league to include cities in the United States and Canada."

Only Jack Kent Cooke…[33]

As the surprise and grandeur of expansion disappeared in the summer of 1966, Quebec's *Val D'Or Star* decided to write a piece on whether or not expansion is good for players. The news organization sat down with NHL star Marcel Pronovost and discussed with him his career, his future and more importantly, the effects that expansion will have on him and the rest of the league. At the very end of the interview, Pronovost insisted that with NHL expansion occurring and the number of jobs that now exist, he's comfortable knowing that he is not too old to earn a modest living playing the sport he loves – especially since jobs are now plentiful in the hockey world.[34]

It is understandable to see how the media had such a large effect on the general opinion on expansion in the mid-1960s. With no Internet, cell phones or other means of obtaining information, the only way to do so was by reading the newspaper each morning. Being the primary information channel, it was easy for news organizations to voice opinions to their readers. Regardless of the intent of any of the published pieces, it is important to realize that many media members were just as skeptical, nervous and confused as many of the fans when NHL expansion occurred.

CHAPTER 5

Expansion Draft

"THIS IS THE YEAR of the great expansion. For the first time, the league will be composed of twelve teams."[35]

With these famous words, Clarence Campbell ushered in the era of expansion. With expansion came six new teams – six empty rosters – that needed to be filled with players. These players, as agreed upon by the Board of Governors, would come from the existing teams. The first two rounds were allocated for goaltenders to be picked. The following 18 rounds would be reserved for skaters, as each new team attempted to become the first one to succeed.

The expansion draft was held in the Queen Elizabeth Hotel ballroom in Montreal. The date was June 6, 1967. In addition to the 10 skaters and one goaltender that each Original Six team was allowed to protect, no expansion team could select a junior player. A junior was defined as a player who was still eligible to play in any junior league in North America, or one who was born after May 30, 1946. However, each expansion team was allowed to draft any player of the Original Six who was left unprotected, even if he was playing professional hockey elsewhere, including the American League, Western League, or Central Professional League. Teams were also allowed to draft any player who was sold to the WHL or CPHL before June 1, 1966.

Each team would pick once per round, with the order as such: Los Angeles, Minnesota, Philadelphia, Pittsburgh, Oakland, and St. Louis.

Each of the new teams drew one of six letters, A through F. The letter chosen determined which picks the team would have in the skaters' draft. For example, Philadelphia chose letter C with their selection. This meant they would pick third in the skaters' draft. Each letter was written on a piece of paper and each of the individual papers was placed in a capsule in the bowl of the Stanley Cup.

The rules for the expansion draft were as follows:

> After each of the first and second rounds the Original
> Six teams would choose one of the players it had
> left unprotected and place him on to their protected
> lists, filling out their rosters again. After the third,
> fourth and fifth rounds the old clubs would not
> be allowed to protect a player. After the sixth and
> all subsequent rounds the teams would continue
> to fill their protected lists. Players who had played
> professionally for the first time in the 1966-67 season
> were ineligible from being picked until their respective
> team had filled their protected list with at least two
> goaltenders and eighteen other players. There were
> many "backroom" deals made so that even players
> who were not protected, would not be drafted by
> mutual agreement.[36]

The expansion draft, often compared to a "rummage sale" by reporters of that era, began with the Los Angeles Kings choosing future Hall of Fame goaltender Terry Sawchuk from the Toronto Maple Leafs. For the Kings, Sawchuk posted an 11-14-6 record, in addition to a 3.07 save percentage. Yet he would play just one year for the Kings before going back to Detroit where his career began.

With the second pick in the draft, the Philadelphia Flyers made a surprise selection, passing on future Hall of Famer Glenn Hall and Canadiens star Charlie Hodge to take Bernie Parent. Parent was a young, promising goaltender who had little success with the Bruins in his first two NHL seasons. When the Bruins left him unprotected, Flyers GM Bud Poile snagged him. The pick, which many fans berated the team about originally, turned out to be a stroke of genius. Parent would go on to play 551 more games in the NHL, winning two Stanley Cups for the Flyers and eventually being elected to the Hockey Hall of Fame.

The St. Louis Blues, picking third, would choose Glenn Hall, who became famous tending the net for the Chicago Blackhawks. Hall would have tremendous success, the best of any expansion draft goaltender in the late 'sixties. In four seasons for the Blues, Hall led them to three consecutive Stanley Cup finals and only once had a goals against average over 2.48. Hall would eventually be inducted into the Hockey Hall of Fame.

The next pick belonged to the Minnesota North Stars, who chose a young goaltender named Cesare Maniago from the New York Rangers. Maniago was named the Central League MVP in the 1964-65 season after playing 67 games for the Minneapolis Bruins, ironically. Maniago would go on to play 513 more NHL games, most of them with the North Stars. In nine seasons in Minnesota, he had five 18-win seasons, all of which came in seasons in which he played just over half the schedule.

Pittsburgh's first pick, Joe Daley of the Detroit Red Wings, played just two full seasons with the Penguins, failing to win more than ten wins in either campaign. He would eventually drop down to the World Hockey Association to play with the Winnipeg Jets.

To close out the first round, the Oakland Seals picked Charlie Hodge, who had great success with the Montreal Canadiens in the 'sixties. Hodge would play just three seasons for the Seals and one for Vancouver before ultimately retiring.

The second and final round of goaltenders consisted of Los Angeles taking Wayne Rutledge, Minnesota taking Gary Bauman, Philadelphia taking Doug Favell, Pittsburgh taking Roy Edwards, Oakland taking Gary Smith and St. Louis taking Don Caley. Of those selected in the second round, only Doug Favell and Gary Smith went on to play more than 240 games. Favell served as a goalie for the Philadelphia Flyers before their Stanley Cup years, while Smith played four seasons for Oakland's franchise before heading to Chicago, Vancouver, Minnesota and finally Winnipeg, where he ended his career.

Of every goalie taken in the 1967 expansion draft, only Bernie Parent made a Hall of Fame career out of his time on an expansion squad. Sawchuk and Hall both created their Hall of Fame images on Original Six teams and were out of their prime by the time expansion happened. Every other goalie selected failed to have a great amount of success with their expansion team.

The first skater selected in the draft was a young Canadien named Gord Labossiere. Labossiere had played just 16 NHL games for the Rangers at that point, but had his rights traded to Montreal. In the American League, Labossiere scored 177 points in just 135 games for the Quebec Aces. Los Angeles believed he would continue that success at the major league level, yet he managed only 106 points in just 199 career NHL games.

The next two players selected were Dave Balon and Jim Roberts by Minnesota and St. Louis, respectively. Balon had a bit more success than Labossiere, scoring 260 points in 434 games, while Roberts trumped both, playing 788 career games after expansion. He also posted 293 points as a defenseman to back it up. All three players were selected from the Montreal Canadiens.

With the fourth pick of the round, the Flyers once again skipped over an older, proven veteran to draft a young, potentially talented player. Sticking with the concept that "defense wins championships," the Flyers drafted a fledgling, 27-year-old defenseman named Ed Van Impe. Van Impe became a solid defensive defenseman for the Flyers, keeping their blueline protected for nine seasons before retiring as a Pittsburgh Penguin. Van Impe would win two Stanley Cups with the Flyers and would be elected to the team's Hall of Fame.

With their first pick in the skater portion of the draft, the Pittsburgh Penguins chose center Earl Ingarfield from the New York Rangers. Ingarfield was a 33-year-old veteran who had accumulated a fair amount of points. However, the veteran forward only managed 90 games with the Penguins before being shipped off to Oakland, where he finished his NHL career.

To finish out the first round, the Seals chose legendary Maple Leafs defenseman Bob Baun to anchor their blueline. After having broken his leg earlier in the game, Baun scored the game-winning goal in overtime of Game 3 of the 1964 Stanley Cup Final, setting up the championship-clinching game for the Maple Leafs. For the Seals, however, he would play just 67 games before moving to the Red Wings, then finally back to Toronto where he would retire.

Toronto fans were not happy that Maple Leafs GM Punch Imlach did not protect Baun. After Baun scored his famous goal to clinch the Cup for Toronto, Imlach was ecstatic and promised that Baun would be an "untouchable" and would be placed on the protected list forever. However, after Imlach found out Baun was helping rookies negotiate their true worth on their contracts, he flipped out.

When reminded by a reporter of his original pledge, Imlach screamed, "Well, shit! I woulda played with ten broken bones. What the f**k's the big deal?"[37]

Round four began with the Kings selecting defenseman Bob Wall from the Detroit Red Wings. Wall was a 24-year-old who had played extremely well in the CPHL. In Los Angeles, he played three seasons of 70 games or more, then left to go down to the CHL. He would go on to play just 70 more NHL games after leaving the Kings.

Minnesota decided to stick with a forward, drafting young guy Ray Cullen, also out of Detroit. Cullen was 26 and had just finished a season in which he put up 16 points in 27 games with the Red Wings. In three years with the North Stars, Cullen would score 162 points in 208 games. He would finish his career the next season in Vancouver.

Philadelphia would draft another defenseman with their fourth pick. This time, it would be Joe Watson, also of the Boston Bruins (the third Bruin in four picks so far for Philadelphia). Watson would prove to be an incredible member of the Flyers' defensive corps, playing 762 NHL games after expansion, 746 of them for the Flyers. Watson would win two Stanley Cups with the Flyers and score 200 more points in his career – not counting the goal he scored against the Soviet Red Army team in 1976.

Pittsburgh would also choose to shore up their blueline with their second choice, as Al MacNeil of the New York Rangers packed up and moved to the Steel City. MacNeil was 32 years old when the 1967-68 season started and would play just 74 games for the Penguins before retiring. His 12 points from the blueline also did very little to help the fledgling new franchise.

Sticking with the defensive scheme of the fourth round, Oakland selected Kent Douglas from the Toronto Maple Leafs. Douglas, 31 years old and hailing from Cobalt, Ontario, would play just a half season for Oakland before moving to Detroit for the remainder of his NHL career. He would play only 145 more games and put up just 63 points in the rest of his NHL career.

To close out the fourth round and the second round of skaters, the St. Louis Blues selected Noel Picard. He would play six seasons anchoring the Blues' blueline, but only played sixty games in three of those six seasons (he was injured twice and was traded in his final season with the Blues). Picard would also become known for tripping Bobby Orr in the 1970 Stanley Cup final, sending Orr flying through the air after he scored the game-winner in overtime.

Round five of the expansion draft began with a young man named Eddie Joyal being drafted by the Los Angeles Kings. Joyal, 27 years old and from St. Albert, Alberta, had already played parts of four seasons in the NHL with the Red Wings and Maple Leafs. The center went on to have a successful career with the Kings, putting up 204 points in 319 games.

The North Stars decided to try and shore up their defense by drafting Bob Woytowich from the Boston Bruins. Having been 27 years old when he was drafted, the Winnipeg, Manitoba native would only play one season with the North Stars before going to Pittsburgh for the next four campaigns. He would finish his NHL career with the Los Angeles Kings before jumping ship to the WHA.

Philadelphia decided to take their first forward of the expansion draft in round five. Brit Selby, who was 22 when drafted, was a left wing for the Toronto Maple Leafs. He would go on to play two years for the Flyers, scoring 53 points in 119 games. He would eventually return to the Maple Leafs, play a couple seasons with the Blues, then move to the WHA to finish his professional career.

Pittsburgh would follow the Flyers and draft another left wing from the Toronto Maple Leafs, Larry Jeffrey. The Goderich, Ontario native never even dressed for the Penguins, crushing all hopes that the high performer from the 1962-63 Pittsburgh Hornets would have that same success in the NHL. Having been 26 years old when he was drafted, Jeffrey would go on to play 122 games with the Rangers, but would only score a petty 13 points.

Bill Hicke, a right winger from the New York Rangers, would go to the Seals with the fifth pick of the round. Hicke would play four seasons for the Oakland organization, putting up 180 points. He would also go on to finish his NHL career with the Penguins. Hicke would play 274 games after the expansion draft, most of them with the Seals.

Ending the fifth round was St. Louis' selection, defenseman Al Arbour. Having been the property of the Toronto Maple Leafs, the 34-year-old Sudbury, Ontario native would play four seasons for the Blues, helping them to shut down opposing forwards. Arbour, of course, would later become the head coach of the New York Islanders when they dominated the league in the 1980s.

Round six began with the Los Angeles Kings choosing a young Lemieux. No, not Mario, of course, but Real Lemieux, who was a 22-year-old right winger who showed a lot of promise in the Ontario Hockey Association and the CPHL. Having been the property of the Detroit Red Wings, Lemieux would play four seasons with the Kings before moving to the New York Rangers and finally the Buffalo Sabres prior to retiring. Lemieux put up 155 points in 482 games after being drafted.

Minnesota would draft a defenseman named Jean-Guy Talbot with their next pick. After the Montreal Canadiens owned him for 13 seasons, the 34-year-old played just four games for the North Stars before moving to the Red Wings and finally the Blues, where he would have a fair amount of success shutting down opposing forwards.

Next on the Philadelphia Flyers' radar was a 29-year-old from Toronto, Ontario. Forward Lou Angotti had tremendous success playing for Michigan Tech in the NCAA and then continued his hockey success in the American League and Central Professional League. Angotti would become the first captain in Philadelphia Flyers' history, yet would leave town after just one year to play for the Penguins. He continued his career with the Blackhawks before retiring as a St. Louis Blue. In 469 games after the expansion draft, Angotti posted 236 points.

Pittsburgh would then choose left wing Ab McDonald from the Detroit Red Wings. McDonald had great talent, while the Canadian, measuring 6-foot-2 and 194 pounds, was just 31 years old. He had played two seasons for the Canadiens, four for the Blackhawks, one for the Bruins and then two for the Red Wings. He was consistently a 40-point scorer in his early years and even put up 56 points in 61 games in 1966-67 for the American League Pittsburgh Hornets. He would play one season in Pittsburgh before moving to St. Louis to play with the Blues.

Choosing their first center of the expansion draft, the Oakland Seals picked Billy Harris, also from the Detroit Red Wings. Harris was 30 years old at the time of the expansion draft, but was a very lanky, scrawny player who had yet to have consistent success at the major league level. Weighing just 157 pounds, yet standing six feet tall, Harris would play just over one season for the Seals before jumping to Pittsburgh, where he would retire in 1969. With the Seals, he compiled 33 points in 81 games.

Closing out the sixth round was St. Louis, yet again. The only team not to have picked a forward in the expansion draft at this point, the Blues once again stuck with strengthening their blueline. Rod Seiling of the New York Rangers had great potential at just 22 years old. He had also shown great promise in the Ontario Hockey Association and with the Rangers. He never played a game for the Blues and was moved to New York shortly after the draft. Seiling became an anchor on the Rangers blueline, playing parts of 12 seasons in the Big Apple. He was subsequently picked up again by St. Louis in 1976. Seiling's numbers after being drafted in 1967 included 52 goals and 286 points in 844 games.

Round seven started with Los Angeles choosing a defenseman from the Bruins, 24-year-old Poul Popiel. Hailing from Denmark, Popiel had a few solid seasons in the American League before being drafted by the Kings. He did not perform as well as they had hoped, though, as the rugged defenseman played in just one NHL game before being sent to

Springfield in the AHL. Later picked up by the Detroit Red Wings, Popiel went on to have a less than exciting NHL career.

The North Stars would choose a right winger from Boston named Wayne Connelly. Being just 27 years old when drafted, the Rouyn-Noranda, Quebec native had already played parts of five NHL seasons, including four with the Bruins, before being drafted by Minnesota. In his first year, he would explode for 35 goals and 56 points – making the Minnesota community ecstatic with optimism. However, after missing many games in year two due to injury and scoring just 14 goals, he was moved to Detroit, where he would spend the next three years with the Red Wings. He would eventually end his NHL career with the Blues before going to the WHA.

Philadelphia, continuing their pursuit of young, promising skaters, drafted Leon Rochefort, a forward from the Montreal Canadiens. He had played with the Quebec Aces, whom the Flyers bought before the expansion draft occurred. Rochefort played two seasons in Philadelphia, scoring 77 points in 139 games. He then moved on to the Los Angeles Kings to end the decade. He played parts of seasons with the Detroit Red Wings, Atlanta Flames, Vancouver Canucks and again with the Montreal Canadiens before retiring in 1976.

Sticking with their belief that older, veteran players would make their team successful, the Penguins drafted 34-year-old Leo Boivin from the Detroit Red Wings. The defenseman had a weak showing with the Penguins, putting up just 40 points in 114 games, before moving to Minnesota. He would retire after his second season with the North Stars.

Oakland would drop back to the blueline and draft a veteran defenseman, Larry Cahan. The blueliner was 33 years old at the time of the expansion draft and had already played for the Maple Leafs and the Rangers in the NHL. He would score 24 points in 72 games with the Seals before being shipped to Los Angeles, where he would finish his NHL career as their captain. He would also play in the WHA before officially retiring from professional hockey.

With the final pick in the seventh round, the St. Louis Blues decided to take the first forward in franchise history. Ron Schock was a 23-year-old center from Chapleau, Ontario. The 5-foot-10, 170-pound Schock had played bits and pieces of three NHL seasons with the Bruins before being drafted by the Blues. In St. Louis, Schock would have a fair amount of success, scoring 57 points in two seasons. He would also be a piece of the two teams that made it to the Stanley Cup final in the first two years of existence. He would eventually be moved to Pittsburgh, would play eight seasons for the Pens, then ended his NHL career as a member of the Buffalo Sabres in 1978.

Round eight was dominated by forwards, as Los Angeles made right wing Terry Gray the first pick of the round. Gray was 29 years old during the expansion draft and had played just four NHL games up to that point. He made a name for himself playing for the Quebec Aces of the AHL, compiling 67 points in the 1964-65 season. For the Kings, Gray would post 28 points in 65 games before going to the CHL to develop. He would play a handful more NHL games, all for the St. Louis Blues, before retiring from professional hockey in 1974.

Minnesota would choose left wing Ted Taylor from the Detroit Red Wings with their pick (the 44th overall pick in the expansion draft). Taylor was 25 years old when he was drafted and had only played 10 NHL games up to that point – spread out over three seasons. With the North Stars, the lack of NHL success would follow Taylor as he played just 31 games before going to the Rochester Americans of the AHL. He would eventually join the Vancouver Canucks of the Western Hockey League and be a part of Vancouver's expansion into the NHL. He would finish his pro career in the WHA for the Houston Aeros.

Philadelphia would venture into Toronto Maple Leafs territory for their eighth pick in the draft, selecting Don Blackburn, a left wing from Kirkland Lake, Ontario. Blackburn only played six NHL games before heading to the Quebec Aces for conditioning and development. The 29-year-old would put up 29 points for the Flyers in their first year, but would ultimately be sent down to the American League in year two before leaving to go to the Rangers. He would be shipped around for the remainder of his NHL career before heading to the WHA, where he would end his pro career.

Noel Price of the Montreal Canadiens would be the next defenseman drafted, this time by the Pittsburgh Penguins. Price was 31 years old when the expansion draft took place, but never had much success in the NHL prior to being selected by Pittsburgh. The Penguins, however, were able to reverse that fortune a bit, as he would play at least 70 games in both seasons in the Steel City. He would even score 53 total points in those two seasons before moving to the Los Angeles Kings. He would retire as an Atlanta Flame in 1976.

Oakland would venture into the Chicago Blackhawks' roster for the next pick, selecting Wally Boyer, a center from Cowan, Manitoba. Boyer had only played two NHL seasons, getting action in just 46 games for the Maple Leafs and 42 games for the Blackhawks. After joining the Seals, he played 74 games and scored 33 points, before moving to the Pittsburgh Penguins. Boyer would score a total of 127 points in 277 games after being drafted in 1967.

Closing out the round, as always, were the St. Louis Blues. They would choose a young center named Terry Crisp. Crisp had played just three games for the Bruins before St. Louis took him, but he couldn't seem to make it in Missouri. After playing in the AHL for a year and playing a year with the Islanders, Crisp was sent to Philadelphia, where he won two Stanley Cups with the franchise. Crisp would retire in 1977 but would also go on to win a Stanley Cup as the head coach of the Calgary Flames in the 1988-89 season.

Los Angeles began the ninth round of the expansion draft by selecting Bryan Campbell from the New York Rangers. The 23-year-old center from Sudbury, Ontario had success in the CPHL with the Memphis Wings and the Omaha Knights. After being drafted by the Kings, though, he struggled early in his NHL career. He moved to Chicago and had a 54-point season, but eventually moved into the WHA, where he became a solid professional forward.

With pick number two in the ninth round, the Minnesota North Stars once again took the defensive route, taking Pete Goegan from the Detroit Red Wings. The 33-year-old defenseman played pieces of NHL seasons with the Red Wings and Rangers before being drafted. However, he would play just 46 games with the North Stars before ending his NHL career.

Philadelphia chose another defenseman, this one being John Miszuk from the Chicago Blackhawks. Hailing from Naliboki, Poland, the

26-year-old had NHL experience with Detroit and Chicago. With the Flyers, he spent two full seasons manning the blue line, before moving on to the Minnesota North Stars. A shutdown defenseman, Miszuk was still able to put up 42 points in 190 games after the expansion draft. He would end his pro career in the WHA.

The Penguins would choose Keith McCreary, a talented left wing from Montreal. He would play five seasons with the Penguins and three with the Atlanta Flames, scoring 131 goals and 240 points in 523 games after being drafted. McCreary would become a regular on the wing for Pittsburgh and became a fan favorite in his city.

Joe Szura was the property of the Montreal Canadiens, but never suited up for the famed Habs. After he was drafted by the Oakland Seals in the ninth round, the center would go on to play 90 games in two seasons with them, scoring 25 points along the way. However, he would make a career playing in the American Hockey League and eventually moved to the WHA before retiring in 1974.

St. Louis decided to continue trying to build their depth at forward, drafting Don McKenney from the Detroit Red Wings. Closing out the second round, McKenney was a regular for the Boston Bruins in the 'fifties and early 'sixties. He moved to the New York Rangers and finally the Maple Leafs and then played one season for the Red Wings. He also split time with the Pittsburgh Hornets. For the Blues, however, he would play just 39 games before moving back to the American League for good.

———————————————————

Only two significant players came out of the tenth round of the expansion draft. Ted Irvine of the Boston Bruins, drafted by the Los Angeles Kings, was one of those two players. He would play three seasons with the Kings before moving to the Rangers and finally the Blues. After the expansion draft, the left winger would put up 331 points in 723 NHL games.

The other player that performed well was Ken Schinkel, who the Pittsburgh Penguins drafted from the New York Rangers. He would play six seasons with the Penguins, consistently scoring over 30 points per year in the Steel City. His numbers after being drafted were 93 goals and 236 points in 371 games.

The other players drafted were left wing Len Lunde by Minnesota, center Garry Peters by Philadelphia, defenseman Bob Lemieux by Oakland and right wing Wayne Rivers by Boston. Peters played 231 more games after being drafted by the Flyers, while Lunde, Lemieux and Rivers each played less than 28 NHL games from the start of the 1967-68 season.

Round eleven was arguably the most successful round in the expansion draft with regards to post-expansion production. Howie Hughes, drafted by the Los Angeles Kings, would go on to play 168 more games, while Dick Cherry – drafted by Philadelphia – played 139 more games. Bob Dillabough played 161 games after being drafted by the Pittsburgh Penguins.

The Minnesota North Stars drafted Bill Goldsworthy out of Boston. Goldsworthy would go on to be one of the most successful players taken in the expansion draft. Playing ten seasons with the North Stars and a couple with the Rangers, Goldsworthy would score 277 goals and 529 points in 738 games – the second most points of any expansion player drafted.

Drafted fifth in the 11th round, J.P. Parise flew to the Bay Area to play with the Oakland Seals. However, he was moved to the Toronto Maple Leafs, then finally the North Stars, where he would spend eight seasons before playing for the New York Islanders. Remarkably, Parise would play 869 games, the most of any player drafted, and would score 590 points (leading all expansion draftees) – a number that includes 236 goals.

Bill Hay also became the first player in the expansion draft to not play an NHL game after being selected. Taken by St. Louis, the center had success with the Chicago Blackhawks after winning the Calder Trophy as the NHL's rookie of the year in the 1959-60 season. However, he never suited up once for the Blues and would subsequently retire after being drafted.

Each of the first four players taken in the 12th round of the expansion draft failed to play more than 80 additional games. Bill Inglis, the center drafted by Los Angeles, would play just 36 more NHL games. Left wing Andre Pronovost, taken by Minnesota, played only eight games after the draft. Philadelphia took defenseman Jean Gauthier, but he would play just 80 games before ending his NHL career. Lastly, center

Art Stratton was taken by Pittsburgh and played well directly after the draft, but after 70 games, his NHL career was done.

The last two players of the round, however, had great success with their respective teams from the start of the 1967-68 season. Ron Harris was a defenseman with the Boston Bruins and was drafted by the Oakland Seals. Though he played just 54 games with the major league Oakland Seals (he played two seasons with the San Francisco Seals in the Western League), he moved to Detroit to play for four years, played a half season in Atlanta, then finished his career in New York with the Rangers. He would play 472 total games after being drafted and put up 110 points from the blueline.

St. Louis would end the 12th round by drafting Darryl Edestrand, a defenseman from Strathroy, Ontario. Playing just a part of his first season with the Blues, he would move through the AHL before finding a home in Pittsburgh. Finishing his NHL career with the Los Angeles Kings, he would play 455 games after being drafted, scoring 34 goals and 124 points.

In round thirteen, Los Angeles drafted left wing Doug Robinson of the New York Rangers, Minnesota took defenseman Elmer Vasko from Chicago, and the Philadelphia Flyers took center Jim Johnson from New York. Pittsburgh's 13th rounder proved to be the most successful of the six, as left wing Val Fonteyne played 349 more NHL games after 1967, including five seasons with the Penguins. Oakland would draft Terry Clancy out of Toronto, while St. Louis would close the round by selecting right wing Norm Beaudin from Detroit.

The 14th round of the expansion draft was very successful for the majority of the new teams. Los Angeles opened the round by drafting left wing Mike Corrigan from the Maple Leafs. He would go on to play seven seasons with the Kings and two each with the Canucks and the Penguins. Corrigan would play 594 total games after being drafted by the Kings. Murray Hall of Chicago was next, as the right-winger was taken by Minnesota. Playing just 126 more games, Hall managed respectable numbers, posting 29 goals and 74 points.

Philadelphia would draft a gem in the 14th round, as Gary Dornhoefer was selected from Boston. He would play a crucial role in Philadelphia's two Stanley Cup championships and would play 11 seasons with the Flyers. Those seasons produced 202 goals and 518 points in 725 games. He became an icon in Philadelphia and after retirement, moved to the broadcast booth for Comcast SportsNet, the regional TV network. He is also a member of the Flyers Hall of Fame.

Pittsburgh's pick, Jeannot Gilbert, never played another game in the NHL after being drafted in 1967. Oakland would take a defenseman, Tracy Pratt with their next pick. Although Pratt played just 34 games with the Seals, he would continue his NHL career until 1977, retiring as a member of the Toronto Maple Leafs. The final draftee of the round was Larry Keenan, a left wing from Toronto, taken by St. Louis. He would play 232 more games in the NHL, posting 102 points along the way.

The only significant players in the 15th round were Bryan Watson of the North Stars and Ron Stewart of the Blues. Watson, a defenseman, would go on to play 716 more NHL games. Stewart would play 389 at center. Other players drafted included Jacques Lemieux (Los Angeles), Forbes Kennedy (Philadelphia), Tom McCarthy (Pittsburgh) and Autry Erickson (Oakland).

Round 16 featured Bill Collins being drafted by the Minnesota North Stars. He would score 311 points in 768 games after expansion. The other successful player from the 16th round was Lowell MacDonald, drafted by the Kings. The right wing would score 379 points in 460 games.

The only other significant players to be drafted in rounds 17 through 20 were Bill Flett, Brent Hughes and Bryan Hextall. Flett, drafted by the Los Angeles Kings, would play five seasons with the Kings, before going to Philadelphia. He would go on to win a Stanley Cup in 1974 with the Flyers – and that was just one part of his post-expansion career that included 202 goals and 417 points.

Hughes was drafted by the Los Angeles Kings, where he spent three seasons. He would go on to play for the Flyers, Blues, Red Wings and Kansas City Scouts, before going to the WHA. Hughes would play 435 NHL games after being drafted. Lastly, Bryan Hextall was drafted by the Oakland Seals. The eighth-to-last pick in the expansion draft, Hextall would score 99 goals and 258 points in 528 games, though he would not play a single game for the Seals. He played in Pittsburgh for five seasons, before joining the Atlanta Flames, the Red Wings and finally, the North Stars. He would retire after the 1975-76 season.

Altogether, all but eight of the 120 players drafted in the 1967 expansion draft continued to play in the NHL. Generally, the six expansion teams were successful with their original picks – picks that would serve the teams well in their immediate future. Whether they were reaching the Stanley Cup final for three consecutive years like the St. Louis Blues or winning two straight Stanley Cups like the Philadelphia Flyers, the expansion draft helped set the foundation for what would become a nationally-recognized sport.

It is difficult to judge which team was the most successful in the expansion draft. Three teams – the Philadelphia Flyers, St. Louis Blues and Los Angeles Kings – all claim to have had the best expansion drafts of any of the six new teams. In fact, Flyers founder Ed Snider even claimed in *The History of the Flyers*, "We had, without question, the best expansion draft of any other team."[38]

Looking at team success, it is easy to say that the St. Louis Blues had the best draft, as they advanced to the first three Stanley Cup finals after The Great Expansion. You could also argue the Flyers had the best draft, as they won a Stanley Cup 15 years prior to any other 1967 expansion team doing so.

The Los Angeles Kings had eight 300-game players of their 20 draft picks, more than any other team: Mike Corrigan, Lowell MacDonald, Bill Flett, Brent Hughes, Dave Balon, Eddie Joyal, Real Lemieux and Ted Irvine. The Flyers and Blues were right behind, though, with seven each. Players such as Rod Seiling and Noel Picard of St. Louis and Bernie Parent and Gary Dornhoefer of Philadelphia helped their respective teams have great success in the years following expansion.

The Kings also had five players with over 200 points, while Philadelphia and St. Louis were right behind with four each. With regards to goal scoring, Minnesota and Los Angeles each had four 100-goal scorers from the expansion draft, while St. Louis and Philly were tied with two.

With regard to longevity, the Flyers had five players dress for more than 500 games – Bernie Parent, Ed van Impe, Joe Watson, Leon

Rochefort and Gary Dornhoefer. The Blues had four, while the Kings had just two. In goaltending, however, there is no question the Flyers had the most successful draft. The Kings and Blues took legendary goalies in Terry Sawchuk and Glenn Hall, while the Flyers took young, promising players in Bernie Parent and Doug Favell. Bernie Parent would go on to have a Hall of Fame career, posting 289 wins after expansion, most of those with the Flyers. He also led them to two consecutive Stanley Cups in the 1970s. Lastly, Parent set a record for most wins in a season that stood until after the lockout, when it was broken by Martin Brodeur (with the help of shootouts).

On the gritty side of the puck, the Flyers and North Stars had the most penalty minutes, as Ed van Impe and Gary Dornhoefer combined for over 2,100 minutes in the sin bin, while Bryan Watson and Bill Goldsworthy together combined for over 2,700 after the expansion draft. However, time spent in the penalty box was not an indicator of on-ice intimidation, as was apparent by the North Stars' lack of success in early years. The Flyers, however, went on to become extremely successful, despite incurring such a high number of penalty minutes.

During the two rounds of the 1967 Amateur Draft (there was no universal entry draft until 1969), the Flyers were the only expansion team to successfully draft a bona fide professional player. Serge Bernier, a right winger drafted fifth overall, would go on to score 197 points in 302 NHL games and 566 points in 417 WHA games. The only other two NHL players to come out of the Amateur Draft were taken by the Toronto Maple Leafs and the Detroit Red Wings.

It is difficult to judge which expansion team had the most successful draft. Based solely on individual stats, many believe the Philadelphia Flyers came out on top (the key draft selections will be discussed in more detail in the upcoming chapters). However, when they won the Stanley Cup, over half of the players they drafted in 1967 had left the team. Therefore, many believe that St. Louis had the best expansion team in their first three years of existence, due to their appearance in three straight Stanley Cup Finals.

Unfortunately, not all of the 1967 expansion teams experienced such quick success.

Oakland Seals

1967-68 Statistics

	Pos	Ht	Wt	Age	GP	G	A	Pts	+/-	PIM
Gerry Ehman	RW	6-0	190	35	73	19	25	44	-5	20
Bill Hicke	RW	5-8	164	29	52	21	19	40	-22	32
Charlie Burns	C	5-11	170	31	73	9	26	35	-14	20
Wally Boyer	C	5-8	165	30	74	13	20	33	0	44
Billy Harris	C	6-0	155	32	62	12	17	29	-6	2
Ted Hampson	C	5-8	173	31	34	8	19	27	-10	4
Larry Cahan	D	6-2	222	34	74	9	15	24	-29	80
Alain Caron	RW	5-9	182	29	58	9	13	22	-22	18
Larry Popein	C	5-10	165	37	47	5	14	19	-17	12
George Swarbrick	RW	5-10	175	25	49	13	5	18	-17	62
John Brenneman	LW	5-10	175	25	49	13	5	18	-9	14
Kent Douglas	D	5-10	180	31	40	4	11	15	-18	80
Aut Erickson	D	6-1	188	30	65	4	11	15	-17	46
Bob Baun	D	5-9	175	31	67	3	10	13	-18	81
Ron Harris	D	5-10	190	25	54	4	6	10	-27	60
Gerry Odrowski	D	5-10	185	29	42	4	6	10	0	10
Mike Laughton	C	6-2	185	23	35	2	6	8	-17	38
Tracy Pratt	D	6-2	195	24	34	0	5	5	-18	90
Joe Szura	C	6-3	185	29	20	1	3	4	-2	10
Bert Marshall	D	6-3	205	24	20	0	4	4	-2	18
Ron Boehm	LW	5-8	160	24	16	2	1	3	-5	10
Tom Thurlby	D	5-10	175	29	20	1	1	2	-6	4
Bob Lemieux	D	6-1	195	23	21	0	1	1	0	4

	Pos	Ht	Wt	Age	GP	W	L	T	GAA	SO
Charlie Hodge	G	5-6	150	34	58	13	29	13	2.86	3
Gary Smith	G	6-4	215	23	21	2	13	4	3.19	1

CHAPTER 6

Oakland/California (Golden) Seals

WHILE NHL EXPANSION WAS deemed to be successful, no team experienced more failure at it than the Oakland Seals. Or the California Golden Seals, as they became known. Hockey was popular and successful at the minor league level in Northern California for years, but fans seemed to become disinterested in the NHL club quickly, leading to a dissolving and total destruction of professional hockey in the Bay Area.

The organization began in Winnipeg in 1955 as the Winnipeg Warriors. The Warriors had great success on the business side, even setting a record for highest attendance at a Western League game. Success continued on the ice as well, as the team won the Lester Patrick Cup in 1956 as the WHL champions, just one year into their existence. Future NHLers such as Noel Price, Fred Shero, Harry Lumley and Ed Johnston played for the Warriors, leading to their time in the major league.

But prior to the 1961-62 season, WHL teams were not doing well financially and were having difficulty affording the constant travel to Winnipeg, which was out of the way compared to the rest of the league's cities. Seemingly overnight, the league relocated the Winnipeg Warriors to San Francisco, where the San Francisco Seals were born. After a mediocre first season in which the Seals garnered 60 points in 70 games, Bud Poile, the head coach of the champion Edmonton Flyers, was hired by Seals management. Using tough, intimidating methods to win games, Poile had just won his third WHL championship with the Flyers.

With Poile running the team, the Seals won their first Lester Patrick Cup as the WHL champions, as they defeated the Seattle Totems. The next season, 1963-64, would be one in which the Seals struggled throughout the season and finished in fourth place. In the playoffs, however, goaltender Bob Perreault and forward Al Nicholson played with superhuman efforts and led the Seals to their second consecutive WHL championship.

As the calendar turned to 1965, the NHL announced they were planning on adding six new teams to their league and rumor had it CBS demanded a team be put in the Bay Area if the NHL was to obtain a national television contract. "Everybody thought that the Bay Area would be as good a market as there was available," said Bill Torrey, a member of the Seals' management staff in the early years. "The year before that, in the Western Hockey League, San Francisco won the championship playing in the Cow Palace. They sold out every game and the ownership group that was put together, a lot of them came from San Francisco as well as Palm Beach, Florida. They were all friends; everybody thought that it would be a great franchise."

There were two bids from Oakland: one from a man named Barry van Gerbig and his investment group and another from Mel Swig, who owned the WHL Seals. Though Swig seemed to be the better choice from a financial standpoint, there was much controversy surrounding him, with rumors pointing to the league's feelings towards his Jewish heritage. A combination of this, along with other factors, led to a belief that Swig would not be a great owner for a Bay Area franchise. The league ultimately rejected his bid.

When all was said and done, Barry van Gerbig – a goaltender for Princeton University and the 1962 U.S. National team – and his ownership group were chosen to be one of the western franchises for the 1967-68 NHL season, along with the Los Angeles Kings. Van Gerbig's ownership group consisted of over 50 different members, all of whom owned a share of the team. Though no one held a majority share of the Seals, the 29-year-old Gerbig was elected to head the partnership.

"Barry was a very good college goalkeeper at Princeton University.

He was on the U.S. National Team as the backup goalkeeper for a couple years," said Torrey. "He had contacts in hockey. He was very close with Bill Jennings of the New York Rangers. He and his brother and five or six friends all loved hockey and were very interested in it."

The manner in which van Gerbig became the head of the Seals is one that happened fortuitously. "I had been very close to Bruce Norris of Detroit and Bill Jennings of the New York Rangers," explained van Gerbig. "I also knew Charlie Adams in Boston and his lawyer, Charlie Mulcahy, was a friend of my father.

"Charlie Mulcahy and I were both working on Wall Street in 1965. One day, we were playing golf when Mulcahy mentioned that the Bruins organization owned an interest in the [WHL's] San Francisco Seals and that they were looking for a partner to take over their interest when the NHL expands."

Though van Gerbig was intrigued, the team was owned by a group of people led by Mel Swig. Swig was an eloquent, kind man who was well respected by other members of the league and members of the media. Above all, he was classy. He also had many political connections that could give the Seals numerous financial opportunities, many of which other owners may not be able to attain. But when van Gerbig became the head of the group, he cut Swig loose – a decision he would later regret.

"A bunch of good people led by Mel Swig owned a minority stake in the minor league franchise," explained van Gerbig. "Swig was a good man and well connected in San Francisco. The league said to us that Mel Swig and his group were 'not acceptable partners.' Mel Swig was a prince of a man. We should have kept him involved in the ownership of the team. There were apparently some [negative] feelings between the Bruins and the Swig group. I think, in hindsight, that was one of the things that prompted the Bruins to approach me about owning the team in the first place."[39]

Van Gerbig's original group included four others – his brother Mickey, Ice Follies owner Virgil Sherrill, musician George Coleman and singer Bing Crosby. Although they were the main partners involved in the Seals, a total of 52 investors were involved at some level, according to then-employee Frank Selke Jr. Among them were Nelson Doubleday, the famous publisher and eventual owner of the New York Mets;

John Brodie, the former San Francisco 49ers quarterback; and Marco Hellman, who owned Hellman's mayonnaise. Each of these members contributed to the original $2 million fee needed to join the National Hockey League, in addition to the other expenses and decisions involved in running the team.

One of the decisions was to determine where to play the home games. The existing arena that the San Francisco Seals played in, the Cow Palace, was not deemed to be an NHL-caliber arena by the league, forcing the ownership group to play in a new arena opened up across the bay in Oakland. This turned out to be a huge mistake.

"We learned quickly that Oakland was just across the bay from San Francisco, but people from San Francisco don't cross the bay for anything," said van Gerbig. "If Jesus Christ came on a donkey over there, they wouldn't come."

"There was a psychological barrier to San Franciscans," a resident of the Bay Area said. "Oakland was like nowhere to them. Anything in Oakland was considered second- or third-class. The people in San Francisco were so smug and pseudo-sophisticated."[40]

"The reaction by the media was pretty much indifferent," said Brad Kurtzberg, author of *Shorthanded: The Untold Story of the Seals*. "They didn't get the coverage that the Raiders were getting or the 49ers or the Giants. The big problem with the fans was the difference in prices between the WHL product and the NHL product and that they now had to cross the bridge to get into Oakland to see the games as opposed to just being in San Francisco. There was no transit system, so you had to drive over the bridge and they just didn't want to do it.

"It wasn't even just the hassle," Kurtzberg continued. "It took longer to get there; the tickets were more expensive. But part of it was the cultural thing, especially back then. San Francisco was considered very cosmopolitan and a very sophisticated culture and city. Oakland was considered very blue-collar and not very cultured – it wasn't the place to be. If you were an upper class San Francisco hockey fan, the idea of going to Oakland for anything was a little bit alien for you. There always seemed to be a hint that there may be some racism in the cultural differences between Oakland and San Francisco that may have played into that."

Yet the ownership group continued to market their team and try to lure fans across the bay to watch the California Seals. "Our marketing strategy was simple," explained van Gerbig. "The minor league team had a nucleus of about 8,000 fans. The strategy was 'we are bringing an NHL team to town and that is a step up. Chicago and Bobby Hull will be coming to town. Detroit and Gordie Howe will be, too'."[41]

After advertising the team and selling season tickets, van Gerbig's next job was to hire a staff. The first man he hired was Rudy Pilous, who was originally the coach of the WHL Seals. Pilous was hired as a team broadcaster and publicist. According to Frank Selke, Pilous was well liked and considered a great management-type. He was considered for the General Manager role, but the prospective coach, Bert Olmstead, refused to be hired if Pilous was running the team.

"Part of Bert's deal was that Rudy had to go," said Selke.

"Bert Olmstead used to think Rudy Pilous was a clown, or a buffoon," said Tim Ryan, the Seals broadcaster. "Bert had him dismissed and he brought in Gordie Fashoway as an assistant coach."[42]

Van Gerbig and his group were sure that they wanted Olmstead in as a head coach, even if it meant Pilous could not be involved in the hockey decisions of the squad. Tim Ryan, however, did not agree with the decision. "Rudy was great with the press. He was gregarious and open with the media," Ryan explained. "Olmstead was a hero because of who he was in Canada, but by nature he was a shy, inward-looking guy who put a lot of pressure on himself to do well. Bert was always short-tempered with 'stupid' questions from the press." As another person put it, "If Olmstead did public relations for Santa Claus, there wouldn't be any Christmas."[43]

Regardless of feelings for their new head coach, though, the organization's next move was to prepare for the expansion draft and the 1967-68 season. Van Gerbig's plan was to scout the Central Hockey League in hopes of finding some rookies that could step in and help the team. As far as the expansion draft, van Gerbig felt helpless about the rules which were mandated to protect the Original Six teams.

"One month before the draft they came up with each team protecting 14 players and one goalie and they rammed this down our throats," van Gerbig said. "We had already paid $1 million and we ended up with the last guys on the bench in the NHL."

This protection of the older teams would affect how the new

teams performed at the box office, thought van Gerbig. After all, if the WHL Seals were just as good as the NHL Seals, why would fans pay exponentially more money to see the new team? "They were right," said van Gerbig on the fans' decision not to pay. "We were charging major league prices for a minor league product."[44]

After the league reneged on their original expansion draft plan and allowed the Original Six teams to protect just eleven players, the Seals desperately tried to ice a solid team, specifically through this expansion draft. In drafting Charlie Hodge with their first pick, Olmstead believed the goaltender would be able to lead the team through the season and to the playoffs with the solid play he showed with the Canadiens. Bob Baun, the superstar defenseman from the Toronto Maple Leafs, was expected to anchor the Seals' blueline for the first season. Future star players J.P. Parise and Bryan Hextall, however, would be traded to Toronto before the season started for Gerry Ehman, a right wing who was expected to have a great NHL career.

"After the expansion draft, most of the experts were picking the Seals to finish first or second in the Western Division," said Brad Kurtzberg. "Most 'experts' thought they had the tools to compete for the Western Division title."

That quest for the inaugural Western Division title got off to a great start, as the California Seals won their first two games against the Flyers and North Stars, respectively, by a combined 11-1 score. They tied the Kings in their third game 2-2 to keep a hold on first place with a 2-0-1 record. But in their fourth game, they suffered their first loss of the season, dropping their first of six straight road games, by a 3-1 score, to the North Stars.

That loss would start a five-game losing streak and be the second game of a 14-game winless streak, in which the Seals would lose to five Original Six teams and tie the other one (Chicago). With their record at 2-11-3, leaving them at the bottom of the league standings, they went on a three-game unbeaten streak in which they would beat the Montreal Canadiens for their first Original Six victory in franchise history.

Just one month into the organization's first season, Barry van Gerbig decided, with the advising of his investment group, to change the name of the team from the California Seals to the Oakland Seals. With efforts to bring the San Francisco crowd over the bridge to Oakland failing, van Gerbig hoped the new name would attract more local fans from Oakland.

Their history would continue with bouts of inconsistency. Included in this inconsistency was a three game winless streak, then a streak in which they won three of six games from the end of November 1967 to mid-December. The second half of December would begin by being shut out by the Minnesota North Stars, commencing a five-game losing streak and an 11-game winless streak – and a stretch in which they won just once in 17 games.

Oakland would sweep a two-game series with the Kings at the end of January, but they would immediately go on a seven-game winless streak, beginning again with a loss to the Minnesota North Stars. Although a three-game winning streak would begin in February, the Seals would quickly revert to their losing ways, winning just two more games at the end of the month before going on a 13-game winless streak to end the season.

The Oakland Seals finished their first season with a horrendous 15-42-17 record for last place in the Western Division and the league. "As the season progressed, Olmstead had trouble dealing with the continued losses," says Brad Kurtzberg in *Shorthanded: The Untold Story of the Seals*. "Winless streaks…didn't help. Olmstead's frustrations showed and he took it out on his players at various times during the season."

"They're just not trying," said Bert Olmstead at one point during the season. "I've tried everything to get them to snap out of it. I've insulted and I've threatened. But they've just quit."

Another time during the season, Olmstead yelled at a reporter, "If I were a player, I don't even know whether I'd want to be associated with this bunch…I'd be tossing a few of them out of that dressing room on their cans. They have no pride. A lot of them are getting the chance of a lifetime and they're reacting like playing in the NHL is a prison sentence."[45]

Olmstead's antics would end later in the season, as he stepped down as head coach and allowed assistant coach Gordie Fashoway to take over. Unfortunately, the losing continued and the Seals, as previously stated, finished last place in the league. In addition to their record, the team averaged about 4,960 fans per game in an arena that seated 12,500. Business was clearly not good, both on and off the ice.

"Obviously that first season was just a disaster," said Brad Kurtzberg. "They changed general managers and coaches right before the entry draft, so they didn't have as much time to prepare as the other teams. Bert Olmstead just picked players he knew, whether he played with them in Toronto or Montreal or players that he had coached in the Western Hockey League the previous year. So they didn't have as much time to thoroughly go over the expansion draft and the entry draft as some of the other teams did."

"Oakland was picked to be the best of the new expansion teams, and unfortunately, they were a total flop on the ice," said Bill Torrey, then the Vice President of the organization. "They were a total flop in the box office.

"The first year it wasn't competitive at all," Torrey continued. "The media in general thought that the Seals had the best team and would be the most successful team. That seemed to be the consensus of opinion. Bert Olmstead thought that it would be the best team of the new expansion teams. Unfortunately, they didn't win. They didn't draw. One problem after another crept up. On top of it all, since they didn't draw, they weren't well financed. By November of the first year, they were even thinking of moving the team to Vancouver."

From Olmstead's standpoint, part of the problem resulted from not knowing what the staff of the team looked like. "I never really knew either [who the owner was]," said Olmstead. "The person I did business with was a guy by the name of Barry van Gerbig. He was a spokesman for a number of shareholders. I don't know what that number was and what their percentage of the team was. I think two guys were brothers that, together, owned 20% of the team. But they were all over the place."

At the end of the season, the van Gerbig group had lost great deals of money and were looking to get out of Oakland as soon as possible. They requested to relocate to Vancouver for the 1968-69 season, as Bill Torrey hinted, but the Board of Governors rejected the request with an 8-4 vote. With no end in sight to the loss of money and failure to produce on the ice, Olmstead, Fashoway, assistant coach Ken Wilson and trainer Bill Gray left the team, bolting from the disaster that was Oakland hockey.

After Olmstead left the team, there was a vacancy in the front office.

That vacancy was filled by Frank Selke Jr. "With Olmstead gone," said Selke, "I was asked by the board if I would consider becoming GM in his place, relinquishing the presidential title and some salary. I agreed on both counts for several reasons, not the least being my conviction we could be better even if I wasn't so sure about selling more tickets."[46]

In the 1968-69 season, the Oakland Seals started their campaign with a four-game winless streak that made the team seem destined to miss the playoffs again. With just four wins in their first 19 games, the Seals were headed back to the cellar, where they simply seemed to belong. Once again, inconsistency would be the story of the Seals, as they went 13-13-4 from the end of November through the start of February – leading to an 18-27-7 record after game 52.

A five-game unbeaten streak would ensue, followed by a 3-3-1 record to end the month. Five losses in seven games would be the prequel to a streak at the end of the season in which the Seals went unbeaten in four of the last five contests. It would bring their season record to 29-36-11, good for 69 points.

Though they had only a moderate year on the ice, it turned out to be one of the best of the expansion teams, as they finished in second place behind the dominant St. Louis Blues. In the playoffs, they would face the fourth place Los Angeles Kings, where they would be upset in seven games. Nonetheless, the team finally qualified for the postseason and was able to bring in a bit more revenue for the ownership group. Though they finished higher in the standings, the team still struggled in the box office and was unable to make any money.

The 1969-70 season would prove to be even worse than the previous year, as they finished the campaign with a 22-40-14 record for 58 points. Though they had an awful .289 winning percentage, they tied the Philadelphia Flyers for fourth place. The tiebreaker was number of wins, leaving the Seals (22) in the playoffs over the Flyers (17). The Seals would face the second place Pittsburgh Penguins in the playoffs, but were once again eliminated in the first round.

When the offseason began, Barry van Gerbig was eager to sell the team. After a couple of failed attempts to sell the team to Puck Inc. and Trans National Communications, van Gerbig was successful in selling the team to Charlie O. Finley, the owner of the Oakland Athletics. Bill Torrey explained the process of the sale to Finley:

"Charlie Finley came much later. There was the van Gerbig group, then they handed the team off to the ones that owned the Harlem Globetrotters. They ran it for six to eight months, then because of a tax ruling on how they purchased their interest in the team, they turned it back to Barry and his group. He didn't really want it the second time.

"They then sold it to a group that included Trans National Communications. That was a holding company from New York that said they were very wealthy. They didn't take to be very wealthy, though. They went belly up. Whitey Ford, the Yankees pitcher, was in that group, along with an executive from the New York Giants football team. They didn't have the money to sustain it for very long.

"They turned it back to Barry a third time. They filed for bankruptcy, then at that point, the bankruptcy judge advised the league that he was not going to select between Charlie Finley – who was one bidder – and the other bidder was a group including [Oakland Raiders owner] Al Davis. They advised the league to call a meeting and have the Board of Governors decide. The vote of the governors was that they preferred Charlie Finley instead of that combined group."

When Finley bought the team for $4,500,000, he changed the name of the team from the Oakland Seals to the Bay Area Seals. The name didn't stick and just two games later, the name became the California Golden Seals.

Before the name was even changed, though, the front office would change dramatically. General Manager Frank Selke Jr. would quit the team, leaving another vacancy in the front office. Bill Torrey would replace him as the head of the team, but would resign less then a month later. Fred Glover, the team's head coach, would become the GM in November for the remainder of the season.

In addition to the off-ice problems, the Seals were also a disaster on the ice. Losing their first five games by a combined 23-7 score and going winless in their first nine games, the Seals were destined to be in the basement from day one. A four-game winning streak from October 30, 1970 to November 11 would give the team some hope, but they would go on a streak in which they won just once in nine games to drop their record to 5-15-2 by the end of November.

Another four-game winning streak in December was simply cancelled out by a five-game losing streak. Though they were on the verge of going on a stretch in which they went .500, from January 29, 1971 to March 14, the Seals won just two games. They would finish the season by losing five of their last six games and ended with a 20-53-5 record for 45 points. The total would place them in seventh place in the newly realigned West Division and last place in the league.

But all hope was not lost. The upcoming NHL amateur draft was featuring a young phenom named Guy Lafleur. With the worst record in the league, the Seals were guaranteed to obtain him. But Lafleur desperately wanted to be a Canadien, and he convinced Canadiens GM Sam Pollock to make a trade with Charlie Finley, one that would haunt the Seals faithful for eternity and ultimately lead to their downfall. In 1970, before the Seals even looked to have ownership of that first pick, the Canadiens sent their first round pick and Ernie Hicke to California for Francois Lacombe and the Seals' first round pick, which ironically turned out to be first overall. Lafleur would go on to become a Hall of Famer, while the Seals pick, Chris Oddleifson, scored just 95 goals in his NHL career. The deal would start another dynasty in Montreal and leave the Seals with nothing but some loose change.

Because of awful financial conditions and an inability to find a suitable owner, the owners began to seek the funds necessary to build a new arena in San Francisco. When those plans failed to come to fruition, the league agreed to allow the team to relocate. However, with a new expansion team having already been placed in Vancouver in the 1970 NHL expansion, the Seals had to find another city in which to relocate.

In 1975 Mel Swig bought the team from van Gerbig and was subsequently persuaded by George Gund, a minority owner of the Seals, to relocate the team to Cleveland for the 1976-77 season. Due to having a successful minor league team for years, the NHL approved the move and the Cleveland Barons were born into the NHL.

But the Barons had just as many problems as the Seals, both on and off the ice. Because the move was not finalized until August 1976, they did not have sufficient time to market the team to the city before the season began. Their home opener had just 8,900 fans at the game, while they only surpassed 10,000 fans in seven of their 40 home games. In fact, average attendance in Cleveland was worse than that in Oakland.

Because of a problem with the stadium's lease, the Barons almost failed to finish the 1977 season – but were given a $1.3 million loan by the league in order to prevent the embarrassment of a team folding while the season was still being played. When the Barons finished in last place and failed to make money, Mel Swig sold his share of the team to George Gund and his brother. After another dreadful season in 1977-78, though, it was clear the Barons were not going to survive in Cleveland.

During some GM meetings at the 1978 NHL draft, Minnesota North Stars GM Lou Nanne was trying to make some deals with Cleveland GM Harry Howell. As he was negotiating a possible trade with Howell, Nanne was pulled into the hall by two peers who were with Minnesota, advising him not to make a move. "You're going to have more players than you can handle," said one to Nanne. "We might buy another team."

When Nanne entered another meeting room to discuss the possibility of buying out the Barons and merging the two struggling teams together, he was encountered by Gordon Gund, who reached out twice to shake Nanne's hand, but missed both times. "Why is this guy playing with me?" Nanne asked himself, to which Gund revealed to him that he was blind.

To continue the odd happenings inside the room, Nanne heard, "Hi, Lou," but did not know where it was coming from. When he looked down, he noticed George Gund lying on a board under a table, smoking a cigar. Asking why he was there, Gund responded that because of his bad back, he remains there to make himself more comfortable. Nanne was then introduced to the Seals' lawyer, who was hiding in the adjacent bathroom and talking through a door, because he did not like the smoke being produced from George Gund under the table. "What am I getting myself into here?" Nanne thought.

Gordon Gund explained that the North Stars were going to purchase the Barons and take half of their players. All that was waiting was the league's approval. Inside the league meeting, however, many GMs were not pleased with the idea. "We can't allow two teams to be put together," one said. [47]

But at the conclusion of the meeting, the move was ultimately approved. The North Stars were allowed to protect 10 players and two goalies from the Barons' roster to bring to their own team. The Barons would be gone by the end of the 1978 draft.

The Seals would be no more in 1976, and when Dennis Maruk (the last member of the Seals active in the NHL) retired in 1989, the organization that began in San Francisco officially was gone. Though numerous fans exist from the days of the Golden Seals, with three franchises currently existing in California, there is little to no chance that the Seals could ever return. With Brad Kurtzberg's book on the Seals having been published, the team's short, illustrious history is now only available in a book or on the Internet, as opposed to an on-ice product, which still exist for the other five Great Expansion franchises.

But as Bert Olmstead said, "It's the story of the Seals. Because I don't know where the hell they went."

Los Angeles Kings

1967-68 Statistics

	Pos	Ht	Wt	Age	GP	G	A	Pts	+/-	PIM
Eddie Joyal	C	6-0	178	27	74	23	34	57	-2	20
Bill Flett	RW	6-1	205	24	73	26	20	46	4	97
Lowell MacDonald	LW	5-11	185	26	74	21	24	45	-11	12
Ted Irvine	LW	6-2	195	23	73	18	22	40	-10	26
Gord Labossiere	C	6-1	190	28	68	13	27	40	6	31
Bill White	D	6-2	195	28	74	11	27	38	17	100
Real Lemieux	LW	5-11	180	23	74	12	23	35	-2	60
Terry Gray	RW	6-0	175	29	65	12	16	28	-3	22
Howie Menard	C	5-8	160	25	35	9	15	24	4	32
Howie Hughes	RW	5-9	180	28	74	9	14	23	1	20
Bob Wall	D	5-10	171	25	71	5	18	23	-9	66
Bryan Campbell	C	6-0	173	23	44	6	15	21	2	16
Brian Smith	LW	5-11	170	27	58	10	9	19	-2	33
Doug Robinson	LW	6-2	197	27	34	9	9	18	4	6
Dale Rolfe	D	6-4	210	27	68	3	13	16	-10	84
Brent Hughes	D	6-0	205	24	44	4	10	14	15	36
Dave Amadio	D	6-1	207	28	58	4	6	10	-10	101
Brian Kilrea	C	5-11	175	33	25	3	5	8	-4	12
Jim Anderson	LW	5-10	165	37	7	1	2	3	-2	2
Jacques Lemieux	D	6-2	190	24	16	0	3	3	3	8
Billy Inglis	C	5-9	160	24	12	1	1	2	-6	0
Jim Murray	D	6-1	165	24	30	0	2	2	-4	14

	Pos	Ht	Wt	Age	GP	W	L	T	GAA	SO
Wayne Rutledge	G	6-2	200	26	45	20	18	4	2.87	2
Terry Sawchuk	G	5-11	195	38	36	11	14	6	3.07	2

CHAPTER 7

Los Angeles Kings

WHEN JACK KENT COOKE was granted an NHL franchise in Los Angeles, Southern California changed forever.

To be honest, Cooke had already changed Southern California. Born in Canada, the entrepreneur had already moved to California and purchased the National Basketball Association's Los Angeles Lakers for an unheard of price of $5 million. He also purchased a portion of the NFL's Washington Redskins. But his first love was hockey and he wanted an NHL franchise.

Los Angeles already had a fairly successful Western Hockey League franchise – the Blades. However, there were numerous bids from Los Angeles. Everyone collectively assumed that Southern California was going to get a team, but the only plausible place to play hockey was the Los Angeles Sports Arena, where the Blades and Lakers played. The city was not too happy putting a third team in the arena, so Cooke had no choice but to threaten to build his own arena – which turned out to be the only credible decision for him to make.

In addition to Cooke, four other bids were being made from others who wanted to own a team in Los Angeles. Dan Reeves, who owned the WHL's Los Angeles team, seemed to be the frontrunner. In fact, Reeves was even encouraged by the NHL to apply for a team, based on his success at the Western League level. Reeves also held the lease to the Los Angeles Arena, the stadium the Blades called home. But Reeves wasn't the only competitor. Other bids included Ralph Wilson, owner of the American Football League's Buffalo Bills and Tony Owens, who was a TV producer at the time.

Of every potential owner, only Jack Kent Cooke promised to build a new arena, which the NHL Board of Governors saw as a plus. "You have to be impressed with anyone who offers to build a new building," said Canadiens owner David Molson.[48] Cooke pitched his vision to the league, which included an arena that rivaled that of the ancient Roman Forum. He wanted the land to include a convention center, a shopping center, a public library and a railroad station. Altogether, he wanted this Forum to be recognized by the entire country for its spectacular appearance and presence as a part of Hollywood.

Cooke would explain to the league the benefits of having a brand new facility compared to using the existing Los Angeles Sports Arena. One advantage was that in a building seating 2,000 more fans than the Sports Arena, there was more potential for larger profit margins. In addition, since Cooke would not be sharing the new building with anyone (at the beginning, at least), the Kings would have first choice of available playing dates, making for fewer conflicts than there would be at the Sports Arena. Considering who controlled the use of the Sports Arena (the Los Angeles Coliseum Commission, who was known for being extremely difficult to deal with), it would prove to be of the utmost importance.

"The Coliseum Commission is supposed to be an administrative body," Cooke said, "But instead the commissioners use it as a power base for themselves personally. I made two applications – one for a long-term lease for the Lakers and a second for the right to sign a lease for hockey if I were awarded an NHL franchise.

"The commissioners rejected both applications and only offered me a two-year lease for the Lakers. When I replied that such a ruling was completely unacceptable, Ernest Debs (a Los Angeles County Supervisor and influential member of the Coliseum Commission) replied – and these were his exact words – 'Take it or leave it'."

Cooke explained that he would simply be forced to build his own place for the franchise. Debs replied sarcastically, "Har, har, har." Cooke gazed at Debs briefly, then said, "Well then I've just decided that I am going to build my own arena!"[49]

After making his presentation to the league, Cooke was granted a franchise on the condition that he built this new arena. Only a few months after being announced as the owner of a new NHL franchise – July 1, to be exact – Cooke announced that he purchased 29.5 acres of land in Inglewood, California. The land used to be a golf course, but for the (relatively) cheap price of just over $4 million, Cooke found a place to build this new temple for the hockey gods.

The arena, he said, would take up about 3.5 acres of the land he purchased. It would seat 16,602 for basketball games; 17,526 for boxing matches; 14,504 for the circus; and 15,048 for the Los Angeles Kings. He immediately hired Charles Luckman, an architect, who had recently designed Madison Square Garden. Cooke would also hire C.L. Peck as the construction company to build the arena.

The construction of the building was financed partially by Atlantic-Richfield Oil, in addition to money from Cooke's pocket. The budget for the construction was $11 million, yet it ultimately wound up costing just over $12 million. The groundbreaking occurred on September 15, 1966 and the building was completed just 15 months later.

Cooke based much of the design of the building from his childhood home, located in Toronto, Ontario on Neville Park Boulevard. He wanted columns and lots of them. He designed "tall, simple, unadorned columns, eighty of them, each 57 feet high, weighing a ton per foot."[50]

"What I want is something 6,000 miles east of here and 2,000 years ago," Cooke said to his designer. "That's the beginning of what I want." The designer drew up the columns to resemble a mixture of ancient Greece and Rome.[51] "The Forum," as Cooke called it from the start, would be shaped as a perfect circle. It would also have a parking lot that could house about 4,000 cars. "Perhaps 200 years from now – or even 2,000," Cooke explained ecstatically, "People will say that The Forum was one of the finest buildings erected during the twentieth century… it's man's greatest tribute to athlete's foot."

When all the dust settled and all the checks had been signed, the costs for the Los Angeles Kings included the $2 million expansion fee; $1 million of indemnity paid to the Blades and the WHL for being a competing team in the same area; $4.02 million for the land; and $12.2

million for the building – a total of over $19 million, an extraordinarily high price for an NHL franchise in the '60s.

"Ever since February 9, 1966, when Jack Kent Cooke was awarded a new National Hockey League franchise, ice hockey has been played at the highest level in a city that rests among the beautiful beaches of the Pacific Ocean," says the Los Angeles Kings media guide. "Wanting his new hockey club to take on an air of royalty, Cooke named his team the 'Kings' and was part of six new teams that would double the size of the NHL from the Original Six franchises to 12 teams, starting with the 1967-68 season. Part of Cooke's plan was to build a new state-of-the-art sports and entertainment facility, which coincided with the Kings opening in Los Angeles that same season. The building was soon dubbed the 'The Fabulous Forum' and became the home for the Kings for the next 32 seasons."[52]

But before even beginning to think about a Stanley Cup, Cooke had to hire a staff that would help not only to create a successful team on the ice, but also create an entertaining and successful operation off the ice. One of the first people that he hired was "Jiggs" McDonald, who would be his play-by-play man for television.

"I don't know how many applicants Jack Kent Cooke had for the job," said McDonald, "But first, I sent in a tape of a senior game of hockey here in Ontario that I was doing at the time. He was going to be in Toronto for soccer meetings. I sent the tape in sometime in the fall of '66, and once we knew that expansion was reality…I got a call in January that I was in the running." McDonald had a strong desire to work for Cooke, having known about his travels and his successes in business and the sports industry. He simply knew that Cooke was going to have success in whatever endeavor he pursued.

"He was going to be in Toronto for whatever this soccer meeting was in '67," McDonald continued. "I was to come meet him there and I did. He explained what he liked and didn't like about the tape. He wanted to know how old these guys were, how big they were, etc. We had a game that weekend, so I sent that tape to him as well. In January I was one of the final five and sometime in February, he told me that it was two…then he wrote and said that he was offering me the job and what the terms were. I sent a telegram that night that I was definitely interested. It would be the middle of the following week, the ides of March, where he called and told me the job was mine."

McDonald was Canadian, though, and American immigration laws were almost as strict as they are today. "When I got the job, we went through a process that I had to apply for a work visa or a green card, at least," he said. "Before they would give me that, Mr. Cooke had to show justifiable reason or cause why he could not or would not hire an American. He had a list of 127 American applicants and proved to immigration that there wasn't an American available to do the job. We went from March until late September until we got our green cards and were able to move."

Convincing United States authorities that only a Canadian could perform this job was just one example of what a powerful and influential man Cooke was in his time. But this power and influence did not translate into a tough, mean demeanor, as many would expect. Cooke was a fun, loving guy who simply loved to be around the hockey rink. He would routinely strap on his skates and hang out with the Kings players before practices. In fact, Terry Sawchuk would consistently stop Cooke's attempts to score on his superstar goaltender. At one point, Cooke finally looked up into the stands and said, "Hey Terry, isn't that your wife sitting up there?" As Sawchuk turned around to look, Cooke, a sports star in college, flipped the puck by the goalie and skated away smiling.

In late September, though, when the preseason began, the Forum was not yet completed and the Kings had to play their home games at both the Los Angeles Memorial Sports Arena and the Long Beach Arena. After the preseason was complete, however, the Kings were ready to begin their inaugural season. Or, so they thought.

Before the 1967-68 season even began, the Los Angeles Kings were being picked by numerous media sources to finish in last place in the newly created West Division. Although they had future Hall of Famer Terry Sawchuk in net and although the Kings had the first pick in every round of the expansion draft, the experts did not believe they had created a good team – one that could compete with the Original Six squads.

Instead of simply brushing off the hockey writers and claiming that his team was fine, Cooke went out and purchased the Springfield

Indians of the American League and took some of their players for the NHL squad. According to Jiggs McDonald, the move gave Cooke and his Kings a fair amount of players. "He got probably five first-line players for his NHL team by the purchase of Springfield," said McDonald.

In addition to adding players, Cooke needed to make sure that his team's head coach was a competent man who could lead a young, inexperienced team to the Stanley Cup. His hope was that in the expansion draft, he would select Toronto Maple Leafs star Red Kelly, who was going to be unprotected and would be retiring from his playing days. Cooke would take control of Kelly's contract and make him the first head coach in Kings history.

Kelly, a left wing and fan favorite in Southern Ontario, already had incredible success in his Hall of Fame career – one that included eight Stanley Cups in 20 seasons with both Detroit and Toronto. Cooke and Kelly had rendezvoused shortly before the expansion draft and discussed their plan to take Kelly and groom him into a big league coach.

In typical Jack Kent Cooke style, Cooke proudly announced his plan to the media and the entire hockey world, explaining that Red Kelly would become a member of his team and stand behind the bench for the first few seasons of NHL hockey in Los Angeles. In fact, he never even considered that someone might take Kelly in the draft prior to the Kings. After all, who would want an overage, high-salary player like Kelly who was most likely going to retire soon anyway?

During the expansion draft, though, the Maple Leafs lost two young unprotected left-wingers early on. Toronto GM Punch Imlach panicked and placed Kelly on the team's protected list after the tenth round, as the league rules allowed, in order to fill up their slowly diminishing depth on the left side of the ice.

Cooke was furious. He accused Imlach of trying to sabotage his attempts to create a successful hockey club, while Imlach was irate that Cooke had even considered speaking with Kelly while he was still a member of the Maple Leafs – let alone that Cooke did it anyway. Imlach and Leafs management complained to NHL president Clarence Campbell and accused Cooke of tampering with a player who was under contract. Imlach said that because Cooke had worked out a hidden agenda with Kelly, the Los Angeles owner should be fined and punished.

After a few days of examining the situation and determining what truly happened, Campbell concluded that no punishment was to be handed down to Cooke, but that if he wanted Red Kelly, he would have to send Los Angeles' 15th pick in the expansion draft to secure the veteran's services behind the Kings bench – which Cooke accepted.

Although the team had their dream head coach, they did not perform incredibly at the beginning of the season, both on the ice and in the box office. In fact, the Kings never had 10,000 fans in attendance before The Forum opened. The fans' consensus reaction to the Los Angeles Kings was not all that positive in the early part of the 1967-68 season. Their reactions to the players were not that positive. Most importantly, their reactions to the prices were not that positive, either.

"Some of the early reaction was that you had Howie Hughes, who had played in the Western League with Seattle. Fans didn't feel that he was NHL-caliber," explained Jiggs McDonald. "The reaction was good when any of the Original Six teams came in. With the Original Six, you were pretty much assured of a pretty good crowd. But season tickets didn't sell all that well. The price difference between the Western League and what the NHL prices were – not that they were high in comparison to today's prices – but it was a huge jump.

"They had indication of all kinds of interest, and the media thought, 'Well, we sold out, we have 14,000 season ticket holders easily.' And of course, when they found out the prices, they were all like, 'Noooooo.' Cooke was counting on the half million Canadians that lived in Southern California at that time to be season ticket holders. It just didn't happen. They would come see Toronto or Montreal, but they weren't going to sell out the building on a season ticket basis. He said it took him a year to recognize that the people only moved there because they didn't like hockey!" McDonald concluded with a laugh.

Regardless of ticket sales, the season continued as the Kings battled for first place. They didn't lose a match until the sixth game of the season. They even beat Chicago in the old Chicago Stadium in their first game against an Original Six squad – it was their third win of the season. In the first month of the season, they went a respectable 4-3-2. They even had a six game road trip that began on the fourth day of the season and their performance on the trip managed to keep them relevant. In November, they had a stretch where they went 6-2, winning three games against Original Six squads, all at home.

On November 9, 1967, the biggest crowd the Kings ever had to date at the Los Angeles Sports Arena showed up to watch the Kings play the Toronto Maple Leafs. After a hard-fought game, the Kings defeated the defending Stanley Cup champs 4-1, solidifying their place among expansion clubs and making Mr. Cooke a very happy man. Ever the showman, he left his perch from where he watched the game, grabbed a Toronto sportswriter and kissed him on both cheeks. He then kissed Jiggs McDonald on the cheek and ran into the dressing room immediately, giving coach Red Kelly a big smooch in front of the entire team. "You're the most wonderful bunch of guys in the world!" screamed Cooke at his players. "I wish you were all my sons!"[53]

But the big news for the Kings occurred on December 30, 1967, when The Forum would host the Kings for the stadium's first NHL game. The Philadelphia Flyers were in town, as were 14,366 fans – the most fans Los Angeles ever had at one game to that point in their history. Although they were shut out 2-0 by the Flyers and although it was the midway point of an eight-game losing streak, there was much optimism among management and Cooke that the Kings would succeed.

With a 16-21-3 record after 40 games, the Kings needed to step up their game if they hoped to make the playoffs. As the season came to a close, the Kings defeated the Flyers in the fourth-to-last game of the season in front of over 14,000 fans at The Forum. The Kings took over first place with the win and were looking to become the first Western Division champions. But in the final three games, the Kings went 0-2-1 to drop down to second place, just one point behind the Flyers.

Qualifying for the playoffs, they faced off against the Minnesota North Stars in the 1968 Western Division quarterfinals. The Kings won the first two games at home, taking a 2-0 series lead over the North Stars. After Minnesota won both of their home games to tie the series, Los Angeles squeaked out a victory in Game 5, taking a 3-2 lead and pushing the North Stars to the edge.

But in Game 6, the North Stars were able to pull out a miraculous overtime victory to send the series back to Los Angeles for Game 7. In The Forum, the North Stars dominated from start to finish, defeating the Kings 9-4 and vaulting themselves into the semifinals against the St. Louis Blues.

Although they failed to make it out of the first round, the first year was far from a failure. "You would have thought that these experts back east would have recognized the advantages in having depth of talent and would have picked my club and the Philadelphia club as the strongest," Cooke explained as the season came to a close.[54]

In their first season, the Kings showed that they were going to beat other teams using their depth – unlike the Original Six teams, who thrived on the strength of their superstars. The Kings had eight players with at least 25 points in the 1967-68 season, including four players with at least 18 goals. Twenty-four-year-old Bill Flett, chosen in the 18th round of the expansion draft from the Toronto Maple Leafs, led the team with 26 goals, while Eddie Joyal, 27, would lead the team with 57 points. Bill White would be the team's physical presence on the blueline, as he posted 100 penalty minutes, second only to Dave Amadio's 101 PIM in year one. White would also contribute 11 goals and 38 points from the back end.

In goal, Terry Sawchuk began the season as the starter, but a young 26-year-old named Wayne Rutledge would wind up playing 45 games for the Kings and posting fairly impressive numbers for an expansion team. He had a 20-18-4 record and posted a 2.87 goals against average in the Kings' inaugural season.

Off the ice, the Kings struggled a bit at the beginning of their season. Before moving into the Forum, the Kings averaged about 6,045 fans per game in 17 games. After building the Forum, however, their attendance swelled to an average of about 9,725 fans per game. Altogether, the Kings averaged about 8,034 fans per game in 37 home games for the season.

Like most expansion teams, the Kings made more money when an Original Six team came to town. In fact, the Kings averaged about 12,560 fans per game when playing against the Original Six teams in the Forum. However, including games played prior to the opening of the Forum, the Kings averaged about 9,289 fans per game when playing against Original Six teams. When comparing attendance to when the Kings played expansion teams, when they garnered an average of just

7,432 fans per game, indications were that there was potential fan interest, even if only in the stars of the league.

At the start of the 1968-69 campaign, the second season of expansion, the Kings experienced in-house problems between the coaching staff and management. "Things became sour with Kelly in the second season," McDonald continued. "[Cooke] barely spoke to Red. Barry Regan, the GM, didn't speak to the coach. He got into the habit of trading first round draft picks.

"When you look back, [the] whole theory was that you give up a future unknown talent for proven talent today. It just doesn't work that way in the NHL, and it was proven by [the Toronto Maple Leafs in 2010]. When Hal Laycoe came in, he was insistent that you don't trade the future. You don't trade a first round pick for anybody. And Cooke fought him and he took him to a room in Montreal the night before the draft, just hammering him. Finally Hal gave in and said, 'Alright Jack, you win.' But he never did the job in Los Angeles."

Regardless of off-ice problems, the team still had a fair amount of success on the ice. Joyal and Flett once again finished 1-2 in points on the team, with Joyal posting 52 and Flett compiling 49 points. They would also be 1-2 in goals, with 33 and 24, respectively. A new goaltender, Gerry Desjardins, was acquired from the Canadiens for two first round picks after Wayne Rutledge ran into trouble with the job. Desjardins would not fare much better, as he posted a pitiful 18-34-6 record with a 3.26 goals against average. Terry Sawchuk was moved back to Detroit for center Jimmy Peters, who would have a 25-point season.

Behind solid play from their skaters, the Kings managed to squeak into the playoffs with the last spot, fourth place. They finished with a mediocre 24-42-10 record, giving up 260 goals through the regular season. Adding to their woes, the Kings won just five road games all season, though they played strong at home, winning 19 games at The Forum. Nonetheless, they were able to qualify for the postseason and a date with the second-place Oakland Seals.

The Kings would upset the Seals in seven games, similar to the North Stars defeating the second-place Kings a year earlier. They would split the first six games, but the Kings would come out on top in Game 7 with a 5-3 score. In the semifinals, however, they would be eliminated in four games by the St. Louis Blues, who were headed to the final for the second consecutive year.

On the business side of the game, the Kings hit the 300,000 mark for attendance in just their second season. However, the Kings averaged only about 8,000 fans per game for the '68-69 season, which is consistent with the number from the first season.

After the antics which occurred during the franchise's second year with regards to Red Kelly and Jack Kent Cooke, Kelly left the organization to take a job with the Pittsburgh Penguins. Without Kelly, the Kings would falter, to say the least. Firing coach Hal Laycoe and bringing in Johnny Wilson as his replacement in the middle of the season would not help the Kings, as they fell to last place in the West Division with a 14-52-10 record. They went through the entire month of February without winning a game. The Kings struggled offensively, scoring just 168 goals all season. Their leading scorer, Ross Lonsberry, scored just 42 points in a 76-game season.

Gerry Desjardins would once again play the majority of the games in net, but new goaltender Denis DeJordy, acquired in exchange for Desjardins and others from Chicago, would lead the team by the end of the season with a 3.24 goals against average. Other players the Kings acquired included Eddie Shack from Boston, Dick Duff from Montreal, and Leon Rochefort from New York.

The Kings went 17 straight games without winning, a stretch spanning from January 29 to March 5, 1970. They had a 10-game winless streak in November and had two separate eight-game losing streaks, in January and February. For more than a month in the new year, they lost 11 consecutive road games. All season, they won just two games away from The Forum. In the seats, the Kings struggled mightily, surpassing the 10,000 mark for attendance just nine times in 38 home games – and never when an expansion team was in town.

In the first three years of expansion the Kings failed to make it to the final, yet Jack Kent Cooke continued to show the world his love of hockey. If you were not a hockey fan, Cooke would simply shove it down your throat to make sure you understood how important the Kings were to him. He believed the Kings could become the hottest ticket in town, which would only happen in 1988 when Wayne Gretzky was brought to the team – but by that point, Cooke was long gone from the hockey scene.

Regardless of superstars and winning traditions, Cooke knew how to promote his team. "We played a preseason game in St. Louis on a Saturday night," Jiggs McDonald explained. "He called on Saturday morning and we had to find a costume store to rent an Indian headdress, a French beret, and something that looks like jets on the blades of a player's skates. When the team arrived in Los Angeles the next day, those players had to come off the plane wearing these costumes. They got off the plane and there was a high school marching band welcoming them to Los Angeles. Cooke was a showman. He knew how to promote."

McDonald also explained that other funny stories happened throughout his time with the Kings, directly a result of Cooke's antics. "The night before the first game ever, they had a party at the Cooke residence. Mr. and Mrs. Cooke hosted the Kings and Lakers. All kinds of alcohol. There was nothing to eat – no sandwiches, no peanuts, not even a chip – there was lots of beer and lots of hard liquor. The next morning, everyone maybe got over served a little bit. Everyone was fine, except for our general manager and his wife. I guess she had a little too much. An actor walked by and she demanded that he sign an autograph for her. He didn't want to do it. She ended up throwing her salad at him – tons of beans everywhere. She was arrested for public mischief or something. That made headlines on opening day for the Kings."

Cooke was also a stern man who knew what he wanted made public and knew what he wanted to remain hidden from the media. At one point, during a Lakers game, he began feeling pain in his throat and his jaw. The pain continued to get worse and Cooke could not bear it anymore. He approached the Lakers team doctor and asked to be examined. The trainer, Robert Kerlan, examined him, then quietly, but quickly, called 9-1-1 and ordered an ambulance to be brought to The Forum as soon as possible. "You've had a coronary," said Kerlan to Cooke. Cooke jumped out of the chair he was laying on and immediately got angry and nervous – but not at his health condition. "Keep everyone away!" Cooke yelled. "Keep those bloody newspaper men out! And radio! And TV!" Not being surprised at Cooke's response to this, Kerlan simply exclaimed, "Jack, for God's sake, lie down and shut up."

Lastly, Cooke was a fan of superstars, especially since he was constantly competing with the glimmer of Hollywood in his backyard. He stunned the basketball world by acquiring NBA superstar Kareem Abdul-Jabbar for the Lakers. Just a few weeks later, he would go into Kings mode, trading defenseman Terry Harper and left wing Dan Maloney to the Red Wings for Marcel Dionne – an emerging superstar. Kings coach Bob Pulford was not a fan of the trade, as the team was already successful. But Cooke knew what he wanted, namely, higher attendance and better business for his precious Kings. Dionne indeed drew more fans and revenue for Cooke, who rewarded the superstar and future Hall of Famer with a $1.5 million contract through five years – an exorbitant sum for a player in those days.

As previously mentioned, Cooke was a stern man who knew what he wanted. In fact, he would often trump his general manager and make hockey decisions, including trades and signings, on his own, without consulting his coaching staff or hockey operations department. As Jiggs McDonald explained, "For trades, he would make calls with the other general manager or the other owner." This contributed to his frequent tensions with members of his organization and ultimately, firings and resignations.

However, it all came to an end as the '70s came to a close. The Kings were bought at the end of the 1979 season by Dr. Jerry Buss, a local real estate tycoon. Buss paid $67.5 million for the team – much more than the $2 million Cooke originally paid for it.

The Kings would later become fairly successful, especially after being bought by Bruce McNall in 1986. When he brought the legendary Wayne Gretzky to town, hockey shot to the top of the charts in Los Angeles for a short period of time. McNall was able to make hockey the hottest ticket in town, in addition to prodding the Kings toward the Stanley Cup final in 1993, the only final they would ever reach.

After stooping as low as bankruptcy court in 1995, the Kings were bought by local entrepreneur Phillip Anschultz and real estate investor Edward P. Roski, who currently own the team. Under their ownership, the Kings stayed under the radar for a while before moving to the Staples Center in downtown Los Angeles, where they currently play. The Kings made it back to the playoffs in 2009-10 after not having made it to the NHL's second season since before the 2004-05 lockout. However, they still have a hill to climb to return to the Stanley Cup final for the first time since 1993. With star players such as Anze Kopitar, Dustin Brown, Jack Johnson and Drew Doughty, the team is reaching a climax it hasn't enjoyed since the Gretzky and Dionne eras.

The tradition of business and on-ice success began with a dream, envisioned by Jack Kent Cooke one day in 1965. That day and that dream turned into one of the most successful of the six expansion teams in 1967 and one of the most storied teams in NHL history. Although the tradition seemed to dissipate for a number of years, it never completely disappeared, as is shown by the Kings' continued strong showings at the gate and on the ice in the new century.

Minnesota North Stars

1967-68 Statistics

	Pos	Ht	Wt	Age	GP	G	A	Pts	+/-	PIM
Wayne Connelly	C	5-10	170	28	74	35	21	56	-32	40
Ray Cullen	C	5-11	180	26	67	28	25	53	-24	18
Andre Boudrais	LW	5-8	165	24	74	18	35	53	-3	42
Dave Balon	LW	5-10	180	29	73	15	32	47	-10	84
Mike McMahon	D	5-11	180	26	74	14	33	47	-13	71
Parker MacDonald	C	5-11	180	34	69	19	23	42	-18	22
Bill Goldsworthy	RW	6-0	190	23	68	14	19	33	-8	68
J.P. Parise	LW	5-9	175	26	43	11	16	27	-10	27
Bob Woytowich	D	6-0	185	26	66	4	17	21	-23	63
Bill Collins	RW	6-1	178	24	71	9	11	20	-16	41
Milan Marcetta	C	6-0	195	31	36	4	13	17	-10	6
Bill Masterton	C	6-0	189	29	38	4	8	12	-4	4
Bob McCord	D	6-1	202	33	70	3	9	12	-10	39
Sandy Fitzpatrick	C	6-1	195	23	18	3	6	9	0	6
Ted Taylor	LW	6-0	175	25	31	3	5	8	-7	34
Bronco Horvath	C	5-11	185	37	14	1	6	7	-6	4
Moose Vasko	D	6-2	200	32	70	1	6	7	-36	45
Duke Harris	RW	5-10	180	25	22	1	4	5	-10	4
Murray Hall	RW	6-0	175	27	17	2	1	3	-7	10
Pete Goegan	D	6-1	195	33	46	1	2	3	-16	30
Bill Plager	D	5-9	175	22	32	0	2	2	-16	30

	Pos	Ht	Wt	Age	GP	W	L	T	GAA	SO
Cesare Maniago	G	6-3	195	29	52	22	16	9	2.77	6
Garry Bauman	G	5-11	175	27	26	4	13	5	3.47	0
Carl Wetzel	G	6-1	170	29	5	1	3	1	4.01	0

CHAPTER 8

Minnesota North Stars

FOR ALMOST AS LONG as hockey has existed in the United States, hockey has existed in the state of Minnesota. The traditions of the University of Minnesota, simply known as "The U," date back to the time of The Great Expansion. In fact, the yearly Mr. Hockey award is awarded to the best high school player in the state. But as popular as hockey was in the state, there was never an attempt to land an NHL team before The Great Expansion.

That all changed in 1966, when a partnership of nine men finally succeeded in bringing NHL hockey to the Twin Cities. The group, led by Walter Bush Jr. and John Driscoll, was awarded a franchise by the NHL to join the league in time for the 1967-68 season. They were formed on June 19, 1965, where they began their pledge to bring major league hockey to Minnesota.

Bush, a prominent lawyer in Minneapolis, was a part owner of the Minneapolis Bruins, a franchise in the Central Professional League. Among his eight partners, one of the men he teamed up with was Bob McNulty, a broadcaster who was popular in Minnesota. Another was Gordon Ritz, a former Yale hockey player and the owner of a construction company. Ritz would help build Minnesota's own hockey temple that would house the NHL squad for years.

The group's bid was one of two from Minnesota. Regardless of quantity, the media and other observers were very skeptical about

Minnesota's chances to land a team. The city was an extremely small television market, which did not bode well with the NHL trying to secure a major TV contract for the 1967-68 season. However, the NHL simply could not turn down a bid from one of the most hockey-rich cities in the United States. Ultimately, the bid from Walter Bush and Co. would prove to be more financially stable, resulting in the group's success.

The league's guidelines insisted that each new expansion team have a stadium that could seat at least 12,500 people. Minneapolis-St. Paul was devoid of that arena. The biggest arena in town was the St. Paul Auditorium, but it would only house 8,500 people at most – well under the league minimum. The only logical option was to build a new, state-of-the-art arena.

Members of the partnership began discussing the idea of a new arena with the Metropolitan Stadium Commission. They wanted an arena placed in Bloomington, a suburb between St. Paul and Minneapolis. In fact, the stadium would be placed directly across the street from the Metropolitan Stadium, where baseball's Minnesota Twins and football's Minnesota Vikings already played.

The commission finally agreed on constructing an arena that would seat 15,000 fans. The building's official name was the Metropolitan Sports Center, but to all involved, it was simply known as the Met Center. The stadium's construction cost about $7 million and was built in just 12 months – ready precisely on time for the team's home opener in October 1967.

The next move was to determine the name for the team. A contest was held throughout Minnesota to gather suggestions for the new NHL franchise. Suggestions included the Lumberjacks, the Norsemen, the Blades, the Mallards, the Puckaroos, the Voyageurs and the Muskies. It was decided to name the team the North Stars, based off a French phrase, "L'Etoile du Nord," meaning "The Star of the North" and based off the state's nickname, the North Star State.

Two groups of businessmen from St. Paul and Minneapolis also held contests to see who could sell the most season tickets. They marketed through the entire city and when they were finished, almost 6,000 season tickets were sold, which ranked the North Stars among the top of the expansion teams.

When the business was almost fully settled, it was time to prepare the on-ice, hockey side of the organization. The first piece of the puzzle was to hire a general manager and a coach. To kill two birds with one stone, the ownership group hired Wren Blair to serve as both. Blair became known for winning two Allan Cups with the Whitby Dunlops of Canada's OHA Senior League, in addition to winning a gold medal at the 1959 World Hockey Championships. However, Blair was most known for being the one who discovered and helped sign Bobby Orr while working for the Boston Bruins.

Blair was hired on May 25, 1966, with the expectation that he would scout the league for a year before expansion to determine which players would most benefit the North Stars in their maiden season. When the expansion draft ended in the summer of 1967, Blair and the North Stars had a team that was expected to finish in the middle of the standings. His strategy when drafting was to choose players who had great defensive strength and could prevent the Original Six clubs from wreaking havoc on offense. No players available through the expansion draft were talented enough to keep up with the likes of the Montreal Canadiens, so the only option was to stick with the idea that defense wins championships.

Ironically, though, the North Stars' first couple seasons were highlighted by their offense and their ability to score goals. Players like Dave Balon, Wayne Connelly and Bill Goldsworthy helped keep the North Stars in many games when the opposing players were throwing pucks past the defense. In net starred Cesare Maniago, who was known through the New York Rangers organization. He had played in the CPHL with the St. Paul Rangers and had a fair amount of success. On the North Stars, he would enjoy similar success early in his career.

When the season opened, the seats in the Met Center were still being installed. Nonetheless, on October 21, when the North Stars held their home opener, almost 13,000 fans attended. Present to witness the game was NHL president Clarence Campbell, who dropped the ceremonial first puck. The game, against the Oakland Seals, was exciting from start to finish, with Bill Goldsworthy scoring the first goal in North Stars history. Ultimately, the Seals fought back and the game ended in a 3-3 tie.

Although defense seemed to become more of a liability, according to the media, Blair was not worried about his team. In fact, Maniago was so sharp in net that he went 188 minutes and 38 seconds in December without letting up a goal. He was so good that midway through the season the North Stars were still fighting for first place, along with the Los Angeles Kings and the Philadelphia Flyers.

The inaugural season was marred, however, in a game against the Oakland Seals on January 13, 1968. Just four minutes into the game, North Stars center Bill Masterton was skating into the offensive zone just after he made a quick pass across the ice to Wayne Connelly. Just as he passed the puck, Oakland's Larry Cahan and Ron Harris ran into Masterton simultaneously. Masterton fell backwards, slamming his head onto the ice. The force of the impact caused his mouth and nose to begin gushing blood. Just before Masterton lost consciousness, he said to an oncoming teammate, "Never again, never again."

Unknown to the players at the time, it would be the last words Masterton would ever utter. He was transported to the emergency room, where doctors diagnosed him with a massive brain hemorrhage. Unable to perform surgery due to the severity of the injury, Masterton passed away just two days later. It was the first time in NHL history that a death occurred directly due to an on-ice event.

Masterton's number 19 was never worn by another North Stars player again, although it was not officially retired until 1987. However, the NHL honored his memory by creating the Bill Masterton Trophy, which is awarded annually to a player who best exhibits dedication, sportsmanship and perseverance in the game of hockey. Masterton was later inducted into the Manitoba Hockey Hall of Fame.

After the tragedy and for the duration of the season, the North Stars struggled with consistency. They tied their franchise opener with the St. Louis Blues, then lost the next two games, including a 6-0 thrashing at the hands of the Oakland Seals. It took them until game five to win their first game, in addition to winning the next one. They even had a four-game unbeaten streak that began on November 2. Unfortunately for them, they immediately fell victim to an eight-game winless streak that lasted until December.

For the remainder of the season, they had a four-game winning streak, then a five-game winless streak, a five-game unbeaten streak, then a four-game losing streak – all in a row. They continued their inconsistency with separate four- and three-game winning streaks at the end of January and the beginning of February. The end of their winning streak brought them back up to .500 for the season, but they immediately went on a streak in which they won just once in nine games in February. The season ended with two consecutive losses to the St. Louis Blues. The North Stars would finish 27-32-15, good for 69 points and fourth place. They would make the playoffs by just two points, but would also miss out on first place by just four points.

In the playoffs, the North Stars would upset the second place Los Angeles Kings in seven games. They were able to take the St. Louis Blues to seven games in the next round, but would ultimately lose. Nonetheless, the North Stars' first season was a success both on and off the ice.

Wayne Connelly led the team with 35 goals and 56 points. Mike McMahon, though, would be the team's anchor on the blueline, posting 47 points in 74 games. Cesare Maniago would share the net with Gary Bauman, but Maniago would lead the team with a 21-17-9 record, six shutouts and a 2.77 goals against average.

The North Stars' second season, however, was a complete disaster. Beginning the season 2-2 was the only bright spot of an otherwise awful season in which the North Stars finished dead last in the league. By New Year's Day in 1969, the team had garnered a pitiful 9-21-6 record for just 24 points through 36 games. They continued losing through the beginning of the calendar year, as they went on an eight-game losing streak, to complete a 14-game winless streak that lasted from December 22, 1968 to January 19, 1969.

The team managed a six-game unbeaten streak, but four of those games ended in ties. Their regular season schedule concluded with a six-game losing streak and a tie with the Los Angeles Kings to end their campaign. The team finished last in the league in goals against with 270, but managed to finish ninth of twelve teams with 189 goals scored, showing a continued strength on the offensive side of the puck.

Minnesota showed impressive depth down the middle, as six players compiled at least 30 points. Seven players ended up with at least 14 goals on the squad's 1968-69 roster. Unfortunately, no member of the team had a positive plus/minus rating, while left wing J.P. Parise was a team worst minus-44.

In goal, Cesare Maniago dropped in productivity, causing the North Stars to use two other goaltenders, Garry Bauman and Fern Rivard. However, neither Bauman nor Rivard could garner one victory throughout the season, so Maniago held down the fort. His final record was 18-34-10 with a 3.30 goals against average – respectable, but not incredible.

Coming back from their last-place season, the North Stars came out weak again in the 1969-70 season, starting with a 4-6 record through November 2. They went on a hot streak in December, bringing their record to 9-9-7, but a streak in December in which they tied and lost every other game for nine games dropped their record to 9-15-13. In fact, from December 11, 1969 to February 28, 1970, the North Stars won just one game.

When March came around, the North Stars were struggling, to say the least, with a 10-30-18 record. An 8-0 victory against the Maple Leafs on March 1 helped spark the team to a streak in which they lost just once in eight games. Although they only garnered one victory in the next six games, they ended the season with a four-game winning streak to make the playoffs, albeit in third place. Their final record: 19-35-22 and 60 points – just two points ahead of the fifth-place Philadelphia Flyers.

In the playoffs, the first place St. Louis Blues would take Minnesota to school, defeating them in six games to advance to the semifinals, en route to another Stanley Cup final berth.

The team continued to struggle on defense, finishing second-to-last in the league (11th) with 257 goals against. But they also finished in the top half of the league in goals for with 224. J.P. Parise had a breakout season, scoring 72 points in 72 games. Bill Goldsworthy also came into his own, as he led the team with 36 goals and posted 65 points. Their depth increased, as nine players compiled 30 points, and eight players scored at least 15 goals.

Cesare Maniago once again tended the net for the majority of the season, but posted a 9-24-16 record in 50 games – including a 3.39 goals against average. Wren Blair also obtained legendary goaltender Lorne "Gump" Worsley from the Montreal Canadiens. Worsley would succeed, albeit briefly, in Bloomington, posting a 5-1-1 record with an impressive 2.65 goals against average. Worsley had a goals against average under 3.00 in three of his last four seasons in Minnesota.

But that may have been one of the only bright spots for Minnesota as the 'eighties and 'nineties rolled around.

In 1978, the Cleveland Barons, formerly the California Golden Seals and the Oakland Seals, merged with the Minnesota North Stars. (Details of the merger from the Cleveland side can be found in Chapter 6 on the Oakland Seals). Some of the owners in the league did not agree with the decision to merge the two teams, but as Montreal GM Sam Pollock said, "Gentlemen, if you get one bag of shit and put it together with another bag of shit, all you get is a bigger bag of shit. Let 'em do it. It will solve a couple of problems for us."[55]

But through all the havoc of combining two teams, the North Stars still had to remain competitive. They believed they had something going and could possibly make a run for the Stanley Cup in the upcoming years. The rules of the merger, as stipulated by the NHL, stated that the North Stars could take 10 players and two goaltenders from the Barons' roster, while Minnesota would take the Barons' place in the Adams Division. In addition, Barons management would take over the daily running of the team, keeping the North Stars name and building.

As the GM, it was Lou Nanne's responsibility to cut the payroll. "Gunds said to me, 'You've got 65 players here under contract and $4.7 million in contracts. You've got to get it down to $2.2 million'," Nanne reminisced.

Nanne would indeed get to work, trading and buying out everyone he could. In the end of his work, he had moved almost 20 players and cut the team's payroll down to $2.5 million in salaries.

"I was feeling real good about cutting off $2 million in salaries and not losing any of the players we wanted," Nanne said. "But I'll never forget, Gordon said, 'So you've got another $300,000 to go.'

"Right then, I knew it was going to be like Harvard Business School working for these guys. It was tremendous experience to work for people like that, because it was an education in economics. It was all bottom line."[56]

The North Stars posted their best season ever in 1982-83, with a 40-24-16 record. But after the 1983-84 season, the North Stars would only finish above .500 once. This led to numerous problems on the ice, in the locker room, in the box office, and most importantly, in the city. In the North Stars' first six seasons, they drew over 3 million fans to the Met Center for their games – an average of more than 15,000 per game.

But in the mid-'eighties, the Gunds wanted to buy more property around the Met Center in order to build a shopping center. Owned by the Metropolitan Sports Facilities Commission, the area was ultimately sold to the group who eventually built the famous Mall of America in Minnesota.

The Gunds were not happy with the decision, determining that if they could not build more around the arena, they wanted to expand the Met Center by adding 40 new luxury suites. They also wanted to expand the arena's concourse, add a restaurant and build a ticket office at the front of the stadium in addition to the suites. The total cost of these improvements would be estimated at $15 million. This money was to be granted by the Commission and the city of Bloomington in a joint decision. The Gunds even promised that if the money were granted, they would sign a 20-year lease to stay in Bloomington. Neither the Commission nor Bloomington wanted to spend the taxpayers' money to upgrade the arena, so the Gunds' proposition was shot down.

Lou Nanne, then the GM of the North Stars, asked the Gunds to build just 20 suites, which would cost $3.5 million, a much more reasonable sum. After debating whether they could sell that many more suites, the Gunds agreed and the work was done. "We put in the 20 suites and we were very successful with them," said Nanne.

But the city of Bloomington was becoming annoyed with the North Stars, who constantly needed help from the taxpayers and the community to fund their operations. In fact, the Target Center, a new arena, was being built in downtown Minneapolis and the North Stars were being pressured to move their operations to the center of Minnesota. The Gunds didn't want to move from Bloomington, even if it were just downtown to Minneapolis. However, the Gunds continued asking Bloomington for money and the city simply kept rejecting their pleas.

"We might as well move to San Jose," the Gunds said. The idea of San Jose was brought up to the Gunds by Art Savage, one of their advisors. He believed that there was a high demand for an NHL team in California, especially since the Oakland franchise fell by the wayside. "The league is going to fight you if you if you try to leave and you might not win," said Nanne. "I know we can win the case," explained Gordon Ritz. "Well, you're going to spend a lot of money and it's going to be a lot of hassle," Nanne continued. "If…we can get an expansion buyer, then you're home free."

Luckily for the North Stars, NHL president John Ziegler and Chicago Blackhawks owner Bill Wirtz – a member of the Board of Governors – agreed with the idea. Their proposal was that the North Stars would be sold for $32 million, every penny of which would go to the Gunds. The new owners would then pay $50 million as a franchise fee to move to San Jose.

American entrepreneur Howard Baldwin would eventually purchase a share of the North Stars from the Gunds, but he would also ask Lou Nanne to stay with the team. Nanne was planning on leaving the industry to get into the money management market. But Baldwin was able to convince Nanne to stick with the organization for a while longer and help him run the team.

One of the first things that occurred with Baldwin in the driver's seat was to meet with Tony Tavares. Tavares worked for Spectacor, an arena management business located in Philadelphia (Spectacor would eventually team up with Comcast to own the Flyers). Nanne was to meet with Tavares, Marv Wolfenson and Harvey Ratner – all part owners of the NBA's Minnesota Timberwolves – the next morning to figure out a plan to move downtown.

"How about the dasher boards?" asked Nanne. Wolfenson didn't understand. "We get significant revenue from advertising on the dasher boards and we want that money…we also need the right to sell the space to whoever we want." "There's no way," Wolfenson said. "You have to sell it to the sponsors we have in the building. I'm not allowing someone else in." "That's OK, provided they buy the dasher boards," Nanne continued. "But say you have Coke and I have Pepsi, you have Burger King and I have McDonald's. When we sell our packages to TV, their cameras shoot the boards along with the action, so we sell the advertiser on the fact that he's getting exposure from the television package in addition to the rink. If you guys don't take the boards, I have to have the right to sell them to my advertisers."[57]

Timberwolves CEO Bob Stein agreed, but Wolfenson could not concede this right to Nanne and his team. The group could never agree on a proposal for how to sell ad space on the dasher boards, so Nanne walked out, as did the North Stars, on the possibility of moving downtown to the Target Center.

In 1990, shopping mall developer Norm Green took over the majority ownership of the team, while Lou Nanne still remained a part of the team's operations. Green had similar ideas to those of the Gunds, including requesting permission from Bloomington to build shops between the Met Center and the Mall of America, extending the concourse of the Met Center and adding suites to the arena. Every idea Green presented was shot down by the city of Bloomington, yet again.

Green continued to become annoyed with the city of Bloomington and knowing that a move downtown was not financially possible, he began to believe that the only way to keep the franchise alive and keep his pockets full was to relocate to another city. "Some people thought it was a personal problem he was going through," said Lou Nanne, "But it was strictly a financial decision."[58]

The first hint that Green wanted to change the image of the North Stars and possibly relocate the team was when he decided to redesign the North Stars' jersey and logo. The logo had recently been voted as one of the best hockey logos of all time, but the starred "N" on the jersey did not make Minnesota's franchise too attractive to other markets – and if they moved, Green surely couldn't take that logo with him.

Switching up the logo seemed to be a test for Green, in order to determine if another city might be interested in housing the North Stars in the near future. His new jersey had some black in it – as fans seemed to gravitate toward black jerseys – and the logo simply said, "Stars," completely ignoring the "North" aspect of the team's name. Nanne believed the "Stars" logo should have been used only as an alternate jersey, but it became the team's full time logo.

In January, 1993, Pat Forciea, who worked for the North Stars, wanted to gauge the fans' opinions on what the North Stars should do. He sent out this letter to all of their season ticket holders:

To North Stars Season Ticket Holders,

As I write this letter, a number of proposals concerning the North Stars are under consideration. The options are being evaluated and the numbers are being crunched, but even the best financial analysis won't tell us what is on the minds of our most valuable asset: the season ticket holders of this franchise. If we are to find the wherewithal to support and nourish championship NHL hockey in Minnesota, it's critical that we have a sense of which solution our most important customers will support.

To be sure, there have been 5,300 of you this year who have supported North Stars hockey at the Met. More than a few have suggested that a seat at the Met Center is the seat of choice for viewing our games. We agree it's a wonderful facility, but it will be difficult for hockey to survive with the limits the Met places on us--a building where the franchise has suffered three years of crippling financial losses. We have made it clear to the City of Bloomington that we need an additional 2,000 seats and a physical link with the Mall. The City of Bloomington has responded--or more accurately—not responded, by demonstrating they have no interest in helping us find a way to stay at the Met Center.

The City of St. Paul currently has two proposals on the table--one of which would involve playing all of our games at the Civic Center and the other would involve playing a portion of our schedule there. While the St. Paul proposals don't address all of the concerns we have about our future, the city's sincere, community-wide effort will certainly have an impact on any decision we eventually make.

We are complimented and grateful for that major undertaking. If this were an emotional decision, it would be an easy call, but we don't have that luxury. We need to investigate St. Paul's demonstrated emotional strength to see if it can be translated into sufficient financial support to make the economics of a move to the Civic Center work.

Clearly, we need to find a situation that solidifies our long-term future in the state. The economics of the game have changed throughout the league and at the Minnesota North

Stars. We have the sixth highest salary outlay of any franchise in the NHL. Among other changes we need to make for next year, our ticket prices need to be adjusted to prices that are competitive with other NHL markets our size.

There have been indications that the current situation at Target Center may create a one-time opportunity to give Bob Gainey the kind of resources he needs to build one of the best teams in the NHL. Norman Green has made it very clear throughout his tenure here that his defining interest lies in fielding the best possible team. We need to find a way to make the numbers support that goal and the answer may lie in finding a way to play in downtown Minneapolis.

The dialogue between the Target Center, the city and the Minnesota North Stars has been thoughtful and sincere. The increased opportunity of corporate partnerships, more luxury boxes and an additional 2,000 seats means the downtown proposal must be looked at seriously. But the question still remains whether you would be willing to occupy one of those seats.

It's important to mention that regardless of where we end up next year, our current season ticket holders will have first choice of seats for the North Stars season. We have been in the hockey business long enough to know that if we don't take the interest of our best customers to heart, the building we play in won't make much difference. The North Stars are looking for your feedback as directly as we can. Please help us create a future you'd like to be part of by filling out the enclosed reply card.

Sincerest Regards,

Pat Forciea

Minnesota North Stars[59]

Fans voted for various venues to house the North Stars, but no decision was made. Ultimately, the team moved to Dallas in 1993, becoming the Dallas Stars. Coincidentally, the logo created by Norm Green was much easier to transfer to Dallas when they moved, proving his idea correct when he wanted to make the North Stars more attractive to potential lucrative hockey markets.

Minnesota North Stars hockey ended in April 1993 as the North Stars lost 5-3 in the final game at the Met Center and the final game in North Stars history. Al Shaver, the team's broadcaster, made the famous final call:

"It's Ludwig, giving it to Dahlen…4, 3, 2, 1…and it's all over. The Stars lose it here, 5-3, and now it's pack-'em up time and on to Dallas. We wish them good luck. And to all the North Stars over the past 26 years, we say thank you, all of you, for so much fine entertainment.

"It's been a pleasure knowing you, Minnesota's loss is definitely a gain for Dallas – and a big one. We thank you, though, from the bottom of our hearts, for all the wonderful nights at the Met Center, when you've given us so much entertainment and you've been such a credit to the community in which you played. We will still remember you as the Minnesota North Stars. Good night, everybody. And goodbye."[60]

As the Minnesota North Stars failed, North Stars booster club president Julie Hammond explained that when Norm Green arrived in Minnesota, he said, "Only an idiot could lose money on hockey in Minnesota."

"Well," Hammond concluded, "I guess he proved that point."[61]

Philadelphia Flyers

1967-68 Statistics

	Pos	Ht	Wt	Age	GP	G	A	Pts	+/-	PIM
Lou Angotti	C	5-9	170	30	70	12	37	49	4	35
Gary Dornhoefer	RW	6-1	190	24	65	13	30	43	6	134
Leon Rochefort	RW	6-0	185	28	74	21	21	42	-1	16
Ed Hoekstra	C	5-11	170	30	70	15	21	36	6	6
Brit Selby	LW	5-10	175	22	56	15	15	30	-3	24
Bill Sutherland	C	5-10	160	33	60	20	9	29	1	6
Don Blackburn	LW	6-0	190	29	67	9	20	29	-2	23
Forbes Kennedy	C	5-8	150	32	73	10	18	28	4	130
Pat Hannigan	LW	5-10	183	31	65	11	15	26	6	36
Claude Laforge	LW	5-9	172	31	63	9	16	25	8	36
John Miszuk	D	6-1	192	27	74	5	17	22	1	79
Joe Watson	D	5-10	185	24	73	5	14	19	12	56
Ed Van Impe	D	5-10	205	27	67	4	13	17	-5	141
Andre Lacroix	C	5-8	175	22	18	6	8	14	0	6
Garry Peters	C	5-10	185	25	31	7	5	12	-2	22
Jean Gauthier	D	6-1	190	30	65	5	7	12	0	74
Larry Zeidel	D	5-11	185	39	57	1	10	11	12	68
Wayne Hicks	RW	5-11	185	30	32	2	7	9	-5	6
Art Stratton	C	5-11	170	32	12	0	4	4	-4	4

	Pos	Ht	Wt	Age	GP	W	L	T	GAA	SO
Bernie Parent	G	5-10	180	22	38	16	17	5	2.48	4
Doug Favell	G	5-10	172	22	37	15	15	6	2.27	4

CHAPTER 9

Philadelphia Flyers

"In any great drama, you need heroes and villains.
The Flyers are both."
– Liev Schreiber, *Broad Street Bullies (HBO Special)*

ACCORDING TO ESPN AND Forbes magazine, the Philadelphia Flyers
are the highest-ranked 1967 expansion franchise in terms of value – and
the third highest in the NHL with a net worth of over $262 million as
of 2009. The closest 1967 expansion franchise to the Flyers is the St.
Louis Blues, with a current value of about $148 million.

And to think – the Flyers almost didn't get awarded an NHL team
in 1966.

Their history of hockey at all levels was very poor and the chances
that the NHL would look highly upon the city for arguably the league's
biggest decision in history were grim.

Philadelphia's first shot at NHL hockey was in 1930, after the
Pittsburgh Pirates began having financial difficulties. Just one year
after receiving the NHL franchise in 1925, Pittsburgh became rampant
with rumors that the team was going to relocate, with Cleveland and
Philadelphia as the potential markets. The final rumor in 1930 was
that the team would move to Atlantic City as a temporary fix while
Cleveland prepared an NHL arena. But when it appeared that this
plan would not come to fruition, Philadelphia was granted control of
the Pirates.

The new team would be named the Quakers and would play their games at the Philadelphia Arena, a 10-year-old, terribly inadequate home. It sat just 6,000 fans, though the team rarely filled it. Just ten days into their inaugural NHL season, the Quakers looked like they were doomed to the same fate as the Pirates. "The Philly hosts look like the weakest force in the circuit on paper," said Leonard Cohen of the *New York Post* at the time. "They're every bit of that on the ice."

"We must make a good start and I will spare no expense to give the fans what they want," said Quakers owner Benny Leonard. "We have other deals in mind which will be consumed if the men we have now fail to deliver." Leonard continued a couple days later, saying, "Once you see them in action, you will say they have the goods. I feel certain Philadelphia hockey fans will like the men who will represent this city in the National League. I want to produce a winning club."[62]

The Quakers averaged just 2,500 fans per night at the decrepit Philadelphia Arena. In January 1931, rumors already started that the team was going to relocate, just one year after coming to Philadelphia. When the Quakers finished the season 4-36-3, it gave them an NHL record for fewest wins and lowest winning percentage in a season (.136). The latter held for over 40 years, until the 1974-75 Washington Capitals posted a .131 percentage, while the former record still stands today.

Prior to the start of the 1931-32 season, the NHL cut ties with the Quakers and suspended the organization for one year, with the apparent intent of relocating them back to Pittsburgh one season later. However, after suspending them annually for five more years, the league officially announced that the franchise would not be brought back to the NHL circuit. NHL hockey in Philadelphia had died, with no apparent hope of coming back to life.

The city held claim to numerous minor-pro and junior hockey teams for the next 30 years, none of which had tremendous success. The Canadian-American Hockey League's Philadelphia Arrows existed from 1927 to 1935, without ever making much noise in the league standings. The Philadelphia Comets of the Tri-State Hockey League existed for just four months between 1932 and 1933, but failed to win a single game in 16 contests.

The Arrows of the Can-Am League were renamed the Ramblers for the 1935-36 season and immediately took over the league, winning the Frank Fontaine Cup as champions that year. They existed until the

1941-42 season, at which time the Philadelphia Falcons were formed and joined the Eastern Amateur Hockey League in 1942. Due to World War II and the folding of every other hockey team in the city, the Falcons were the only major hockey team left in Philadelphia at that time.

But the Falcons wound up folding as well in 1946, giving way to the next Philadelphia hockey team, the American Hockey League's Philadelphia Rockets. This team was even worse than the Quakers, finishing 5-52-7 for a .133 winning percentage. The team would cease operations in 1949. The Falcons came back for one season in 1951-52, but would close shop once again at the conclusion of the campaign. The Philadelphia Ramblers were reborn in 1955, this time in the Eastern Hockey League. The team had more success than any prior Philadelphia hockey team, as they lasted nine years until they folded after the 1963-64 season.

With the end of the Ramblers came the end of Philadelphia hockey – at least for a few years. But when the 1964 season ended, no one could have guessed that the next hockey team in Philadelphia would be one of the most successful in NHL history.

Ed Snider's parents owned a grocery-store chain that had great success in Washington DC. After he graduated from the University of Maryland, Snider became a partner with Edge Ltd, a successful Philadelphia record company. The young man made a great deal of money in the record business. Snider, along with brother-in-law Earl Foreman and builder Jerry Wolman, bought shares in the Philadelphia Eagles football club – Snider owned seven percent of the team and acted as the organization's treasurer. To do so, he moved from Washington to Philadelphia.

One night while having a cocktail with Juggy Gayles, a sales manager for Carlton Records, Gayles relayed some information that confused Snider a bit. "Look, I've got an extra ticket to the Garden tonight, the Rangers are playing Montreal," his friend explained. "What's that all about?" replied Snider. "It's a National Hockey League game," his friend said. "Would you like to go with me?"

Snider fell in love with the game immediately. But more importantly, it was the play of Rangers goaltender Gump Worsley that caught Snider's attention. "Maybe it was the fact that he didn't look like an athlete or that he wasn't wearing a mask, I'm not sure," Snider later explained. "But I know I was fascinated[63]…It was, without question, the greatest spectator sport I had ever seen." [64]

Snider had no idea that the NHL was planning to add six teams to their league or he would have acted immediately. "There was nothing in the Philadelphia papers about the NHL's plans for expansion," said Snider. "As far as the papers here, the NHL didn't even exist."

When Snider's banker and buddy Bill Putnam came to say he was leaving to move to Los Angeles, Snider was shocked. "He said, 'I'm going to work for Jack Cooke on the coast…Jack owns the Lakers and he has a piece of the Redskins and all of these sports properties'," Snider recalled Putnam saying. "'He's going to try to get a franchise…in the National Hockey League'."[65]

Later that year, Snider was in Boston watching the Celtics play the Philadelphia 76ers in an NBA game. When he exited the arena after the game's completion, he saw hundreds of people lined up at the box office. When he asked his friend what the people were waiting for, the friend responded that they were trying to buy tickets for the Boston Bruins. "Are they in the playoffs or something?" Snider asked his friend. "Oh, no, they're in last place," the friend responded. "They put 1,000 tickets on sale on game day. Those are the only tickets you can get."

"The game in New York and that Boston ticket line left an indelible impression," Snider said years later.[66]

In March 1965, when the NHL was preparing to accept applications from around the continent for six additions to the league, Snider's old buddy Bill Putnam was helping Jack Kent Cooke develop a bid for an NHL squad to appear in Los Angeles by 1967. Putnam became friends with Cooke while working at JP Morgan. Cooke came to Putnam to help him buy out his partner at the Washington Redskins in an attempt to become the majority owner. When that plan failed, Putnam helped Cooke purchase the Los Angeles Lakers. After Cooke informed him of the attempt to land an NHL team, Putnam was intrigued. "I decided sports was more fun than banking," Putnam said.[67]

When Putnam informed Snider of his happenings and that numerous professional hockey teams were for sale to be added to the NHL, Snider ruminated for a bit and approached Wolman, his partner at the Eagles, and asked whether they should apply for an NHL squad and build an arena. When Wolman agreed with the idea, Snider was ecstatic. "With his reputation as a developer and entrepreneur and my ideas, we went forward," Snider remembered. "It became my project."[68]

"I was scared to death that it might not [succeed]," Snider said in an interview with the author. "It was a combination of applying for the hockey club and building the Spectrum – building an arena for both hockey and basketball. I felt confident that the combination would be a success."

Snider immediately got in contact with Bill Jennings, who headed the expansion committee and owned the New York Rangers. After asking what Philadelphia's chances would be if they applied for a team, Jennings acknowledged that they were then the fourth-largest market in the United States. However, he could not get over the fact that Philadelphia's history of hockey was extremely weak. Snider insisted that Philadelphia would be a great town for the sport and that the fans would never turn their back on a major league team once it showed up. After a lengthy conversation, Snider agreed to apply for the team and paid a $10,000 application fee on the condition that the bid would remain a secret.

"We didn't want competition," Snider explained. "There must have been ten groups that had expressed interest in the Eagles when Wolman bought them, driving up the price. I knew Cooke…already had competition for the L.A. franchise…Nobody else in Philadelphia seemed to be aware that the NHL was even expanding. That's the way I wanted to keep it."[69]

The potential ownership group went to various banks to secure the funds necessary to buy a new franchise. "None of them were interested," said Lou Scheinfeld, then the Vice President of the ownership group. "What is it, soccer?" the banks asked. When they were informed it would be a hockey team, they responded, "Hockey will never go over in Philadelphia." But the group finally found a bank willing to help – the last one they visited. The bank's vice president had played hockey and decided to support the ownership group in their bid to land a major league franchise in the City of Brotherly Love.[70]

"I went to the head of city council…Paul Dortona…and he loved the idea. He took me right in to see Mayor Tate," said Snider.[71] "I knew where to build [the arena] because I was involved in the development of the stadium for the Phillies and the Eagles. I told the mayor we would pluck it right there in the parking lot and it would be added revenues to the complex…Mayor Tate loved the idea. He called the city solicitor and the city finance director and right on the spot, he said, 'Let's get the legal work done and figure out the finance work'."

After discussing the idea with the Mayor and the other heads of the city, Snider requested that the mayor call and send a letter to both Clarence Campbell and Bill Jennings to explain what Snider had done and to ensure that Philadelphia was a viable city for expansion. "He did that while I was sitting there," Snider said.[72]

The ownership group was a long shot among every other city applying for a team. In addition, Philadelphia was hardly on the NHL's radar after what happened last time the city was granted entrance into the prestigious league. The group was adamant, though and they continued to work towards securing the league's choice. Snider, realizing that with the amount of work he had with the potential hockey team and the work he already had with the Eagles, called on Bill Putnam to come back to Philadelphia to work with the hockey team. "He told me that the job with Cooke was not working out the way he thought it would," said Snider. "I told him I had the perfect opportunity for him."

Putnam became the president of Philadelphia Hockey Team, Inc. (the name of the group vying for this NHL bid). Putnam, along with Jerry Schiff, Wolman and Snider, owned 91% of the team (Putnam owned 25%, while Schiff, Wolman and Snider each owned 22%) and numerous other investors held the other 9%.

The job duties were divided up as such: Wolman was in charge of financing and constructing the new sports arena. Snider made sure the project continued progressing through the city's higher-ups. Putnam followed up on the team's application and kept in contact with the men atop the NHL.

The group sent a brochure to the NHL advertising Philadelphia as a potential hockey town, according to Jay Greenberg in *Full Spectrum*. "On the cover was a picture of a hockey player in a red and grey uniform, with a yellow Liberty Bell in a circle on the front of the jersey," Greenberg writes. "Entitled 'The NHL in Philadelphia,' it blamed the city's past hockey failures on the poor facilities. The brochure emphasized the area's 5.5- million population and the base of established spectator support for the other major league teams."[73]

But after Wolman and Putnam presented the blueprints for the arena, in addition to their bid for the league, Putnam recalls a less-than-excited reaction from the NHL Board of Governors. "I remember Norris pounding his fist on the table and saying, 'Philadelphia is a lousy sports town'." Putnam said. "But they did seem impressed with the arena proposal. I was hopeful, but I wouldn't say I was optimistic."[74] Putnam was so sure the bid would fail, he remembers telling his wife on February 9th that when Bill Jennings called, he would once again be out of business. But when the phone rang, the voice on the other line simply said, "You're in."

Snider believed Philadelphia would love hockey as much as he did. "I just had this belief that if you're a regular guy and know what regular guys like, you can't be wrong," he explained.[75] Within an hour of the announcement that Philadelphia was getting a franchise, the Eagles' receptionist began getting calls from fans interested in buying season tickets for the new hockey team.

After being granted the franchise, the next step was to present the expansion fee of $2 million in cash to the league. It was to be done on the same day, June 30, by every member of the new division as their ticket into the NHL. Wolman and Schiff both withdrew from the team's bid, which left Snider with a 60% share of the team and beer executive Joe Scott (who bought into the team) with 15%. Bill Putnam, still serving as the team's president, owned a 25% share of the team. This left Snider basically on his own to get the money, quite a task for the budding entrepreneur.

Snider already had remortgaged his house and borrowed $75,000 from two banks in order to pay Wolman and Schiff for their shares of the team, leaving him few other options to raise the extra money needed for the expansion fee. Half of the fee was coming from a loan from Fidelity Bank, while Wolman promised to provide the other half. When Wolman began having financial problems and backed out, the group was in trouble. "It was seven to ten days before the money was due that Jerry told me he didn't have it," Snider recalled.[76]

Together, Snider and Putnam sold three years of broadcast rights for $350,000 and borrowed $150,000 from friends. They still were $500,000 short and their luck was running out. Banks were rejecting their loan requests and they had already borrowed from all the friends they could find. Saturday, June 3 came, with the money still missing. The check was due in Montreal on Monday. Snider had a call in to associate Bill Fishman, president of ARA Services, a Philadelphia-based service management company. Fishman needed to use his personal stock in the company as collateral for a loan and needed to wait until Monday to get a response from Provident Bank, from whom he requested the money. "I didn't wait," Snider said. "I called [Provident executive] Roger Hillas at home. I got him off his lawn mower. He came to the phone and said he would do it."[77]

The money was set and the due date was upon them. Snider was at the bank, ready to wire the money to Montreal, when the lights in the bank went out. The power was out in a 15,000-square-mile area stretching from New Jersey to Maryland and as far west as Harrisburg, Pennsylvania. Snider was completely stunned and unable to get the money to Clarence Campbell and the NHL owners. "Putnam was up there in his [Montreal] hotel room dying," Snider recalled. "He can't get in touch with me or anybody...I was thinking that after all we'd been through, they were going to give the franchise to somebody else."[78]

Somehow, word got to Bill Jennings about the power outage, so the owners waited, albeit impatiently, for a check from Philadelphia to appear before them. When the power was restored near midday, Snider wired the money through New York and to the Royal Bank of Canada to Scheinfeld and Putnam. The duo went into the meeting room where Clarence Campbell was waiting, expecting an ecstatic, smiling president. "I still remember Clarence Campbell sitting there with this dour look on his face saying, 'Do you have the check'?" Scheinfeld remembers. "He didn't say 'welcome' or 'happy to have you' or 'congratulations' or anything."

"He didn't even say thank you," Putnam says. Then Toronto Maple Leafs owner Stafford Smythe, the recipient of the check, piped up and chortled, "The way this thing has gone, this will probably bounce."[79]

"The whole history of how this franchise started is amazing," Snider said years later with a smile.[80]

Giving the new sports arena a name was the next step in the line of the Philadelphia hockey club. Lou Scheinfeld recalls someone bringing up the word "Spectrum," to his intrigue. "For the presentation to Snider," he said, "We worked out this thing that the *SP* would stand for sports, the *E* for entertainment, *C* for concerts and circuses, *T* for theatrics, *R* for recreation and relaxation and *UM* for auditorium, stadium, etc."[81]

The next move was to begin piecing together the hockey operations side of the organization and putting a successful product on the ice. Snider hired Keith Allen as the team's first head coach and Bud Poile as the club's first general manager. The two would scout the league for an entire year prior to the expansion draft. Snider would further help the team by purchasing the Quebec Aces, giving the Flyers rights to numerous minor league players that would eventually contribute at the major league level.

The players the Flyers drafted proved to be some of the best available – Bernie Parent, Gary Dornhoefer, Joe Watson, Ed Van Impe and more. But those players weren't so happy to be drafted at the time. "Talk about disappointment," said Watson. "I had to look on the map to see where the heck this Philadelphia was," said Dornhoefer. "Playing for an expansion team didn't really thrill me," expressed Van Impe.

The fans didn't seem too thrilled either. The city held a parade for the team and drove them from City Hall, down Broad Street, to the Spectrum. But the only problem was that no one showed up. "You'll be in Baltimore by Christmas," yelled one fan as the team sat through a summertime drive through inner city Philadelphia.

Contrary to what fans and the experts had predicted, the Flyers' first season was extremely successful. "I never had any doubts that we'd have a very fine club," said Putnam. "I knew right from the time we first put a team together at the draft meeting in Montreal last June."[82]

Toward the end of the season, though, a piece of the roof blew off the Spectrum. The team had to go on the road for the last few weeks of the season, losing the revenue from ticket sales. To make matters worse, they had to refund the fans' money, "which I didn't have," confessed Snider. In fact, reports stated the Flyers lost over $400,000 because of the accident. But the banks, knowing Snider's great history of financial success, gave him the money he needed, while the insurance company reluctantly paid for the cost of repairing the roof.[83]

Nonetheless, the team was the first to claim the title in the newly formed West Division. They played the third place Blues in the first round of the playoffs. Though they played in front of almost sellout crowds, the team couldn't seem to withstand St. Louis' rough-and-tumble style of play, mixed with strong defense and incredible goaltending. The Flyers ultimately bowed out in seven games, while the Blues went on to face off against the Montreal Canadiens in the Stanley Cup Final.

In their second season, the Flyers faltered for the majority of the regular season, despite having stellar play from goaltender Bernie Parent. Going 1-5-2 in October and compiling a combined seven wins from December to the end of February, the Flyers looked destined to miss the playoffs for the first time, but a 7-2-5 record in March, including going undefeated at home, led them into the postseason with a third place finish. They would once again face the Blues, who had finished in first place this time around.

But the Blues swept the Flyers in four games, dominating from start to finish. The Flyers simply couldn't keep up with St. Louis' combination of speed, grit and all-around talent. They were intimidated from the start and Snider was not a happy camper. He instructed Bud Poile to trade for, sign and draft tough, gritty players that could beat up on their opponents. "We realized that we would have to become tougher, stronger and bigger," said Snider. "We may not be able to win a lot of games as we're growing, but we certainly didn't have to get beat up. So we decided that no team would ever intimidate us ever again."[84]

One of the players that Poile acquired was a young kid named Bobby Clarke, who was drafted in the second round in the 1969 NHL Amateur Draft. Clarke was an extremely talented player from the Flin Flon Bombers, yet there were questions about his NHL longevity due to his diabetes. But the Flyers were not actually the only team desiring his services. After selecting Clarke, another team came to the Flyers and offered a couple players for Clarke, to which Poile responded, "No way."

Though the Flyers missed the playoffs in the 1969-70 season, they returned to the postseason in the '70-71 season, being swept by the more dominant Original Six team, the Chicago Blackhawks, in the first round. Goaltender Bernie Parent was moved to Toronto in late January, while the Flyers acquired Rick MacLeish from the Boston Bruins – one of the big pieces that would launch the Flyers to glory just a few years later. In that summer's amateur draft, the Flyers were able to pick up Bill Clement and Bob Kelly, two players that would play pivotal roles in the Flyers' "Bad Boys" image.

The last piece of the puzzle was hiring Fred Shero as the head coach. Shero, known by many as "The Fog," brought the team together and installed a Russian style of play that he studied for years. This style called for puck possession, crisscrossing forwards, cycling the puck in the offensive zone and transitioning into numerous odd-man rushes up the ice. Mixed with their intimidation method, the style allowed the Flyers to succeed. Even though they missed the playoffs in 1971-72, the next season proved to be the breakout year for the fledgling franchise.

The team fought its way to 37 wins, good for second place in the West Division behind the Chicago Blackhawks (the divisions were realigned after the league expanded in 1970). They advanced to the semifinals for the first time in franchise history after defeating the Minnesota North Stars 4-2. But the team fell to the Montreal Canadiens, who would go on to win the Stanley Cup.

Nonetheless, the stage was set. The Philadelphia Flyers were tough and had a new nickname to go along with their style of play: "The Broad Street Bullies". Five of their players had over 150 PIM in the 1972-73 season, while both Clarke and MacLeish reached the 100-point scoring plateau. Clarke was awarded the Hart Memorial Trophy as the league MVP – the first expansion player to have achieved this honor.

"Keith Allen and Mr. Snider…went out and drafted [Dave] Schultz, [Don] Saleski and [Andre] Dupont," said Clarke. "All of us were tough. We were tough enough to play physically with these other teams. In those days, you could intimidate the other teams. Once we did that, our skill players could go out there and play. We got [Bill] Barber and MacLeish and suddenly we were a great team."[85]

Reacquired in a trade, goaltender Bernie Parent returned to Philadelphia in order to lead them to the Stanley Cup that fans believed was awaiting them at the end of May. Reporters and opposing fans were concerned that the team was simply a bunch of goons who were incapable of playing smart, efficient hockey. But Coach Shero explained their style of play. "We have no Rocket Richards on this team," he said. "Hitting is our game. Besides, eighteen choirboys never won the Stanley Cup."[86]

"In the past, when I've seen violence occur in concentrated doses, it's been a club policy," said NHL President Clarence Campbell. "Either conscious or a matter of toleration. There have been times when this police-type operation has been deemed successful. Obviously, nobody on the Philadelphia club is trying to stop it. The Flyers are an attractive team with some very outstanding players. They may intimidate a weak opponent, but they'll never intimidate a strong one."[87]

In fact, Campbell was spot on. Though they finished with a 50-16-12 record and won the West Division, their opponents in the Stanley Cup Final were the Boston Bruins – a team they historically had trouble beating. The Flyers hadn't even won a game in Boston in six years. With Boston having home advantage, the Flyers had to win at least one game in Boston Garden to have a chance to claim the Cup.

Behind Jack Adams-winning coach Shero and Vezina Trophy-winning Bernie Parent, the Flyers rallied in Boston from a Game 1 loss, as captain Bobby Clarke scored in overtime of Game 2 to even the series. The Flyers won the next two contests in Philadelphia with Parent playing two stellar games, giving up a total of just three goals in those two games. Game 5 was a rout in which the Bruins scored five goals, but when they returned to Philadelphia for Game 6, the Flyers' good luck charm was in the house.

Legendary singer Kate Smith – whose recorded rendition of "God Bless America" became a good luck charm in Philadelphia – made a surprise personal appearance at the Spectrum to serenade the crowd before the puck was dropped. The crowd went nuts, and the Flyers responded, coming out to an early 1-0 lead in front of a sold-out crowd of over 17,000 fans. After Parent shut down the Boston Bruins for three straight periods, the Flyers held on to defeat Boston 1-0 to clinch the series, with Hall of Fame announcer Gene Hart screaming his famous line, "Ladies and gentlemen, the Flyers are going to win the Stanley Cup! The Flyers win the Stanley Cup! The Flyers win the Stanley Cup! The Flyers have won the Stanley Cup!"

With a league MVP, a top coach, a top goalie, a committed owner and a great supporting cast, the Flyers went from expansion franchise to NHL Champion in just seven short years. Though the media had various explanations as to how the Flyers rose to glory, Ed Snider believes he knows the true cause of their success. "Seven of our players from that [expansion] draft played on our Stanley Cup team," he explained. "Usually, in an expansion draft, once you become successful, the players you got in that draft are mostly gone. But our guys played a major role in our winning the Cup."[88]

Montreal Canadiens Hall of Fame goaltender Ken Dryden has his theory as to why the team succeeded as well. "The Flyers figured out the system, played it to cynical perfection and won," Dryden wrote in his book, *The Game*. "Penalized more than anyone else but far less than they might be, with the league as unintended co-conspirator, they benefited hugely from the informal penalty ceiling and the league's commitment not to appear to intervene in a game's outcome."[89]

The league did not believe the Flyers were truly the best team and others called the champions frauds, because as many pointed out, it takes more than just seven years to build a championship team from nothing. The team did not mind, though. Instead, they took it as a challenge. After acquiring Reggie Leach from California, the team went on another run and defeated the Buffalo Sabres in the first Stanley Cup Final since 1926 to feature two post-1967 expansion teams. The win gave the Flyers their second consecutive Stanley Cup – and a place in hockey history as the first expansion team to win the coveted trophy, let alone twice.

Some may call the Flyers "Bad Boys" and others may question their tactics. But as Bobby Clarke cracked, "Tell me – if we're so bad, why haven't they locked us up?"[90]

Though the entire team was successful in the early years, Snider credits much of the winning to the team's leader. "I don't know of any bad deal that Keith Allen ever made," Snider said. "The combination of our drafting and the trades that we made – particularly the trades that Keith made – built us into a powerhouse. Quite frankly, I think we would've won maybe two or three more Cups in a row if Bernie Parent didn't get injured and have to leave the game." The Flyers have had their share of success, though they have never won the Stanley Cup since that second championship in 1975. They have reached the Stanley Cup Final eight times in their history, including six times after 1975 and once as recent as 2010, when they lost to the Chicago Blackhawks. But as previously mentioned, the Flyers are now one of the most valuable and successful hockey franchises in the world.

And Mr. Snider knows the fans and the city should be credited with the success.

"This city is a hockey city. And it became a hockey city in the early years," he said. "When you look at the success at this franchise, it's also interesting to note that when *The Hockey News* graded expansion in 1967, of the six teams, we were voted 'Least Likely to Succeed'…Naturally, I was scared to death when they said that, because I thought we were going to succeed. I put everything I owned in to put this franchise together. And I thought, 'Holy cow, what happens if it doesn't succeed?' So the excitement of knowing that we have a very, very successful franchise – we won the Cup in our 7th year in existence."

Many critics of the Broad Street Bullies cite that the Flyers only won because they were tough and were able to brawl their way to victory. But when Snider hears that, he becomes angry at the illogical conclusion. "You can't win games by fighting," he said emphatically. "We had three Hall of Famers on that team – the *Hockey* Hall of Fame: Bob Clarke, Bill Barber and Bernie Parent. Parent was a phenomenal goaltender. Clarke was one of the best, if not the best player in the league. Bill Barber was a fantastic left wing. We rounded it out with guys that were tremendously balanced. Reggie Leach set records. Rick MacLeish was an outstanding winger. We had very strong defensive defenseman.

"The bottom line is the league was always rough. We had stick fights in the old days. I'll never forget there was a stick fight in our first year [between Larry Zeidel and Eddie Shack]; I never saw anything like it in my life. They're carving each other up with sticks in a fight. The league was always violent. We were beat up like crazy in our first year by the St. Louis Blues – the Plager brothers, Noel Picard. They terrorized us in the playoffs – sucker punched us. We got the hell beat out of us, because we had smaller guys. I said we were never going to have that happen to us again. So we started drafting some tougher guys and we became tougher than anybody else. But before the Broad Street Bullies there were the Big, Bad Bruins. So that's a bunch of crap."

Snider was later elected to the Hockey Hall of Fame and was named by Philadelphia as the city's greatest sports mover and shaker. Though he merged the team with Comcast-Spectacor – a subsidiary of Comcast Corporation – in 1996, he still owns 34 percent of the team and remains the chairman of the Flyers, the NBA's 76ers, the Wells Fargo Center and the Spectrum. But he takes great pride in his Flyers and the impact they've had on the game.

"Knowing that we are the most successful of those six teams in expansion, several of which no longer exist, is very satisfying."[91]

Pittsburgh Penguins

1967-68 Statistics

	Pos	Ht	Wt	Age	GP	G	A	Pts	+/-	PIM
Andy Bathgate	RW	6-0	180	35	74	20	39	59	-11	55
Ab McDonald	LW	6-3	192	31	74	22	21	43	-4	38
Ken Schinkel	RW	5-10	172	35	57	14	25	39	-10	19
Art Stratton	C	5-11	170	32	58	15	21	37	-6	16
Earl Ingarfield	C	5-11	185	33	50	15	22	37	-7	12
Val Fonteyne	LW	5-10	160	34	69	6	28	34	-23	0
Gene Ubriaco	LW	5-8	157	30	65	18	15	33	-13	16
Noel Price	D	6-0	190	32	70	6	27	33	-7	48
Paul Andrea	RW	5-10	174	26	65	11	21	32	-2	2
Billy Dea	LW	5-8	175	34	73	16	12	28	-15	6
Keith McCreary	RW	5-10	180	27	70	14	12	26	-3	44
Leo Boivin	D	5-8	183	35	73	9	13	22	-15	74
Bob Dillabough	C	5-10	180	26	47	7	12	19	-7	18
Bob Rivard	C	5-8	155	28	27	5	12	17	0	4
Bill Speer	D	5-11	205	25	68	3	13	16	-14	44
George Konik	D	5-11	190	30	52	7	8	15	-9	26
Al MacNeil	D	5-10	183	32	74	2	10	12	-6	58
Wayne Hicks	RW	5-11	185	30	15	4	7	11	2	2
Dick Mattiussi	D	5-10	185	29	32	0	2	2	-9	18
Dunc McCallum	D	6-1	193	27	32	0	2	2	-2	36

	Pos	Ht	Wt	Age	GP	W	L	T	GAA	SO
Les Binkley	G	6-0	175	33	54	20	24	10	2.88	6
Hank Bassen	G	5-10	180	35	25	7	10	3	2.86	1

CHAPTER 10

Pittsburgh Penguins

AFTER LOSING THEIR NHL team in 1930 to cross-state rival Philadelphia, Pittsburgh became a hockey-devoid city for more than half a decade.

But you can't blame the league for taking the Pittsburgh Pirates away from the Steel City. The year of the Great Depression, the Pirates went a disastrous 5-36-3 – and it was not an aberration. The team's five years of operations were simply horrid. Their record for wins in a season was 19, as they hit that mark in both 1926 and 1928. The most points they had in a season was 46, in 1928. They squeaked into the playoffs twice, but lost in the first round both times.

After Pittsburgh departed from the NHL's radar, they brought a team into the American League, one level of professional hockey below the National Hockey League. The Hornets, as the team was called, had a fair amount of success from the time the team was brought into existence in 1936. The team even won two Calder Cups in the '50s. In 1952, they finished with 46 wins and 95 points, leading the AHL in both categories. Ironically, neither the AHL president nor the Calder Cup were present when the team won – it had to be presented to them at a later time when they were travelling back to Pittsburgh.

But the Hornets returned to the Calder Cup final the next season, falling to the Cleveland Barons in seven games. In 1955, the Hornets again finished first in the league with 70 points. They trudged through the playoffs and defeated the Buffalo Bisons in the final in six games to earn the organization's second Calder Cup.

However, when the city decided to tear down the Duquesne Gardens, the team's arena, in order to build an apartment complex, the Hornets were homeless and forced to fold.

With the new, state of the art Civic Arena having been built in downtown Pittsburgh in 1961, the team finally had a place to play and they returned to the professional hockey circuit. In its comeback season, the team faltered, going 10-58-2 and finishing at the bottom of the league standings. Just six years later, though, in the 1966-67 season, the Hornets dominated the league, winning the regular season title and their third Calder Cup, after sweeping the Rochester Americans in four games.

When 1965 arrived and the NHL announced they were doubling the size of their league, Pittsburgh immediately became a front-runner for a franchise. The sports scene in Pittsburgh was what it looks like now, sans the Penguins. Baseball's Pirates consistently sold out most of their stadium, while the NFL's Steelers were as popular as they are in the 21st century. But it was hockey that gave people the thrill of action and entertainment unlike any other attraction. As Bruce Cooper explains, "the AHL was again as comfortable and familiar a feature of the Pittsburgh sports scene as the National League Pirates or NFL Steelers."[92] So it seemed logical that Pittsburgh should be guaranteed an NHL team.

As expected, Pittsburgh made a bid for an NHL franchise. Unlike Minnesota, Los Angeles and Oakland, only one group applied for the team. The group was led by Jack E. MacGregor, a Pennsylvania State Senator and Peter Block, a businessman and former classmate of MacGregor's. "Pittsburgh was going through a second renaissance," McGregor said. "I was able to enlist the financial support of the major Pittsburgh families using the NHL as an urban renewal tool. We had a large investor group of about 22. That was the emphasis made with the league – turning around, getting fan momentum. We had a good representation of Pittsburgh in our investment group. Pittsburgh is a great sports town, with the Steelers and the Pirates."

The group's bid focused on the new Civic Arena. "The biggest problem we faced, after getting the investors' support, was the need to comply with the NHL minimum seating capacity standard," McGregor said. The arena housed 10,732, but would be revamped to seat 12,508, just barely over the 12,500 minimum the league required.

"Getting the architects and engineers to decide how to expand the [arena] was one problem," McGregor continued. "Convincing the county government, owner of the Civic Arena, to pay for the expansion, was another big challenge. But we were successful in both."

The most attractive part of the new arena was its retractable roof. It measured 415 feet in diameter, 2,950 tons and 170,000 square feet, had eight "leaves", each of which were pie-shaped. Six of the leaves could be lifted back in under two and a half minutes, revealing the beautiful Western Pennsylvania sky. This feature enabled hockey to be played under the stars in Pittsburgh, which sounded like an incredible idea (though never utilized). The arena was also built in such a way that no support beams obstructed the view of fans, no matter where they were seated.

Regardless of the new arena, however, the rumor was that Pittsburgh was ranked seventh among the other cities vying for an NHL franchise for the 1967-68 season. The league wanted two teams in the west, two in the mid-west and two in the east. Los Angeles and Oakland received bids on the West Coast, St. Louis and Minnesota received the mid-west bids, while Philadelphia and Buffalo seemed to be the front-runners to become the East Coast teams.

Buffalo, being near Canada and having numerous Canadian and American hockey fans in the vicinity, seemed to be the more logical business decision for the league. "[Bruce and Jim Norris] were leaning towards Buffalo. Philadelphia was assured one of the eastern teams, and our main competition was Buffalo. Toronto and Boston had already declared for Buffalo, so getting the Norris' [approval] was key," said McGregor.

McGregor, ever the smart lawyer, realized that if Norris was planning on voting for Buffalo to get a team, it would have a tremendous impact on the votes of the other members of the league. In an attempt to overturn Norris' decision, McGregor recruited Art Rooney, then-owner of the NFL's Pittsburgh Steelers. Rooney contributed greatly to McGregor's political campaigns and also had mutual friends with Norris in the horse racing business.

After Rooney was convinced, he immediately took action per McGregor's request. "He played a key role," McGregor continued. "Art would not be an investor, he was a one sport plus horse-racing guy. But he agreed to help. He knew the two half brothers, Bruce Norris, owner of the Detroit Red Wings and Jim Norris, owner of the Blackhawks. Art wanted me to be present when he talked to them on the phone. It happened in a New York hotel room, where we happened to be on separate business trips. Art called them and said, 'I understand you're leaning toward Buffalo in the expansion process. I want you to know that it would be personally embarrassing to me if Pittsburgh was passed over. We have a nice, young man here that is going to help Pittsburgh.' And he leaned hard on them. He turned them right before my very eyes."

Rooney successfully convinced every member to vote for Jack McGregor's bid to be welcomed into the NHL. After granted entry to the league, McGregor's group paid the $2 million entry fee, plus $750,000, which included an upgrade the Civic Arena and an indemnification fee to Bruce Norris, who owned the Pittsburgh Hornets. McGregor was named the President and CEO of the Penguins by his investor group – he had a 12.5 percent share of the team, which was the most among the investors.

To determine the name of the arena, all McGregor had to do was look at the Civic Arena. Shaped like an igloo, the building quickly took on the nickname, "The Igloo". And when The Igloo came to be, it was only logical what was to follow – the Pittsburgh Penguins.

But many fans were skeptical of McGregor's reasons for wanting to own a team. Numerous citizens believed it was just a political stunt to be reelected in the Pennsylvania State Senate. "People are allowed to speculate," McGregor laughed. "My Senate district, which I won in 1962, was a two for one Democrat margin. Since then, the boundary lines have been redistricting. Mine was redistricted into a fairly safe Republican seat. "According to the polls, I was not in trouble, politically. Politics probably played a role in that I was known through politics and it certainly played a role in trying to convince these large Pittsburgh families to join our investment groups. But I don't recall ever thinking that it would be good or bad or indifferent politically to me if I got the franchise."

In reality, Jack McGregor had the desire to own a sports team for another reason. "It was the challenge of it all. I've long been a sports fan – not a hockey fan – but I was a huge Pirates fan," he explained. "I'm an entrepreneur at heart. Subsequently, I started a minor league baseball team in Connecticut. It was an entrepreneurial opportunity. In the Senate, I was one of the legislative champions of a package of bills that would assist Pittsburgh in its urban renewal. It just seemed to be a good thing to go after."

Another object McGregor went after was the NHL's prized trophy. He secured the Stanley Cup to be brought to Pittsburgh in March 1966 as a marketing stunt. He would parade the famed trophy around the city in an attempt to garner interest in his new NHL squad and to drive up the number of season tickets sold at The Igloo. It even played well in McGregor's political career, regardless of his original intention. "We paraded the Stanley Cup around town for two days," he explained. "I was reelected in November 1966 and in October 1967 the Pittsburgh Penguins commenced play in the NHL."

But before the Penguins could begin playing, they would need a front office staff that would begin stocking the team with talent taken from the six existing teams. McGregor immediately gravitated toward John "Jack" Riley, the president of the American League. "He was recommended by Clarence Campbell," said McGregor. "He was president of the American League and through that knew something about Pittsburgh, in following the Hornets. He was sure to be a savvy hockey man."

Riley played pro hockey in the AHL in the '40s, but became an executive when he was just 26 years old. Riley was a GM in the Eastern League and the AHL before becoming the league's president in 1965. But when he was approached about joining the ranks of the NHL for the first time in his career, there was no chance he was going to reject the offer.

"I had been General Managing the Rochester Americans in the American League for five years and at that time, they asked me about being the commissioner of the league," said Riley. "I accepted it and after the second year, they were looking for people to come into the NHL. I had an offer from St. Louis. I was interviewed by Philadelphia and the Penguins. I decided I was going to take a big league job because

I was better off financially, in addition to it being my goal at the time. I had a three-year contract with the AHL and I asked if they would let me out of the last year of the contract, which they did. So I accepted the Penguins' offer."

Riley's first act as GM of the Penguins was to hire a coach – George "Red" Sullivan was the man. Sullivan was a former NHL player, competing for over a decade with Boston, Chicago and New York. He also coached the Rangers for three years, from 1962-1965. "Red had coached the New York Rangers and played for them," said Riley. "I was a friend of his and I had followed his career. He was a fiery type of coach and I thought he was the right man for the job at that time. I signed him the year before and we scouted. I knew the AHL pretty well and he scouted the Western League. And of course, he knew the NHL well, which was a plus for us."

Most impressively, the 5-foot-10, 160-pound Ontario native established an AHL record when he posted 30 goals and 89 assists for 119 points in 69 games. That record would stand for over 30 years.

However, his records were not going to build the Pittsburgh Penguins into a Stanley Cup contender. Sullivan knew that the task at hand was going to be the toughest, yet most exhilarating of his career. Teamed with Riley, he would immediately begin scouting the league for the expansion draft and leafing through pages of available free agents to sign, in order to develop young prospects for his squad.

Throughout the expansion draft, the Penguins would select nine former New York Rangers – Earl Ingerfield, Ken Schinkel, Al MacNeil, Noel Price, Val Fonteyne, Art Stratton, Mel Pearson, Billy Dea and Andy Bathgate. Riley would then trade for three more former Blueshirts, moving Larry Jeffrey to New York for Paul Andrea, Dunc McCallum and George Konik. When all was said and done, 12 of those on the Pittsburgh roster had played on Broadway at some point. "I think it was a coincidence," Riley said, "Plus the fact that Red knew a lot of these players. He played with them and he coached them. He had a good 'in' there. We didn't get the best of the draft, either; we drafted fifth. But I thought we had a competitive club."

Of the twelve former Rangers who would suit up for the Penguins, Andy Bathgate was the most surprising. "Going into the 17th round, I noticed that Andy Bathgate, the fading superstar of the New York

Rangers, was still available," McGregor said. "He was expensive, another reason why he had not been selected. But I felt he had a year or two left in him and should be worth the investment.

"I told Jack Riley…'Let's go for Andy Bathgate'."

"He's going to be pricey," Riley responded (Bathgate's salary was $75,000 annually), "and how could we do that to the Rangers? He's one of their marquee players."

"Let me worry about the cost," McGregor said. He would later reason, "As for the Rangers I explained that Bill Jennings has become a good friend and a beer afterwards should smooth things over. I felt Bill wouldn't mind losing old blades for new skaters."

When Riley announced that Bathgate would be switching jerseys and moving across the state line, the fans and reporters were stunned that such a move would be made. It seemed everyone was electrified – except for Bill Jennings. "I went straight to Bill after the draft and he said, 'You don't have to explain or apologize. I thought it was a smart move.' I got lucky," McGregor concluded. "It didn't even cost me a beer!"[93]

Although the $75,000 price tag for Bathgate seemed worthwhile to McGregor, one man does not make a team. The remainder of the team was filled with a mixture of veterans and young players. Included in the veterans was Ab (Alvin Brian) McDonald, drafted from the Detroit Red Wings. McDonald, a 31-year-old, nine-year veteran of the league, played for the Hornets when they won the Calder Cup a year earlier. He would ultimately be Red Sullivan's choice for the Pittsburgh Penguins' first captain. Unfortunately, he did not produce and would be traded to St. Louis after the end of the inaugural season.

Another player, defenseman Leo Boivin, was a 5-foot-7 hard hitter from Detroit. He was a 15-year NHL veteran and would contribute as a solid anchor on the Pens' blueline. Other players include winger Gene Ubriaco, a 29-year-old former Hershey Bear, who would eventually become a coach of the Penguins after his playing years ended; and 27-year-old NHL veteran Keith McCreary, a winger who had just nine NHL games under his belt when he was drafted, but would play just under five season with the Penguins. Ironically, he would be taken from Pittsburgh in an expansion draft when the Atlanta Flames joined the league in 1972.

The two goaltenders the Penguins selected in the expansion draft were Joe Daley and Roy Edwards. Daley was 23 when he was drafted from the Detroit Red Wings. He was also a former Pittsburgh Hornet. He would spend the first season in the AHL with the Baltimore Clippers and would play 38 games for the Penguins in the 1968-69 and 1969-70 seasons. He would also be lost in an expansion draft to the Buffalo Sabres in 1970.

Edwards was a 29-year-old goalkeeper taken from the Chicago Blackhawks. He did not even last long enough in Pittsburgh to see the first puck drop, as he was traded to the Red Wings during training camp for Hank Bassen, a 35-year-old goaltender who had 132 games under his belt. Ironically, neither goalie selected by the Penguins in the 1967 expansion draft would play a single game in the inaugural expansion season in the Steel City.

Bassen had also played in the AHL and the WHL. He played for the Hornets for five seasons prior to expansion and had led the Hornets to a Calder Cup the year before the Penguins came into existence. In fact, his playoff stats would include a 1.67 goals against average, a number that led the league.

The Pittsburgh AHL hero was hoping to become the number one goaltender for the newly born Penguins when their inaugural season began. However, a young "prospect" named Les Binkley surprised coach Red Sullivan in training camp and won the starting job. Although Binkley was a rookie, he was 33 years old. Never having been in the NHL, Binkley was signed nine months prior to the expansion draft when Penguins management bought his contract from the Cleveland Barons of the AHL, then loaned him to the Western League's San Diego Gulls for the 1966-67 season to develop. In season one, Binkley would play the majority of Pittsburgh's games, going 20-24-10, compiling six shutouts and a 2.88 goals against average. Bassen would play just 25 games and would retire at the end of the season.

But the Penguins were lacking young talent and were the oldest team in the league when the 1967-68 season was ready to begin; the average age of the Penguins was 32. "Everybody had a different strategy," said Riley. "But the owners in Pittsburgh wanted the best team, regardless of age, in that first year." However, history had proven that teams comprised only of older veterans typically did not perform as well as others.

The day had finally arrived – October 11, 1967. It had been 37 years since the lights were turned out in Duquesne Gardens, metaphorically related to the lights being turned out on NHL hockey in Pittsburgh. It had been six months since the Hornets had ended their 26-year drought by winning the Calder Cup. But NHL hockey in Pittsburgh was back – to stay.

Clarence Campbell and Jack McGregor together dropped the ceremonial first puck, then left the ice as the 1967-68 season began against the Montreal Canadiens. McGregor took that first puck, had it bronzed, and kept it on his desk. He still uses it as a paperweight to this day.

But on the ice, there were no paperweights, as bodies were thrown around in a rough and tumble style game. At 7:06 of the third period, just over two hours after Campbell and McGregor left the ice, Andy Bathgate scored the first NHL goal in Penguins history by putting the puck past Rogie Vachon – the first NHL goal for a Pittsburgh-based team since 1930, when James "Bud" Jarvis pocketed the last goal for the Pittsburgh Pirates. Unfortunately for the Penguins, they lost that opening game by a score of 2-1, leaving the Canadiens with their first win of the season.

In their second game, the Penguins would gather the first tie in their short history, evening the Minnesota North Stars 3-3, with Bathgate scoring all three goals – the first hat trick for the Penguins. It was also the first and only time in NHL history the same player scored a team's first four goals. But three nights later, on October 18, the Penguins would be victorious for the first time, defeating the Chicago Blackhawks 4-2 at the Igloo.

Unfortunately, it would be the only win over an Original Six team the Penguins would garner until December. The first month of their season was mediocre, as they finished with a 3-6-1 record. However, they bounced back in November, as they went on two three-game unbeaten streaks and went 6-3-2 to finish November at .500. December proved to be problematic, as did January, as the Penguins compiled a combined 8-15-4 record in those two months.

In February, the Pens would start off bright, but end badly. March was the opposite, as they began by winning just twice in the first ten games. However, they finished with a five-game unbeaten streak. The streak would bring their final record to a dismal 27-34-13, good for 67 points and fifth place in the new expansion division. Fifth, however, was just two points out of a playoff spot and just six points out of first place.

The Penguins finished the inaugural season with a 15-12-10 record at the Igloo – not quite great, but not awful either. But the story of the first season was the return of Andy Bathgate and his continued success in the NHL. He led the first-year Penguins with 20 goals and 59 points in their first season. He also led all expansion team players in points and was the only expansion player to be in the top 20 in league scoring.

The injury bug also drove the Penguins to the bottom of the standings. Bathgate's linemate, Earl Ingerfield, suffered a fractured kneecap in February, leading to a dreary record down the stretch. Defenseman Ken Schinkel, who played in the All Star Game that year, fell victim to a cracked ankle after stepping in front of a Bobby Orr slapshot in January. Goaltender Les Binkley broke his finger on March 2 and was unavailable until the final week of the season – too late for the Penguins to claim a spot in the postseason.

Though in the playoff race at one point, the Penguins suffered in the standings once hit by this injury bug. St. Louis and Minnesota were able to make up lost time, while the Pens could do nothing but watch their playoff hopes flicker away and fade at the last minute.

––––––––––––––

At the end of the 1967-68 season, McGregor and his group had invested their cash in a professional soccer team and were already unable to deal with the financial responsibility of owning an NHL squad as well. Because of this, Jack McGregor and his investors sold their piece of the Pittsburgh Penguins to Donald H. Parsons, a lawyer and banker located in Detroit. Parsons and his group bought 80 percent of the club and took over control of the Penguins. Jack McGregor explained the story:

"We ran out of money, the Penguins. The families who had supported the initial round of financing and were prepared to finance a second round, were led down the garden path to the Pittsburgh Phantoms in the new National Soccer Association by one of our partners in the Penguins."

"There were the same investors in the hockey team that there were in the soccer team," said Jack Riley. "The minute the soccer team started losing, they just left it and let it die. It cost them a lot of money. I guess they didn't have enough for both businesses."

"I talked to Art Rooney about it and he urged me not to join the group, that we had our hands full with the Penguins," McGregor continued, "So I decided against joining them. They had assembled poorly managed people and were ridiculed in the press. They lasted just one season. Most of the Pittsburgh families that I keep referencing joined the Phantoms in the investment group, and they were the objects of a lot of ridicule for the way it was managed. We knew we would need additional cash and finances. When we did need cash, the same, reliable Pittsburgh families were no longer available. So we were forced to go to the outside. Parsons was then the head of a very successful banking empire in Michigan, and crazy about hockey. The word got out that control was for sale, and Parsons called me. We hit it off, and it worked out all right."

The move was not supported by Henry Hillman, one of the members of McGregor's original investment group. But McGregor did what he thought was best for the group. Unfortunately, McGregor's foresight was not as keen as Hillman's. "Henry, as usual, turned out to be right," said McGregor some time later. "Parsons, while a good guy, was not strong enough financially to be a long-term player. The Penguins had to be sold by Parsons in another short three years."[94]

Before Parsons could sell his share of the team, though, the Penguins would start up another chance to make the Stanley Cup playoffs. The 1968-69 season began with much optimism from the Penguins' side. In fact, the first bit of optimism started when the Penguins bought John Arbour and Jean Pronovost from the Boston Bruins shortly after the playoffs ended. Arbour, a defenseman, would play just 17 games for the Penguins, but Pronovost, a left-winger, became a superstar in the Steel City. Pronovost would become the Penguins all-time leading goal and points scorer, posting 316 goals and 603 points in 753 games (also a team record at the time). In fact, the Shawnigan Falls, Quebec native would remain the leading scorer until Mario Lemieux in the 1990s.

With Pronovost leading the team at the start of the 1968-69 season, the Penguins began optimistically, as they tied two Original Six teams in the opening two games of the campaign. However, their luck went downhill when they were shutout by the Philadelphia Flyers on October 17, 1968, by a 3-0 score. That would lead to a stretch in which the Penguins would win just twice in 14 games. In fact, by November 20, their record was 2-12-2, last place in the league.

They would rocket back up the standings briefly, though, as they won three of five games and went on a six-game unbeaten streak to end November, raising their record to 5-12-5. Two five- and three-game losing streaks ended 1968, and as the calendar year turned, their luck did not improve. Jack Riley picked up Billy Harris and Jean-Guy Lagace from the Seals and Canadiens, respectively, but neither was able to help as he hoped they would. As the Penguins continued to stay at the bottom of the league standings through January, Riley traded Leo Boivin to the North Stars in exchange for Duane Rupp. He also moved Earl Ingarfield, Dick Mattiussi and Gene Ubriaco to Oakland for Tracy Pratt, George Swarbrick and Bryan Watson.

These players failed to help the team's efforts, though, as a nine-game winless streak from January 16 to February 2, mixed with a five-game winless streak throughout February, sealed the Penguins' fate for the second straight season. Though they once again ended the season on a hot streak (five wins and a tie in the last six games), the Penguins finished with a 20-45-11 record, 51 points and tied for last place in the league.

Even worse than their embarrassing season, the Penguins' average attendance at the Igloo dropped from 7,407 per game in 1967-68 to 6,008 per game in 1968-69. Les Binkley would have a terrible season, going 10-31-8 with a 3.29 goals against average. On the flip side, Keith McCreary was the only Penguin to reach the 20-goal mark, as he finished the season with 25. Schinkel played in the All Star Game for the second consecutive year and led all Pittsburgh players with 52 points.

In an unusual stunt to attempt to bolster their attendance, the

Penguins purchased a live penguin and attempted to teach it to skate. For two months, intense sessions were held teaching the young bird to move across the ice. Just after the debut of the penguin was scheduled, it contracted pneumonia and passed away. Though sadly humorous, this Penguin was a perfect metaphor for Pittsburgh's NHL success – or lack thereof – in the first few years of their post-expansion history.

Before the 1969-70 season could begin, Jack Riley moved Red Sullivan to the scouting staff and replaced him behind the bench with Red Kelly, who was coaching the Los Angeles Kings at the time. Kelly was inducted into the Hockey Hall of Fame on opening night of the 1969-70 season at the Igloo – a great tribute to a great player until he retired from playing in 1967.

Riley brought in Dean Prentice, a 37-year-old left wing from the Detroit Red Wings in hopes that the veteran's presence would lead the Penguins to the playoffs for the first time. But the biggest acquisition of the season came in May, immediately after the playoffs ended. Riley sent Andy Bathgate again to the Vancouver Canucks of the WHL, in addition to John Arbour and Paul Andrea in exchange for a young player named Bryan Hextall. Originally taken in the expansion draft by Oakland, the 28-year-old center was the son of the last player to score a Stanley Cup-winning goal for the Rangers (in 1940), but was even more talented than his famous dad. Hextall would have great success in his first season, scoring 31 points and posting 87 PIM in 66 games. In goal, Riley would bring in Al Smith, who would go on to play the majority of the Penguins' games during the regular season.

However, as the campaign began, optimism and hope quickly faded to anger and disappointment, as the 0-3-3 start to the season turned into a 2-7-3 record and finally a 9-16-5 record by mid-December. The team would win 12 games over the next two months and would once again fall victim to inconsistency, as they went on a ten-game winless streak, dropping their record to 23-36-11 with just six games remaining. They would only win three of the last six games to finish with a 26-38-12 record, but due to the horrendous drop off from the previous season by the Kings and the Flyers, the Penguins were able to clinch second place with 64 points, albeit 22 points behind the first place Blues.

In the first round, the Penguins would face the fourth place Oakland Seals, who were also appearing in their first NHL postseason. Though the Penguins went 2-3-3 against the Seals in the regular season, they were adequately prepared by coach Red Kelly, who led the Penguins to a four-game sweep over Oakland, in which the Penguins gave up just six goals and scored 13 in four games.

The Conference Finals, however, would feature a matchup between the St. Louis Blues and the Pittsburgh Penguins. The Penguins had won just one game against the Blues all year, as the Scotty Bowman-led Blues ravaged the West Division. After dropping the first two games in St. Louis, the Penguins won their first two games in the Igloo by 3-2 and 2-1 scores. Even at two games apiece, the Blues would come out flying in Game 5, shutting out the Pens 5-0. In Game 6, the Blues took a lead and held on for dear life, as the Penguins failed to jump back in the series. The final score was 4-3, and it sent the Blues back to the final for the third straight year and sent the Penguins back to the golf course, with which they had been so finely acquainted for the past two years.

After the postseason, the team would have to mourn one of their own, as third-round draft pick Michel Briere, taken in the 1969 NHL Amateur Draft, was injured in a car crash. After spending a year in the hospital, Briere passed away, leaving an emotional hole in the Penguins organization. The Steel City was extremely fond of Briere, as he scored five goals in the playoffs, including the series winner against Oakland in overtime of Game 4. He totaled eight points in ten playoff games for the Penguins in his rookie season. The Penguins would go on to retire Briere's "21", making it the only number to be retired until Mario Lemieux's was raised to the rafters decades later.

Although the Penguins failed to reach the Stanley Cup final, *The Hockey News* honored the team by naming Red Kelly the coach of the year. The year was far from a failure, even though the team failed to reach the 7,000-fan attendance mark for the second straight season.

The team would continue to have a reasonable amount of success, even reaching the playoffs in seven of eight seasons from 1975 to 1982. In 1983 and 1984, however, the team fell to the depths of the league and compiled the worst record of any team in both seasons. The selection of Mario Lemieux with the first pick in the 1984 Entry Draft would prove to be a franchise-changing move, as he would go on to lead the team to two Stanley Cups in 1991 and 1992.

The Pens would yet again succumb to financial and on-ice pressures, falling again to the bottom of the league standings at the turn of the millennium. The trade of Jaromir Jagr to the Washington Capitals was the catalyst that sent the Penguins home in early April 2002 for the first time in 12 seasons. They continued to slump, finishing last in the league in the 2003-04 season and reaching the point of declaring bankruptcy just before the lockout in 2004-05 (the second time, after previously declaring in 1975). The Penguins had the worst attendance in the league the season before the lockout, averaging just 11,877 fans per game.

But one-time franchise savior Mario Lemieux would come back into the limelight, purchasing the franchise and putting them back on the NHL map. Selecting goaltender Marc-Andre Fleury first overall in 2003, center Evgeni Malkin second overall in 2004 and center Sidney Crosby first overall in 2005 would help bring the Penguins back from obscurity and ultimately lead them to their third Stanley Cup in the 2008-09 season.

As the Penguins and owner Mario Lemieux look to the future, their new arena, the Consol Energy Center, replaced the Igloo for the 2010-11 season. What started out as a hip, retractable dome, state-of-the-art arena in the 1960s would eventually become obsolete, leading to a move across the street, signifying new life and new success for the Pittsburgh Penguins – success that eluded them in their first few decades after becoming one of six cities to be honored with an NHL expansion franchise.

St. Louis Blues

1967-68 Statistics

	Pos	Ht	Wt	Age	GP	G	A	Pts	+/-	PIM
Red Berenson	C	6-0	185	28	55	22	29	51	-8	22
Gerry Melnyk	C	5-10	165	33	73	15	35	50	-11	14
Jimmy Roberts	D	5-10	185	27	74	14	23	37	-8	66
Frank St. Marseille	RW	5-11	180	28	57	16	16	32	11	12
Terry Crisp	C	5-10	180	24	73	9	20	29	9	10
Don McKenny	C	5-11	160	33	39	9	20	29	1	4
Bill McCreary	LW	5-10	172	33	70	13	13	26	2	22
Gary Sabourin	RW	5-11	180	24	50	13	10	23	11	50
Larry Keenan	LW	5-11	175	27	40	12	8	20	-7	4
Barclay Plager	D	5-11	175	26	49	5	15	20	4	153
Ron Schock	C	5-11	180	24	55	9	9	18	-17	17
Fred Hucul	D	5-10	170	36	43	2	13	15	-3	30
Tim Ecclestone	LW	5-10	195	20	50	6	8	14	1	16
Ron Stewart	RW	6-1	197	35	19	7	5	12	-7	11
Al Arbour	D	6-0	180	35	74	1	10	11	-6	50
Noel Picard	D	6-1	185	29	66	1	10	11	-4	142
Craig Cameron	RW	6-0	200	22	32	7	2	9	2	8
Dickie Moore	LW	5-10	168	37	27	5	3	8	-8	9
Wayne Rivers	RW	5-9	177	25	22	4	4	8	-2	8
Ron Attwell	RW	6-0	185	32	18	1	7	8	-9	6
Bob Plager	D	5-11	195	24	53	2	5	7	-11	86
Jean-Guy Talbot	D	5-11	170	35	23	0	4	4	3	2
Gord Kannegiesser	D	6-0	190	22	19	0	1	1	-3	13

	Pos	Ht	Wt	Age	GP	W	L	T	GAA	SO
Glenn Hall	G	5-11	180	36	49	19	21	9	2.48	5
Seth Martin	G	5-11	180	34	30	8	10	7	2.59	1

CHAPTER 11

St. Louis Blues

No EXPANSION TEAM HAS had the highs and lows of the St. Louis Blues – highs in which fans, players and staff of the team believed they were the best team in the world. Lows, to the extent that it makes fans wonder, "Are we ever going to see a Stanley Cup in this town?" There also has been no other team that was granted a franchise so nonchalantly as the Blues. St. Louis was the first city to be granted a franchise for the 1967-68 season, but was the last franchise to pay the entrance fee, the last to be named and the last to have its ownership assembled.

At the Board of Governors meeting in February 1966, St. Louis was awarded a conditional franchise. Conditional, that is, that a suitable owner would emerge in the next couple of months. This was because the old, decrepit St. Louis Arena was owned by Blackhawks owners Arthur Wirtz and James Norris. The arena was built in 1929 for the annual National Dairy Show, but had not been used since. The two wanted to get rid of the arena while still making a profit on the building. They cornered the Board of Governors and convinced everyone to vote for a franchise in St. Louis, on the assumption that the new owner would buy the arena from the two men in addition to paying the $2 million expansion fee. "St. Louis is an attractive NHL area but somebody has to come up with a franchise bid," said Jim Norris. "I don't want to rent the rink to whoever wants in the NHL. I want to sell it."[95]

When the league announced that St. Louis was awarded a conditional franchise and was looking for a suitable, financially strong owner, a young, 28-year-old man named Sid Salomon III was hanging out at a country club in St. Louis. He was a huge hockey fan and a well-respected citizen, due to his relationship with his father, Sid Salomon Jr.

Salomon Jr. was a well-known insurance salesman who started his own company, Sidney Salomon Jr. and Associates, Inc. He was also a politician and served as the treasurer of the Democratic National Committee. His political connections remained when he became the chairman of John F. Kennedy's presidential campaign in 1960. He also owned parts of the St. Louis Browns and St. Louis Cardinals baseball teams. When Sid III heard the news that the NHL wanted an owner for an NHL franchise in Missouri, he almost fell into the country club's pool.

Sid III met with his father, who put together a bid in less than two months. Salomon Jr. bought the St. Louis Arena for $4 million from Wirtz and Norris. The Salomons would also pay numerous startup costs and expenses, including the $2 million expansion fee. Salomon Jr. created the Missouri Arena Corporation (MAC), which owned the Arena, the land and the team. Salomon Jr. also became the president of the new company. He wanted the arena to be renovated and refurbished, in order to convert it from an old, dusty building into a quality, state of the art NHL arena.

The building was so old that when Salomon Jr. first walked through the building, he found newspapers on the floor from the 1930s. He decided that he would spend every penny turning the arena into a suitable home for a hockey team. His checkbook opened and did not close until the St. Louis Arena was new and state of the art, seating 14,200 fans. When all was said and done, Salomon Jr. paid about $8 million for the St. Louis franchise, including the costs of purchasing and renovating the arena.

"[My son] started thinking about it three or four years ago," Salomon Jr. said at the time, "And he finally got me interested in the project a couple of months back. At first, I hoped some other group in St. Louis would take the lead, and we could go in as minority owners – say 10%. But no other group stepped forward, so we…formed our syndicate and made our bid."[96]

Though Salomon Jr. was the lead investor, he gave control of the team to his son, Sid III. His idea was that the team would give young Sid the team in order to keep himself busy. He allowed Sid to take complete control of all decisions, including all hockey operations and business dilemmas. Knowing that he had just 18 months to hire a staff and build a team that could compete with the other 11 teams, Sid III hired Lynn Patrick, who had worked in the Boston Bruins organization, as the team's coach and general manager. Sid knew that because he had no farm team, no knowledge of management and no chance to succeed on his own, a man like Patrick, with an incredible hockey pedigree, could help bring his team success.

Patrick's first moves were offering jobs to Cliff Fletcher and Scotty Bowman, who were both working with the Montreal Canadiens at the time. Both accepted job offers to serve as Lynn's assistants behind the bench and in the front office. Their jobs would be to scout every player in the league and in the minors who could possibly be available when the NHL held the expansion draft in June 1967.

"We scouted every pro player in the business at least five times," said Patrick, "So that when we went to the [expansion] draft we would not make any silly mistakes. We knew who and what we were after."[97]

At the expansion draft, Patrick and Co. based their draft strategy on how the Original Six teams were built, in an attempt to defend against them. Because of the list of players available, there was no possible way the group could draft a team talented enough to beat teams like the Canadiens and Maple Leafs on skill alone. They needed to build a team that could shut things down and slow their opponents enough to score some goals. Bowman knew that playing wide-open hockey against his former team would kill their chances. Building through solid defense and talented goaltending would enable the Blues to have some success against the powerhouses that already existed.

"We were looking for a goalie and defense," said Bowman. "We wanted to draft players that could play more than one spot...we wanted to buy ourselves some time so that we would have a team that could keep us in contention while we were building our younger players to the point where they could move into the big time," said Bowman.

With the expansion draft completed, the group was confident in their abilities and their choices, but they were still not convinced they had what it took to challenge for the Stanley Cup right out of the gate.

"The Original Six teams gave us nothing," said Glenn Hall. "They gave us older guys who couldn't play anymore and some young kids who were never going to play."[98]

As soon as the draft ended, Bowman and Patrick decided to trade Rod Seiling, whom they drafted in the fourth round, to the New York Rangers for defenseman Bob Plager and right wing Gary Sabourin, in addition to Tim Ecclestone and Gord Kannegiesser, two amateur players. In addition to draft picks Noel Picard and Al Arbour, the Blues would have three tough, strong, yet talented defensemen. "Nobody will be pushing us around," exclaimed an ecstatic Bowman.[99]

Now that the tough side of the team was defined and established, Bowman and Patrick's next moves were to improve the team's raw skill. After the Blues began the season 1-5-2, Bowman traded the Blues leading scorer – Ron Stewart – and Ron Atwell to the New York Rangers for Barclay Plager and forward Red Berenson – two players from Bowman's 1958-59 junior team that went to the Memorial Cup. In addition, Bowman would now have both Plager brothers on his blueline, a move that would prove to be stifling to opposing players.

After 15 games, when the Blues were a pitiful 4-9-2, Lynn Patrick stepped down from the head coach position to concentrate on his duties in the front office. Scotty Bowman replaced him behind the bench and took control of the team. Bowman's first goal was to set the psychological tone of his squad and remind them that they were not as talented as they thought.

"There are twenty guys in here who probably have twenty different ways to make out the lineup," Bowman said in the locker room one night. "I suppose you all have a better way to shuffle this deck and come up with a winning hand. But let me tell you this, gentlemen: You can't shuffle deuces and threes!"[100]

When Bowman took over, the Blues' luck improved and they slowly started to get on the winning track. Along with those wins came fan excitement and support. The building sold more tickets and the players were ecstatic. "It was tough to build into good teams," said Glenn Hall. "But the people must have accepted it. It had to be either old guys or young guys."[101]

Regardless of the team's success, though, the fans were not showing up as Salomon had hoped. Though the Blues had one of the highest attendance numbers of the new teams in year one, they still only averaged about 8,900 fans per game.

Bowman stressed the idea of overachieving and tried to coerce his players into doing so. He informed veterans that just because they had experience, they were not necessarily a lock for the roster each night. And just because a young player was drafted early, doesn't mean they were assured of a spot on the NHL squad. He believed that by succeeding on the ice, the Blues could bring respectability to the division and the idea of expansion.

Halfway through the season, the Blues were slowly climbing up the standings and had a 14-20-3 record. In the midst of a four-game unbeaten streak, Bowman saw an opportunity to shore up his team for a playoff run. He signed three defensemen, including Jean-Guy Talbot, who made a huge impact on the team with his shutdown abilities.

The move worked as Bowman expected, as the Blues went on a seven-game unbeaten streak and raced through the remainder of the season on a hot streak. Though they lost three consecutive games in the middle of March, the Blues won three of their last four games, giving them a 27-31-16 record and 70 points for the year, just one ahead of the fourth place North Stars.

Red Berenson rocketed through the season after being acquired by Bowman, scoring 51 points in 55 games, while players such as Gerry Melnyk and Don McKenney had great impact up front. On the blueline, Jim Roberts and the Plager brothers anchored the defense and other stellar players such as Noel Picard and Al Arbour prevented opposing players from getting anywhere close to Glenn Hall – who ended the first season with a 2.48 goals against average.

Prior to the playoffs, Bowman convinced Canadiens legend Dickie Moore to come out of retirement and play for the Blues. Moore took the reigns himself and averaged just under a point per game throughout the playoffs. He helped lead the Blues to a seven-game series win over the Philadelphia Flyers and a date with the Minnesota North Stars in the semifinals.

Before the semifinals started, *The Hockey News* named Bowman the coach of the year. The award motivated Bowman even more, allowing him to enthusiastically coach his team through the grinding series. Four of the seven semifinals games went into overtime, a record that still stands. The Blues went down 2-1 in games and were headed toward a deep hole when they were down 3-0 in Game 4. However, Dickie Moore once again took a stranglehold on the team and scored a goal and an assist in one minute, making the score 3-2. Bowman held one of his better players, Gary Sabourin, on the bench throughout the third period because he wasn't playing well, in hopes Sabourin would get the message and improve. Bowman pulled Glenn Hall and when Jim Roberts scored with 11 seconds left in the third period, the game was tied and went into overtime. In the extra session, Bowman let Sabourin loose and allowed him on the ice, after which he took a feed from Terry Crisp and scored the game-winner to even the series.

The Blues would go on to win the series in seven games and set a date with Bowman's old Montreal Canadiens in the Stanley Cup final. As the final started, it was clear that the Blues were grossly outmatched by the powerful Canadiens, but were not going down without a fight. Losing two of the first three games in overtime and the other one by just one goal, the Blues were faced with a 3-0 series deficit. Though Glenn Hall played exemplary in goal, the Canadiens were simply too talented to allow the Blues to win – let along four games in a row. Montreal won the Stanley Cup with a 3-2 final score in Game 4.

"It was a heartbreaker to see," wrote journalist Red Burnett at the time. "A number of Hall's saves were seemingly impossible. Experts walked out of the Forum convinced no other goaltender had performed so brilliantly in a losing cause."

Glenn Hall was named the Conn Smythe Trophy winner as the playoff MVP, to which legendary Canadiens coach Toe Blake – who retired in the post-game celebration – agreed with the decision. "St. Louis got great goaltending and, because of it, were rarely behind in the score for any length of time in the games," Blake said. "That meant they didn't have to open up. They could play their right, checking style and wait for the breaks. They stayed on top of us with their checking. We didn't get a chance to really break out against them."[102]

"It was simply that we weren't good enough," said Cliff Fletcher. "You certainly can't compare the Blues to the Canadiens in those days, because there was such a tremendous gap in the talent between the teams."

The season was anything but a failure, from the Blues' standpoint.

After all, they made the Stanley Cup final in their inaugural season and gave the Canadiens a tough time in a losing effort.

"I think you have to give the majority of the success to Lynn Patrick and Scotty Bowman," Fletcher continued. "The quality of the talent available to the expansion teams at the time was marginal. They did a great job of bringing in quality, seasoned veterans, combined with the good fortune of having excellent goaltending."

Fletcher also attributed the success of the team to the way in which they drafted. "We picked up some solid NHL veterans," he said. "We made a great trade with the Rangers to acquire Red Baron, who became an instant star, from being a part-time player with the Rangers. Doug Harvey played, Dickie Moore, just on and on. It definitely helped our club out once we got into the playoffs. We had a lot of players who had a lot of rings and could help us out once the playoffs came along."[103]

One of the turning points of the first season came after Dickie Moore joined the team late in the 1968 regular season. After a young player threw his jersey on the ground allowing the Blues' musical note logo to hit the floor, Moore grabbed the player by the throat and slammed him against the locker. "In Montreal," he screamed, "The sweater has never hit the floor! That's your life – the crest. Respect it!"

That lesson on respect was mixed with Bowman's incredible hockey knowledge and motivational abilities to bring the Blues to success. "Scotty was a winner," said Jim Roberts. "I think, as a team, we just as well could have been losers as well as winners. He was the guy that made us a winner. He wouldn't let us go off the line, day or night. He was on us every day. It was a special group of guys...the chemistry all kind of came together."[104]

After the Blues made the final in 1968 and began preparations for the 1968-69 season, the St. Louis Arena was expanded to hold 18,000 people – a shrewd move, considering the Blues rarely, if ever, sold out in their inaugural season. The move worked like a charm, as the team sold out every game for the next seven seasons. Their attendance would become the best in the entire league – *including* the Original Six teams.

The 1968-69 season began with a nine-game streak in which they won and lost every other game, leading to a 4-5-0 record. When their record reached 6-6-1 at the beginning of November 1968, St. Louis went on a 12-game unbeaten streak, bringing their record to 11-6-8 and taking hold of first place in the West Division by a large margin. Throughout the rest of the season, behind stellar play from Glenn Hall and newly acquired Jacques Plante, the Blues dominated the expansion teams, reaching a 32-16-12 record by mid-February 1969. Although they were winless in 11 of their last 16 games of the season, the Blues still managed to finish atop the West Division with a 37-25-14 record. This gave them 88 points, a huge margin over of the second place Seals, who compiled 69 points.

Red Berenson would dominate the West Division's scoring, posting 82 points in 76 games, while Gary Sabourin had a solid year with 48 points. Hall had a 2.17 goals against average while Jacques Plante had an unbelievable 1.96 goals against average, allowing both to share the Vezina Trophy as the goaltending tandem with the fewest goals against. On the blueline, the Plager brothers, along with Noel Picard and Doug Harvey, would once again anchor the team and give opposing teams significant offensive problems whenever they met.

The Blues swept the Flyers in the first round of the playoffs and the Kings in the second round to reach the final with much more ease than the previous year. However, in the final, they once again lost to an incredibly strong Montreal squad in four games, this time only scoring three goals in the process. Even Plante's 1.43 goals against average in the postseason could not lead St. Louis to the Stanley Cup they so desired.

During the 1969-70 season, the Blues had another incredible campaign, dominating the West Division from start to finish. They finished the season with a 37-27-12 record, despite Glenn Hall having retired at the end of the previous season, then returning halfway through the next. The Blues finished with 86 points, more than 22 points ahead of the second place Penguins. Center Phil Goyette had an incredible season, scoring 78 points and winning the Lady Byng Trophy after posting just 16 penalty minutes. Red Berenson continued his stellar Blues career with 72 points in 67 games. In goal, Hall had only a moderate season, going 7-8-3 with a 2.91 goals against average. However, Plante once again stymied opposing forwards with a 2.19 goals against average while newly acquired Ernie Wakely posted a 2.11 goals against average in 30 games played.

In the playoffs, the Blues defeated the Minnesota North Stars in six games, then defeated the Pittsburgh Penguins by the same series score to advance to their third straight Stanley Cup final. This time, against the Boston Bruins, the Blues were outmatched even more so than they were against the Canadiens in the two previous finals. With Bobby Orr and Phil Esposito entering their primes and taking a hold of the NHL, the Blues could do nothing but watch Bobby Orr jump through the air after scoring the game-winning goal in overtime of Game 4.

Although the Blues failed to win a Stanley Cup during their first three years, and to this date have still not succeeded in their attempts to lift the hallowed trophy, their early years were extremely successful, arguably more than any other expansion franchise. "I think we really represented expansion very, very well," said Glenn Hall. "Had it not been represented well, I think it would have been more difficult for people to accept it."[105]

The Blues were hot in those days. They were the ticket that everyone in St. Louis desired. Fans adored the players and the players adored their owner, Sid Salomon III, since Salomon treated the players like close family members. *Sports Illustrated* explained this relationship in a 1969 article: "Salomon's tender loving care notoriously extends to the Blues players. Any man who does something to enhance the team's name - scores three goals in a game, makes the All-Star team, plays a major role in a key victory - gets a gold wristwatch. Not any gold wristwatch, mind you, but a $750 Patek Philippe."[106]

Red Berenson scored six goals in a game against the Flyers in November 1968. "In New York or Montreal, all you'd get would be a handshake," said Berenson, who was a former member of both teams. Yet Berenson was awarded a brand new 1969 Chevrolet with a canoe on top and a shotgun inside, courtesy of his generous owner.

Even coach Scotty Bowman understood the generosity of Salomon and appreciated it. "Whenever we're on the coast, Mr. Salomon wants me to take the players out to dinner at some real nice restaurant," said Bowman at the time. "The players still get their meal money – the dinner is on Mr. Salomon."[107]

"We had a great relationship with the owners of the team," said Bowman, who again reminisced in a 2010 interview. "They treated our players first-class. At the end of the season – they owned a hotel in

Hollywood, Florida – we went down there for ten days. They invited all the players and their families down there. It was a great gesture. It was just like a family atmosphere and they treated us like such."

"Today I make $35,000, which is $15,000 more than I ever earned in my best year in Montreal," said Jacques Plante during his tenure with the Blues. "To tell you the truth, I never dreamed of getting a salary like this…I still cannot believe this is really happening to me…with other teams, there is a wall between the owners and players. That is not true here…they are interested in us not just as hockey players, but as human beings. So we put out extra for them."[108]

"It was unique compared to what was going on in the league," said Glenn Hall. "You were just like cattle, bought and sold and auctioned off. The only way we could return the favor to the Salomons was to go out and give a good effort every night."[109]

But Salomon's generosity was met with contempt from other owners and managers in the league. "I think the Salomons are on very thin ice with that kind of stuff," said Punch Imlach. "From a management point of view, it's bad. It puts every other club in the league in an impossible competitive position."[110] Knowing that his ways were respected and admired in St. Louis, Salomon was not afraid to fight back. "I think Mr. Imlach owes us an apology," explained Salomon. "We're not trying to tell or show anyone else how to run their clubs. We paid $2 million for this franchise and we're entitled to run it the way we please."[111]

Though the city loved the team and consistently filled the arena, hints arose in the early 1970s that the Salomons were having financial problems. "They say we got [the franchise] for $2 million, a bargain," said Sid III in a 1970 interview with *Sports Illustrated*. "But remember this, we spent another $8 million for our building and improvements. That's a big investment. We don't know if we'll be able to compete well enough in the future to make it pay off."[112]

Numerous variables contributed to the continued financial troubles that begat the Salomon family in the 1970s. In August 1972, Crown Life Insurance, a major sponsor of the Blues, ended their relationship with the team, costing Salomon a great deal of money. He filed a $1.6 million suit against the company, but ultimately lost the case, with it having also paid enormous legal fees.

In 1975, he demanded to be allowed to destroy part of a forest near the St. Louis Arena in order to add over 1,000 parking spaces. The city was not a fan of the proposal and after receiving much criticism from the public, the family withdrew it from the city council.

The Salomons sent a letter to the *St. Louis Post Dispatch* in July 1975 explaining the main issues with the team that were leading to the family's financial downfall. The first was the cost of the arena and the maintenance costs required to upkeep the building. Although the cost of the arena and the numerous renovations through the years were financed by MAC, Salomon explained that because the building was not air conditioned, it could only be used in cold weather and he was therefore unable to make a profit from the building in the summer. The maintenance costs were sky high as well, leaving him with more debt than he imagined. The family also cited high city and state taxes as a major cause for their downfall. The average NHL team at the time paid just 4.5 percent tax to their city and state, while the Salomons paid 9.5 percent on behalf of the Blues – a number that had cost the family an extra $5 million since the franchise's inception.

Adding to the financial problems was the rival Kiel Auditorium, which housed numerous shows and concerts throughout the year. Though the St. Louis Arena was a much nicer building, the Auditorium had rent prices that were much lower than market price and much too low to be making a significant profit. This caused the Salomons to miss out on numerous business and entrepreneur opportunities, thereby making it even more difficult to meet their debt obligations.

Lastly, according to the Salomons, St. Louis' government did not support the Blues and were unwilling to help the team during difficult times. Many other American and Canadian cities encouraged and supported professional sports teams because of the tax money they brought in. When the Salomons asked for the same type of support, however, they were met with glares, anger and denials by city officials.

"It was increasingly difficult for the Blues to operate competitively in St. Louis, and future planning for our operation might well be affected," explained Salomon. "MAC has not shown an operating profit since it had begun operation in 1967…and in the most recent year ending June 30, 1975, our cash flow loss was very substantial."[113]

Salmon hinted that the team might have to relocate if it couldn't find a financial arrangement with St. Louis. The fans were shocked when, in 1976, the NHL gave the family permission to search for a buyer or another city to which to move. "If we had our choice, we'd prefer to stay in St. Louis," said Blues attorney Jim Cullen. "The hockey team itself is making a profit, but we're losing money on the building and we're losing more on the building than we're making on the team... We are trying to make it clear that we cannot continue to operate under the present conditions."[114]

In 1977, the team was forced to let Lynn Patrick go in order to cut money from the payroll. The moves continued, as various members of the Blues staff were released on short notice. "Too much money was tied up in deferred contracts to early Blues stars," said a former employee of the team. "That too much money was lost in paying off all the various coaches who had been fired and that the Blues took their customers for granted after reaching the sell-out point."[115]

In addition to Sid III's financial issues, his interference in the team's hockey operations became overbearing. "Sid Salomon III was an awful meddler," said Hockey Hall of Famer Jimmy Devellano, who worked with the Blues as a scout at the time of the team's inception. "He couldn't keep good managers and coaches because of his constant meddling. Sid was a good person, but he just didn't know hockey. His interference caused a lot of turmoil in St. Louis, and it cost the Salomons dearly."[116]

After years of financial turmoil and "he-said, she-said" disputes, Salomon and the Blues reached a deal with Ralston-Purina Co., a pet food company headquartered in St. Louis. The deal would give Ralston control of the organization and the St. Louis arena for a petty $8.8 million, much less than the Salomons actually put into the team in the first few years of existence.

"If the Salomons had a fault, it was that they tried too hard to please everybody," said *St. Louis Post Dispatch* writer Jeff Myers after the sale. "They were obsessed with making the Arena a comfortable, visually exciting place to watch a hockey game, and obsessed with putting a winning team on the ice. The Salomons cared."[117]

When Sid Jr. died of a heart attack in 1986 at age 76 and Sid III succumbed to cancer in 1988 at age 51, former Blues broadcaster Dan Kelly summed up Sid Jr.'s small investment in 1967: "[St. Louis] had such great early success, that I think the Salomons thought it would be easy…when Sid Jr. moved to Florida, I think he was most sad to leave the hockey team that he gave so much to build. He really did love the Blues. I think he died of a broken heart."[118]

CHAPTER 12

Competitive Imbalance

NHL MANAGEMENT IS NOT clueless.

This may be a revelation, considering the constant criticism of current Commissioner Gary Bettman and the NHL front office. But league management knows what it is doing and it always has.

For example, when six new teams are brought into a league where the existing six teams are already dominant, there is going to be a competitive imbalance. This is why the league decided to split the old and new teams by division to ensure that the playoffs were run symmetrically and to guarantee that an expansion team would always be in the Stanley Cup Final. The assumption was that this would create interest in the six new cities.

"You want to give the expansion teams a chance of credibility," said former NHL President John Ziegler. "If no team was going to be in the Stanley Cup for many years or have a number of games in the playoffs, it would just be a lousy business situation...Even to this day, as my old friend Bill Wirtz used to say, the three secrets of success are season tickets, season tickets and season tickets. The way you sell season tickets is by being in the playoffs.

"If you look at the teams whose attendance go down and down and down every year, they don't make the playoffs. Once they start making the playoffs, you see their season ticket sales go up. In order to give the six new teams a foundation, you wanted to have four of them in the playoffs every year."

Ziegler – who was working as a member of the Detroit Red Wings' Board of Governors at the time – knew, along with Clarence Campbell, that the league had to ensure that the format of the new NHL would be efficient, both financially and on the ice. They had to determine how an expansion draft would be structured, what the schedule would look like, and a way to keep the new teams competitive while not penalizing the more experienced and more talented Original Six teams.

"The most difficult issues to deal with at the board level are the competitive issues," said Ziegler. "These include players and scheduling – a balanced schedule vs. an unbalanced schedule, how the playoffs are structured. The issue of acquisition of players was always a difficult issue. Of course, the drafting of an expansion draft was a formidable task. And it went through many, many drafts."

The urgent need for playoff hockey is supported by a study performed in 2007 by BirdWatchersAnonymous.com (an Atlanta Thrashers blog) to show the relationship between playoff wins per season and financial success since The Great Expansion.[119] "It seems that a long playoff run can be very important to building or solidifying the fan base," the researcher writes. "I suspect that a good long playoff run has a powerful intensifying effect on fan loyalty. It can turn casual fans into more ardent supporters and it may induce occasional attendees to become season ticket holders."

The study explained that there is a correlation between playoff games won per year and financial success. In plain English, the more playoff wins a team has per season, the stronger their market tends to become. The results of the study show that the teams with the most playoff success – Montreal with 5.7 playoff wins per year, Colorado with 5.6, Edmonton with 5.4 and Dallas with 5.0 – have never been in serious danger of folding or relocating and for that matter have never had severe financial problems.

The New Jersey Devils, Philadelphia Flyers, Boston Bruins and Carolina Hurricanes round out the top eight teams in playoff wins per season, and most have therefore never been in true danger of relocation or bankruptcy. The teams on the bottom of the list – Cleveland and Kansas City with zero playoff wins – no longer exist. Other teams with fewer than two playoff wins per season include the Quebec Nordiques, Winnipeg Jets, Hartford Whalers and Phoenix Coyotes – three of which are no longer in existence and one which has encountered financial difficulties.

An important rule always taught in mathematical statistics is that correlation does not equal causation. This means that although the two factors (playoff success and market strength) are correlated, it does not necessarily mean playoff success causes the city to be a stronger NHL market. But in 1967, the NHL didn't need a statistical analysis to understand that playoff success seemed to be beneficial to the financial strength of an NHL team. This is the reason the NHL decided to place all six expansion teams into one division. Four of those teams would be guaranteed to make the playoffs. It also assured at least one of those teams a berth in the Stanley Cup final.

In the 1967-68 campaign, the first season after expansion, the top five teams in the league were all Original Six teams – led by the Montreal Canadiens. The Detroit Red Wings finished 11th in the league after an awful season and failed to beat out Philadelphia, the top expansion team in the first season. However, six of the bottom seven teams in the league were expansion teams, with Oakland finishing in last place with 47 points.

Every expansion team finished under the league average of 74 points in the '67-68 season and the Flyers led all six newcomers with 73. In fact, the Flyers didn't even have a winning record, yet still managed to win the West Division. A points percentage of .487 was all that was required to beat out the second-place Los Angeles Kings in the West Division. In the Original Six division, the top two teams had points percentages above .600, while Montreal led the league with 94 points and a .635 points percentage. This shows the huge imbalance in competition after expansion.

There are numerous other statistics which show how poorly matched the new West Division was compared to the more experienced East. The expansion teams each had an average of 207 goals against for the inaugural season, or an average of about 2.8 goals against per game. Original Six teams gave up about 203 goals each for the season, averaging 2.74 goals against per game – not much of a defensive difference. However, if you remove the stats of the Detroit Red Wings, who gave up an inordinate number of goals in expansion's inaugural season, the Original "Five" teams finished with an average of 192.8 goals against for the season and an average of 2.6 per game – a fairly significant difference from the 2.8 allowed by the expansion teams per game.

Offensively there was an even greater gap between the two divisions. Original Six teams scored an average of 231.2 goals each for the season, averaging 3.12 goals per game. The expansion teams scored about 181.5 goals each on average during the season, averaging to about 2.45 goals per game. This showed a huge gap between the two divisions in terms of offensive skill and raw talent on each squad.

Even more convincing, every major regular season award in the 1967-68 season was won by a member of an Original Six team. Of all the league leaders in offensive categories (goals, assists, points and plus/minus), only one player from an expansion team finished among the top five – Wayne Connelly (who scored 35 goals for the Minnesota North Stars). The only category that included more than one expansion team player – and was dominated by the expansion teams, for that matter – was penalty minutes, in which four of the top five leaders belonged to expansion team players.

This increase in penalty minutes for the league and for the expansion teams showed a change in the style of play for the expansion teams. "In order to get some sense of competition, the expansion teams had to load up on minor leaguers," said hockey historian Stan Fischler. "A lot of these guys couldn't keep up and that's what led to this brawling – dirty hockey – that really wasn't the case before expansion. That's why the Flyers became the Broad Street Bullies. This was their one way of keeping up.

"Eventually, you had so much hooking, holding and hacking and brawling. And the brawling, it was purely a product of expansion. It was frowned upon by guys who liked their hockey the way it was. Obviously in Philadelphia, they loved that. Anybody who went to an expansion game from an expansion city, all he wanted to do was to see his team win. He didn't [care] how it won, one way or another. So if they won by brawling, all the better!"

According to Fischler, the Original Six teams "were appalled" with the new type of game born after expansion. "It's like you drive a Rolls Royce your whole life, then suddenly you're driving a Yugo," Fischler offered as a metaphor. "It's not the same, is it? So that was the feeling, 'What kind of [game] are we watching now'?"

Expansion team goaltenders generally had problems as well. This could be a result of being a member of an inferior team, but just as well could be due to these goaltenders not being nearly as talented as the keepers on the Original Six squads. The average save percentage for Original Six goalies was .911 in the 1967-68 season, while the average save percentage for expansion teams was .898 – and that was while facing the less competitive expansion teams more often as opposed to the Original Six for the majority of the first few seasons.

But expansion teams are not always doomed to failure. They are weak when they first join the league because, similar to a team that is going through a rebuilding process, the expansion team lacks prospects and the luxury of players in their prime. Other teams are not willing to part with their star players during the expansion draft, however after a few years, expansion teams often find success. The Arizona Diamondbacks of Major League Baseball won the World Series in 2001, just three years after their inception. In 1996, the National Football League's Jacksonville Jaguars and Carolina Panthers came within one win of the Super Bowl – each in just their second year in the league.

Hockey and football are similar sports from a building standpoint, in that each requires a large number of players to be successful. It has been proven in the NBA that with just one or two high-caliber players, a team can come within reach of a championship. LeBron James and Mo Williams proved this with the Cleveland Cavaliers in the mid-2000s, as did Kobe Bryant with the Los Angeles Lakers in 2009 and 2010. In hockey, teams cannot succeed with just a few dominant players. The Washington Capitals had an incredible season in 2009-10, being led by forwards Alexander Ovechkin and Nicklas Backstrom and defenseman Mike Green. However, they have not yet won a Stanley Cup as of the 2009-10 season. Successful hockey teams are built through great goaltending, solid defense, and four lines of forwards that can both score and prevent goals from being scored.

The 1968-69 NHL season showed even more of a division of the old and new teams, with the St. Louis Blues being the exception. All of the Original Six teams finished among the top seven in the league, while five of the expansion teams finished from eighth to twelfth. The Canadiens and Bruins dominated the league, finishing with 103 and 100 points, respectively, to lead the league. Aside from the Blues, the expansion teams remained well below the league average of 76 points, with Oakland finishing in second place in the West Division with 69. Offensive production among expansion teams was still down, as each had less than the league average of 227 goals. St. Louis dominated the league's defense, allowing 40 goals less than the second-ranked Rangers.

Off the ice, all of the major awards were swept by Original Six players except for the Vezina Trophy, which was shared by Glenn Hall and Jacques Plante of the St. Louis Blues. In the offensive categories, expansion team players did not rank in the top five in goals, assists, points or plus/minus that season, yet the expansion teams still managed to place players atop the league leaders for penalty minutes. Among league All-Star teams, Glenn Hall was the only expansion player to be named to a team, making him the first player on an expansion squad to be so honored, after the new clubs were blanked in the 1967-68 season.

The 1969-70 season was the year the young Boston Bruins finally became a powerhouse team. Anchored by Bobby Orr and Phil Esposito, Boston led the league with 99 points and soared into the playoffs. The Original Six teams once again staked claim to six of the top seven spots in the league, with St. Louis finishing sixth. Every expansion team but the Blues again finished with less than the league average of 76 points, yet offense began to rise, as both the Minnesota North Stars and the St. Louis Blues finished with more goals than the league average of 221. However, defense seemed nonexistent, as five of the six expansion teams soared above the league average in goals against.

Although the Original Six teams staked claim to all the major awards for the second time in three seasons, a few expansion players – Tommy Williams and Phil Goyette – found themselves among the league leaders in assists. Goyette even finished with 78 points, fourth among forwards behind Orr, Esposito and Stan Mikita. Penalty minute totals again were dominated by the expansion teams, while the All-Star teams were all about the Original Six.

That spring, the Bruins proved to be too much for the Blues, as the Bruins beat up on the still fledgling expansion team in four games – ending with the famous Bobby Orr overtime goal. Though the Bobby Orr goal, and the subsequent photograph, was portrayed as one of the greatest moments in NHL history, media members such as Stan Fischler were not impressed with the victory because of the imbalance of competition between the two clubs. "The media resented the fact that the game was diluted terribly, because they went from six to 12 teams. Where the hell were these [extra] guys coming from? They were coming from the minors. So you had a sham Stanley Cup final in '68, '69, and '70."

Fischler often asks people how Bobby Orr's goal was scored. When they respond that Orr was flying through the air, Fischler becomes irate and red with anger. "No, bullshit!" he yelled. "He wasn't flying through the air when he scored the goal. He scored the goal, and then this idiot defenseman on St. Louis, Noel Picard – who couldn't skate worth a shit – tripped him."

Fischler makes a bold statement that would make a Bruins fan become teary-eyed. "That goal is the phoniest goal in the history of sports," he exclaimed emphatically. "They played a two-bit team, loaded with guys who were over the hill. To put a guy like Noel Picard – you could've put a cigar-store Indian in front of that net and he'd have been better than Picard. It was a joke. And of course, the 1970 Bruins Stanley Cup, that was like an American League team they were playing. Everybody was making a big deal – Bobby Orr flying through the air – that's bullshit! Phony!"

Apart from the feelings of the media, the on-ice product changed. Before expansion, gameplay was wide open and fast. Two games that exhibit this style specifically were in April 1954 and 1955, when the Detroit Red Wings and Montreal Canadiens faced off in consecutive Game 7's in the Stanley Cup Final. In each of the final games, there were no pretty moves, no fancy stickhandling and for sure no bone crunching checks that fans currently expect. Rough play was barely existent, as was evident in the 1954 Game 7, when a player accidentally ran into the opposing goaltender. Instead of starting a huge brawl, as was typical after expansion, the player simply got up and skated back toward the bench, with no punches thrown on either side. It was just part of the game.

Game 7 of the 1964 Stanley Cup Final featured the Toronto Maple Leafs and Detroit Red Wings. This game also exhibited a style of play similar to other games of that era. Players spread out and skated used the entire ice surface – but not in the same formations that appeared after expansion. On the offensive rush, players stayed on opposite sides of the ice, skating full speed toward the opposing goalie. There was no crowding of the net or fancy criss-crossing that now occurs. Players moved up the ice, remaining in position, sometimes passing the puck and shooting at the net, as opposed to setting up in the zone, which is common today. Play was continuous with few battles in the corners, no vicious crosschecks and a minimum of dirty plays.

Another example of this style was Game 5 of the 1965 Stanley Cup Final between the Chicago Blackhawks and the Montreal Canadiens. Teams didn't seem to rely on specific formations or strategies common in today's game. The job of the defensemen wasn't to move around from zone to zone, rather, to remain in their position and make sure the puck did not get too close to their own net.

While checking always existed, it traditionally only occurred in a direct attempt to separate an opposing player from the puck. If a check seemed imminent, but the puck was passed away quickly, the oncoming checker simply turned and went toward the new puck carrier. There was no checking just for the sake of creating reckless collisions with other players on the ice, which seemed to become prevalent at the onset of expansion.

Prior to expansion, defensemen seemed to converge on the puck carrier instead of playing in a defensive zone system. This often left other offensive players open on the opposite side of the zone. Goaltending was also much different before expansion, as goalies rarely left their crease to play the puck or challenge a shooter. When a goaltender held the puck for a faceoff, it was generally because he physically could not move the puck away from himself, as opposed to holding it for the sake of stopping play. Perhaps this change was due to the inexperience on the expansion teams and their subsequent fears of being dragged into a wide-open game, in which they would be unable to compete.

After expansion, Original Six players immediately noticed the change in every part of the game. "There's no question that, first of all, the intensity changed," said Rod Seiling, then a member of the New York Rangers. "You went from playing teams 12 to 14 times a year to half that. So the rivalries you once had and the animosity that built up – because familiarity sometimes breeds contempt – [were gone]. Sometimes things get a little hot under the collar, so quite often you could deal with it the next night or within a week. Now, that could be months. That level, that intensity disappeared. Also, of course, on the expansion teams, the quality of those teams was very low, so when you were playing some of those teams, there was some difference in the competition level, obviously."

"I think obviously it took away from the product of the game for sure," said Paul Henderson, who played for both the Detroit Red Wings and Toronto Maple Leafs in the 1967-68 season. "The new teams coming in, none of them were nearly as formidable as the teams already there…The whole idea was to play defensive hockey and keep the score as close as possible to try to get a tie or a win out of it…when you played them, people expected it to be a sort of a feast. We didn't take the game quite as seriously and we didn't need to. We obviously were going to get more scoring chances, because they just didn't have the ability at that point for the first couple years."

Expansion also caused teams to change the way they manage themselves and their rosters, according to former New York Ranger Vic Hadfield. Before expansion, he observed, teams would have just one goaltender on their roster. But when the league expanded, it allowed room for six new goaltending jobs. With so many potential NHLers fighting for so few jobs, expansion teams began keeping two goaltenders on the roster in order to encourage the starter to remain focused and sharp. If he knew there was a backup waiting to take his place, perhaps he would perform better on a nightly basis.

Hadfield also noticed a decline in the respect level between players – a problem that remains in today's NHL. "When there were only six teams, we kind of policed it ourselves. It was between all the fellows," said Hadfield. "There were no masks, no helmets. People respected the other players in the league as much as they wanted to beat them anyway they could. But there was still a tremendous amount of respect. So you kept your stick down. You were always told and taught, 'this is how you play the game. When you go into the corner, you keep your stick down and on the ice. You hit the individual with your shoulder, knock him off balance and with your stick on the ice. You can walk out of the corner, make a pass to your teammates and move the puck up the ice. You don't see that today. Sticks are up high and there's no respect. Now they have helmets on and facemasks, so the respect is not there as it was in the '60s and the early '70s. I think the players are much bigger and faster today than they ever were, but I'm talking about respect."

According to Hadfield, this respect issue also stretched to the treatment of the officials during the course of a game. During the previously mentioned Blackhawks-Canadiens game in 1965, there were numerous penalties handed out. Never once did a player complain to the referee or yell toward an official for a call. When a penalty was called or a play was blown dead, the players simply skated toward the bench or the faceoff circle. Players given penalties sometimes asked the ref a question, but it was always in a calm manner with more curiosity than anger.

Regardless of respect, players on the Original Six teams never changed their style of play when they played an expansion team. As Seiling notes, although the Original Six teams may not have felt the need to be as sharp for contests against an expansion team, the style never changed. "We always had a pretty good hockey club, especially from '65 on, in New York," said Hadfield. "With [coach] Emile Francis involved, we put in a system that we stuck to, no matter who we were going to be playing. Players were taught at an early age when they came to the big club and they were able to fit in pretty well. We didn't change it, though.

"We respected the other team and we respected the players. They may not have had the NHL experience that some of the other teams and other players had, but they certainly tried and made up for it with real good efforts. You don't want to be critical of these guys. They were given an opportunity to play and they took advantage of it, which is certainly good for the game of hockey."

Paul Henderson noticed that teams had a different mindset in those types of games, however. "You definitely could take more chances," Henderson explained. "If you were playing against the Montreal Canadiens, you had to be aware. I mean, they had some pretty fantastic hockey players. But when you play the Oakland Seals...they may have one or two players you may be concerned about. I think everybody [took more chances], there's no question about it."

Players also were immediately able to see the fledgling clubs' potential to succeed in the league. "The expansion teams – in fact, some of those who did quite well –kept the games quite close and played a tighter style of play," said Seiling. "They identified that they could not get into an open game [with the Original Six] and hope to win against the firepower that the Original Six teams had for the most part."

Henderson also believed that the players' job security also increased with expansion. "More job security? Oh absolutely," said Henderson. "You had six more teams, so you just doubled your job security." The excitement of competition in the playoffs also decreased, according to Henderson. "I mean, how many years did it take for the expansion teams to win Stanley Cups? How long after Philly did it take for another one? So that answers the question right there."

This idea of parity has always been a problem in the NHL, from the time of 1967 expansion, even to modern days. From 1976 to 1988, the Stanley Cup belonged to just three teams. But since 1994, the Stanley Cup has been won by ten different clubs. Since the 2005 NHL lockout, no team has repeated as Stanley Cup champions.

"While it might seem unfair that cities like Raleigh, North Carolina and Tampa, Florida have enjoyed more Cup success than Toronto the last few decades, we like spreading the wealth," said *Sports Illustrated*.

Traditional hockey fans complain that with new teams, there is far too much parity and that hockey is wasted in smaller markets. Others gripe that there are now too many teams. After all, why does a sport once referred to by the media as a "small, regional sport," need 30 teams throughout North America?

"Some fans in Montreal, Chicago and Boston might long for the good ol' days," concludes *Sports Illustrated*. "But having too many teams certainly beats having too few."[120]

NHL Standings, 1967-68

Team	GP	W	L	T	Pts
1. Montreal Canadiens	74	42	22	10	94
2. New York Rangers	74	39	23	12	90
3. Boston Bruins	74	37	27	10	84
4. Chicago Black Hawks	74	32	26	16	80
5. Toronto Maple Leafs	74	33	31	10	76
6. Philadelphia Flyers	74	31	32	11	73
7. Los Angeles Kings	74	31	33	10	72
8. St. Louis Blues	74	27	31	16	70
9. Minnesota North Stars	74	27	34	13	67
10. Pittsburgh Penguins	74	27	34	13	67
11. Detroit Red Wings	74	27	35	12	66
12. Oakland Seals	74	15	42	17	47

NHL Standings, 1975-76

Team	GP	W	L	T	Pts
1. Montreal Canadiens	**80**	**58**	**11**	**11**	**127**
2. Philadelphia Flyers	80	51	13	16	118
3. Boston Bruins	**80**	**48**	**15**	**17**	**113**
4. Buffalo Sabres	80	46	21	13	105
5. New York Islanders	80	42	21	17	101
6. Los Angeles Kings	80	38	33	9	85
7. Toronto Maple Leafs	**80**	**34**	**31**	**15**	**83**
8. Pittsburgh Penguins	80	35	33	12	82
9. Calgary Flames	80	35	33	12	82
10. Chicago Blackhawks	**80**	**32**	**30**	**18**	**82**
11. Vancouver Canucks	80	33	32	15	81
12. St. Louis Blues	80	29	37	14	72
13. New York Rangers	**80**	**29**	**42**	**9**	**67**
14. California Golden Seals	80	26	42	11	65
15. Detroit Red Wings	**80**	**26**	**44**	**10**	**62**
16. Minnesota North Stars	80	20	53	7	47
17. Kansas City Scouts	80	12	56	12	36
18. Washington Capitals	80	11	59	10	32

CHAPTER 13

Competitive Equality

IN THE PREVIOUS CHAPTER, the idea of a competitive imbalance was discussed, in addition to former NHL players explaining how different the expansion teams were from the Original Six teams with respect to talent and performance. The expansion teams had to become more competitive at some point over the next couple decades. Regardless of the Philadelphia Flyers winning the Stanley Cup in 1974, no 1967 expansion team won the Stanley Cup again until 1991 when the Pittsburgh Penguins, led by Mario Lemieux and Jaromir Jagr, lifted the silver mug.

But through the 1970s, the Original Six teams dominated – at least until the latter part of the decade. Looking at numerous stats, it is possible to see a window in which the expansion teams seemed to have a breakout party. From 1967 to 1974, all expansion teams (except the Flyers) seemed to be destined to fall victim to the dominance of the Original Six. But as the decade continued, the expansion teams began climbing the standings and joining the ranks of the Original Six teams atop the league standings and statistical leaders. This culminated with the 1975-1976 season in which, although the Stanley Cup was won by the Montreal Canadiens, the Original Six teams no longer sat atop the league without serious competition.

Additional expansion of the league throughout the 1970s also contributed to the improvement of the 1967 expansion teams, mixed with a continuous diluting of the Original Six teams when future expansion drafts were held. In fact, from 1967 to 1974, there were four expansion drafts to build 12 teams, including 250 players taken from Original Six teams, an average of almost 42 players per team. So it should not be surprising that the Original Six teams lost significant talent and found parity with the 1967 expansion teams in just eight years.

In addition to expansion drafts, it is commonly known that General Managers consider the best (and cheapest) way to build and develop a team is to properly draft players through the NHL Entry Draft. In the '60s and '70s, there was no NHL Entry Draft, only universal Amateur Drafts, which began in 1969, when the Montreal Canadiens drafted right wing Rejean Houle and left wing Marc Tardif with the top two picks – players who would combine to score over 800 points and score over 350 goals in over 1,150 games in their combined careers. As the seasons passed, expansion teams became much more adept at identifying and selecting future talent in each Amateur Draft.

During that first amateur draft, one future Hall of Famer and five future All-Stars (defined here as playing in the league All-Star game) were selected. Hall of Famer Bobby Clarke was selected by the Philadelphia Flyers in the second round. Two of the five All-Stars – Ron Stackhouse of the Seals and Butch Goring of the Kings – were selected by expansion teams. This means that 50% of "great" players (defined here as being either a future Hall of Famer or future All-Star) selected in the 1969 amateur draft were chosen by expansion teams.

In the 1970 amateur draft, two future Hall of Famers and eight future All-Stars were selected. One of the Hall of Famers (Gilbert Perreault of the Sabres) and four of the All-Stars (Dale Tallon, Vancouver Canucks; Greg Polis, Pittsburgh; Bill Clement, Philadelphia; and Al McDonough, Los Angeles) were selected by expansion teams, giving them another 50% share of the significant future talent in the draft.

The 1971 amateur draft featured such legendary players as Guy Lafleur, Marcel Dionne and Larry Robinson. However, none of these players were drafted by expansion teams. Of the seven future All-Stars drafted, just four of those were taken by expansion teams, making just 40% of future greats drafted the property of expansion teams.

But in 1972, the luck of the expansion teams began to turn for the better. Bill Barber, a future Hall of Famer and Stanley Cup winner was drafted in the first round by the Philadelphia Flyers, while eight of the nine All-Stars taken were drafted by expansion teams. These players included Billy Harris of the New York Islanders, Jim Schoenfeld of the Buffalo Sabres and Bob Nystrom, also of the New York Islanders. Altogether, of eleven future greats selected in the draft, nine were taken by expansion teams, making for a huge jump to an 82% success rate for new teams.

The trend continued in 1973 as future Hall of Famer Denis Potvin was selected by the New York Islanders, in addition to the two other Hall of Famers selected by Original Six teams. Ten future All-Stars were selected, seven of them by expansion teams – a 70% success rate for expansion teams. That number shot up again to 79% in 1974, and again rose to 83% in 1975. It shows the skill of the scouts on the expansion teams, resulting in better development of their draft prospects.

The rise of the expansion teams in the standings became obvious as the decade continued. In 1970-71, St. Louis and Philadelphia were the only two expansion teams to finish in the top seven in the league. The next season, only Minnesota was able to claim a part of the top half of the league. In both the 1972-73 and the 1973-74 seasons, just two expansion teams finished in the top seven (Buffalo and Minnesota in the former, Philadelphia and Los Angeles in the latter).

But the 1974-75 season brought new life to the expansion teams with the Philadelphia Flyers winning the Stanley Cup, bringing hope back to the newer teams and showing it *is* possible to win against competition that may appear to be more talented on paper. With the success of the Flyers inspiring new teams, Buffalo, Pittsburgh, Philadelphia and Los Angeles all finished in the top seven, marking the first time that the majority of the top half of the league standings was made up of expansion teams. The next two seasons also featured four expansion teams in the top seven, with Philadelphia, New York Islanders, Buffalo and Los Angeles becoming the league's elite.

Another statistic that increased as the expansion teams improved was offensive totals. From 1970 to 1974, there were an average of about 6.24 goals scored per game. From 1975 to 1977, that number increased to about 6.77 goals per game. Expansion players also began to take over the leaders of offensive categories. In the first two seasons of the 1970s, no expansion players were among the top five in goals or points, however in 1972-73, Bobby Clarke and Rick MacLeish of the Philadelphia Flyers finished in the top five in points, while MacLeish and Bill Flett finished in the top five in goals. The big victory for the expansion teams, however, was Philadelphia's Bobby Clarke winning the Hart Trophy as the league MVP – the first time for any expansion player in the league's history.

1973-74 was an aberration, as the dominance of the Boston Bruins had them with four players among the top five in points (Clarke was the other). But nonetheless, Buffalo's Rick Martin and Minnesota's Bill Goldsworthy were among the top five league leaders in goals, showing a growing strength among expansion teams in scoring. Bernie Parent of the Philadelphia Flyers also showed that the new teams were not going to go down without a fight, as he won the Vezina Trophy as the league's top goaltender (for giving up the fewest goals against). The only other expansion players to win the award at the time were Glenn Hall and Jacques Plante (who had both already established careers for themselves before being selected by an expansion squad in the draft).

In 1974-75 the expansion teams once again showed weakness by not having a single player in the top five in points and just one player (Martin) in the top five in goals. Nonetheless, Bobby Clarke once again won the Hart Trophy as the league MVP, while Parent won his second Vezina.

During the breakout season of 1975-76, the offensive numbers increased, as four of the league's top five goal scorers were from expansion teams, including Philadelphia Flyers Reggie Leach, who led the league with 61. The only non-expansion player to be among the top five was Montreal Canadien Guy Lafleur. Four of the top five points scorers were also from expansion teams, as Bobby Clarke led the new teams with 119 points, six behind league leader Lafleur. Clarke won his third Hart Trophy, while New York Islanders defenseman Denis Potvin won the Norris Trophy, becoming the first player outside Philadelphia to win a major award, not including the Vezina.

In the last season examined, 1976-77, two expansion players were in the top five in goals (Marcel Dionne of Los Angeles and Rick MacLeish of Philadelphia) and four players were in the top five in points (Dionne and MacLeish finished second and fourth, while Gilbert Perrault and

Tim Young tied for fifth in the league). However, no expansion player won a major award.

Goaltending also improved, which is a testament to the improved defense in the NHL. When rated by goals against average, just one of the top five goaltenders was from an expansion team each year from 1970-71 to 1972-73. That number increased to two in 1973-74, then doubled to four for the next two seasons. In 1976-77, three expansion goaltenders were in the top five in goals against average.

In the 1970s, some analysts complained that the expansion teams played rougher hockey and took many more penalties than the league was used to. If this is true, then one can conclude that the top five players in the penalty minute category should consistently be from expansion teams. This was true to an extent, as in 1971-72, four of the top five were from newer teams and in 1972-73 and 1973-74, the top five most penalized players were from expansion teams (seven of the top 10 were from the Philadelphia Flyers). The number began to decrease after the Flyers won their first Stanley Cup, however, as it dropped to three in each of the 1974-75 and 1975-76 seasons and even went down to two in the 1976-77. This suggests a decrease in the amount of rough play by newer teams, due to their increased level of talent, enabling them to keep up with the Original Six teams, playing faster, cleaner hockey.

Any time the NHL expands, an imbalance of competition between the existing teams and the new teams will result – particularly when those new teams make up half of the expanded league as it did in 1967. However, after just eight years, it is notable to see the balance of talent between most NHL teams. This can be attributed to numerous factors, including successful amateur drafts, smart trades, better development and more efficient coaching. Regardless of the actual reason, it is comforting to know, from both a financial and competitive standpoint, that any expansion team entering the NHL has the potential of being competitive given proper management, scouting and drafting, as the Flyers proved by winning a Stanley Cup in just their seventh year of existence.

CHAPTER 14

Comparing Expansion in Professional Sports

THE NATIONAL HOCKEY LEAGUE was not the first professional sports league to expand. One of the tendencies of devoted sports fans is that they often forget about the existence of leagues they do not follow. In order to judge the success of NHL expansion, it is crucial to look at league expansions around the same time period in other professional sports. Comparing and contrasting the processes, drafts and successes behind the expansions of the major professional leagues in North America can help one understand the most effective methods of expansion. Major League Baseball (MLB) consists of 30 teams – 16 in the National League and 14 in the American League. The National Football league (NFL) consists 32 teams, 16 in each the National Football Conference and the American Football Conference. The National Basketball Association (NBA) consists of 30 teams, 15 each in the Western and Eastern Conferences. Today, the NHL consists of the same number of teams as the NBA.

Although all professional sports leagues have expanded significantly since the 1960s, the NHL was the last of the four leagues to do so nationwide. The fact that the league is arguably the least popular and least profitable of the four can be attributed to this delay in expansion. Expansion in professional sports leagues does not guarantee failure or success in any way. The NFL learned this decades ago when their initial expansion decisions laid the foundation for one of the most financially successful sports leagues in the world.

Expansion in the National Football League

In 1933, the NFL was formed with ten teams: the New York Giants, Chicago Bears, Green Bay Packers, Pittsburgh Steelers, Chicago Cardinals, Philadelphia Eagles, Boston Redskins, Brooklyn Dodgers, Cincinnati Reds and Portsmouth Spartans. Over the next 20 years, some teams moved, while at the same time, the league expanded across the country. By 1953, the NFL had 16 teams, stretching from Philadelphia to Los Angeles.

In 1960, the NFL began expanding and realigning their conferences in an attempt to grow the game and retain a competitive balance. The Dallas Cowboys, now one of the wealthiest sports team in the United States, joined the NFL, while the American Football League came into existence in an attempt to compete with the NFL and become the world's top football league. Teams such as the Minnesota Vikings, San Diego Chargers, Kansas City Chiefs, Atlanta Falcons and Miami Dolphins were formed and joined one of the two leagues, causing salaries to skyrocket and pushing both leagues closer to the financial brink.

In 1970, when all hope seemed gone, the NFL and AFL wisely decided to merge. Each of the nine AFL teams joined the NFL, and the current NFC and AFC conferences were formed, consisting of 12 franchises in each conference. In fact, of the 26 NFL teams existing in 1970, all but three – the Houston Oilers, Los Angeles Rams and the Baltimore Colts (they are now in Tennessee, Indianapolis and St. Louis, respectively) – still remain in their original cities. The league subsequently became financially sound, making more money than any other professional sports league in North America.

But according to Al Davis, then the AFL Commissioner and currently the owner of the Oakland Raiders, the rival league created what became known as "babysitters." League representatives created relationships with college football players at times when NFL teams were not permitted to do so. These relationships would attempt to convince college prospects to join the AFL, resulting in NFL teams wasting both draft selections and money. (Both leagues often drafted the same player, but with the previous relationships already established by AFL representatives, NFL teams were often left with an unsigned contract in hand). This was a blatant attempt by the AFL to send the NFL into financial trouble. The AFL's plan worked for a while, until the NFL learned of it and subsequently changed their regulations to lure these bright prospects to their league using the same tactics.

But the AFL management did everything they could to ensure they received the best future football stars. In one case, the league wanted to sign Memphis tackle Harry Schuh, who was one of the top college football prospects in the country. The league constructed a master plan to sneak Schuh to a remote location to convince him to sign with the AFL. Al Davis went to Schuh's hotel in Las Vegas and retrieved a key to his room from the front desk. Davis then noticed Rams "babysitter" Harp Pool watching him and reporting his presence back to the Rams. "We had to pull an escapade," Davis says now. "We had to get him out of the hotel." Immediately, Davis stalled and acted as a decoy and distraction – all the while, two of Davis' assistants quietly escorted Schuh out the back door of his hotel and to the airport. The three men took Schuh to Hawaii, as he requested, before officially signing with the Raiders.[121]

In 1960, LSU's Billy Cannon, a Heisman Trophy-winning running back who was certain to have a superstar professional career, appeared to have signed with two teams – the Dallas Cowboys of the NFL and the Houston Oilers of the AFL. NFL Commissioner, Pete Rozelle, cancelled the Cowboys' signing, stating that the Cowboys were not yet formally approved as an NFL franchise. However, Cannon subsequently signed with the Oilers, who drafted him first overall. The ordeal ended in a court of law, where Cannon was allowed to choose where he wanted to play. Ultimately, he chose the AFL and led the Oilers to two AFL Championships. "If Rozelle had left me alone," said former Cowboys president Tex Schramm in his biography, "The NFL and the Cowboys would have ended up with Billy Cannon."

Also in 1960, Hall of Fame tackle Ron Mix was graduating from University of Southern California. He was drafted in the first round by the reigning NFL Champions, the Baltimore Colts, but was also chosen by the Boston Patriots of the AFL. Mix's true desire was to play for the Colts alongside Johnny Unitas, Lenny Moore and Raymond Berry in order to have the best chance to win an NFL Championship. Mix said that if he were going to play in the East, it was only going to be for the Colts. Knowing that the success of their league was more important than trying to sabotage rivals in the competing conference, the Patriots traded Mix's rights to the Los Angeles Chargers after he showed an interest in playing in the West, near his alma mater.

The Colts offered a $7,500 per year salary with a $1,000 signing bonus. The Chargers offered a $17,000 per year contract which included a $5,000 signing bonus – huge money in 1960. Trying to leverage his worth, Mix asked the Colts for a $12,000 salary. Colts owner Carroll Rosenbloom "told me I was asking for 'Johnny Unitas money,' and that high a contract would disrupt the team's salary structure," Mix recalled. "I wanted to play in the NFL, but I wanted to be treated somewhat fairly." The AFL did just that –Mix became one of just 20 players to play in every year of the AFL's existence.[122]

But the AFL and NFL eventually worked out their differences and merged in 1970, creating a dynasty of successful sports business that still exists today. With the AFL making $36 million over five years from NBC and the NFL making $28.2 million over two years from CBS, television was creating a windfall for every owner of the league. This calculated to about $900,000 per AFL team and $1 million per NFL team – fairly even. With the two leagues merged together, the new NFL would financially dominate the other major professional sports leagues in the country. "I never thought we would get that far, actually," said Art Modell, who owned the NFL's Browns at the time. "I thought [the AFL] was a good league and had good names among players, coaches and owners. They were well-coached teams. I believed it would be nice to get together and merge for the good of pro football."[123]

Immediately following the merger, the NFL continued its expansion in 1967 by adding the New Orleans Saints to the league. Over the next ten years, the Cincinnati Bengals, Seattle Seahawks and Tampa Bay Buccaneers joined the league while the Boston Patriots relocated to Foxboro, Massachusetts and became the New England Patriots. In the 1980s, expansion temporarily ceased as team relocation became more prevalent. However in the 1990s, expansion continued once again, as the Jacksonville Jaguars and Carolina Panthers joined in 1995 and the

Cleveland Browns in 1999. The last NFL expansion team entered the league in 2002, when the Houston Texans began NFL play.

Expansion in the National Basketball Association

The NBA did not exist until 1949, as it was previously known as the Basketball Association of America (BAA). Just before the midway point of the century, ten teams from the rival National Basketball League joined the BAA, ultimately becoming the NBA as it is known today. Although nine teams dropped from the NBA over the next four years, the league never considered expansion. From 1954 to 1960, four teams relocated, but no new franchises were allowed to join.

But in the 1960s, the league added two franchises in Chicago (one of which moved to Baltimore) and one each in San Diego, Seattle, Milwaukee and Phoenix. In 1970, Buffalo, Cleveland and Portland joined the league, expanding the NBA to 17 teams aligned in four divisions. Expansion continued when the New Orleans Jazz joined the league in 1974, but the turning point came in 1976 when the rival American Basketball Association merged with the NBA, adding the Denver Nuggets, Indiana Pacers, New York Nets and San Antonio Spurs.

The NBA and ABA originally attempted to merge in 1970, after 13 of 17 NBA owners voted to work with the rival league. However, when the agreement was reached, the NBA Players Association, headed by the Milwaukee Bucks' Oscar Robertson, filed an antitrust suit against the league in a case known as *Robertson v. National Basketball Association*. The Players Association was claiming that with heavy free agency restrictions already in place, a merger would further erode an NBA player's negotiating leverage. The U.S. Congress took action in 1972, creating a bill that would allow the merger to take place. However, the bill favored the owners and the Senate failed to pass it. In 1973, another bill was created, which also did not pass.

The Oscar Robertson suit dragged until 1976, when the case was finally settled. After years of discussions and planning on the part of the two leagues, the court allowed the merger to finally commence. Interleague exhibition games began, creating a friendly relationship that ultimately resulted in numerous ABA teams joining the NBA.

As an interesting side note, when the NBA accepted four of the six ABA teams into the league in 1976, the Kentucky Colonels and the Spirits of St. Louis were left out. However, they were offered $3.3 million as a settlement, which was accepted by the Colonels, but the Spirits of St. Louis owners did not want just a few million. Instead, they struck what was then a minor deal with the league, giving the St. Louis owners a fraction of the NBA's television contract money for the rest of their lives. However, television coverage of the NBA grew, giving St. Louis franchise owners the most television revenue, even though they had no team. Their total earnings were $186 million between 1976 and 2008. Although the NBA tried to buy the owners out in 1982, they declined, opting instead for the continued TV money. In 2007, the NBA extended the contract eight additional years, as agreed in the original deal in the 1970s. Due to the great foresight of the St. Louis owners and their belief in the future of TV, they currently earn about $14.57 million per season from the contract, even though they have no team.

Expansion continued as seven teams joined the NBA between 1980 and 1997, with the Charlotte Bobcats becoming the final franchise to join the league in 2004. After the Bobcats joined, the NBA changed their expansion draft rules. Since they were the only team entering the league at the time, the expansion draft would not be as extensive as that of the NHL in 1967 when the size of that league doubled. However, the NBA had to assure Charlotte a chance to succeed without penalizing the existing teams. The Bobcats, who needed to select at least 14 players in the draft, were only allowed to select a maximum of one player from each team. The 29 existing teams were allowed to protect at most eight players on their roster. The draft continued until the Bobcats had a full roster. To protect the Bobcats from signing big name free agents, the NBA imposed a salary cap on Charlotte which was just 66% of the league cap for the team's first season. In their second season, they would be allowed to spend up to 75% of the league salary cap. The Bobcats would have full salary cap privileges in their third year in the league.

Like the NHL in 1967 (and later), the NBA allowed teams to make trades with the Bobcats in exchange for an agreement that Charlotte would not select certain players in the draft. This allowed the Bobcats to stock up on talent and prospects without actually losing a member of their organization. Unlike the NHL, however, the NBA forbade a team from reacquiring a player lost in the expansion draft (unless the player was put on waivers) until one calendar year had passed from the date of the draft. This was to allow the Bobcats to use every player they selected in order to maximize their potential for success.

The same general plan was used in the 1966 NBA expansion draft, with existing teams allowed to protect eight players. However, the Chicago Bulls were not pleased, being the newcomers to the NBA, and requested that the number be dropped from eight to seven. In exchange, they agreed to select last in each round of the upcoming college draft (now known as the NBA Draft). This shows similarities between both the NBA and the NHL in their attempts to keep the existing teams strong, while still providing new expansion squads with the tools needed to succeed. Ironically, those tools did not work too well the following year for the NBA. In the 1967 expansion draft, every player selected played four seasons or less with the team which drafted them. Each of those players was either moved to another team or retired from professional basketball.

Expansion continued to be a viable option for the NBA through the 1980s, as *Los Angeles Times* writer Chris Baker explains in his April 1987 article entitled *A Look At Expansion in the NBA*. He discusses the expansion fees for NBA franchises, which have skyrocketed over the years. In 1970, Buffalo, Cleveland and Portland each paid $3.15 million to enter the league. Four years later, the New Orleans Jazz paid almost double that – $6.15 million. In the 1980s, the Dallas Mavericks paid $12 million, yet just seven years later, *Fortune Magazine* said the team was worth three times that. Therefore, the NBA decided that, as of 1987, the price for an expansion team would be $32.5 million, $7.5 million more than the media had been estimating six months earlier. "The price was based on a number of factors," explained NBA assistant general counsel Bill Jemas. "We looked at recent franchise sales and we compared the potential income for a new franchise to expenses. We wanted to get a number that the team could afford to live under."[124]

However, the lofty price tag did not scare potential franchise owners from professional basketball. It actually intrigued more investors, since it created the perception of an NBA franchise being very valuable and desirable. Rather than require a low expansion fee just to get 20 players, as the NHL did, the NBA made owners understand that this was not just a check they were going to throw around. They were investing in something of significant value – an NBA team.

Fast forward now to 2011. As reported by the *Seattle Post-Intelligencer* in 2008, NBA owners are not opposed to expansion as are many fans and journalists. After the Seattle Supersonics relocated to Oklahoma City and renamed themselves the Thunder, owners had already speculated that there would be numerous expansion applications from the Seattle area to replace the team that was recently lost. This type of speculation dated back to 2002 when the Charlotte Hornets moved to New Orleans. NBA commissioner David Stern swore that Charlotte would be granted a new franchise within three years if they were able to build a new arena. The arena was built and, subsequently, the Charlotte Bobcats came to existence less than three years later.

Though many owners claim they favor the idea of expansion, it is likely due to some easy cash being generated. However, Stern and a majority of NBA owners instituted a philosophy that they would much rather relocate a financially struggling team than add a new, unproven, expansion team. (Ironically, the NHL makes this same claim, as will be discussed in Chapter 15). Dallas Mavericks owner Mark Cuban agrees with this.

"I would always vote against expansion because expansion's the worst economic move a league like the NBA can make," he explained. "Expansion is nothing more than a loan because whatever [a new owner would] give you [in expansion fees], you pay them back in equity ownership of the NBA and share of the TV money. So it's like saying, 'Hey, buy my house for $300 million and I'll pay you back $26 million a year out of the TV money for buying my house.' For some reason, I was the only one who could figure out that was a bad deal and so I voted against it [in Charlotte] and everybody else voted for it."[125]

Although the NBA seems to have mixed opinions regarding future league expansion, numerous rumors indicate that the league is interested in expanding internationally to countries like China, Russia and throughout Europe. Talk that the NBA was serious about international exposure began when the league created an NBA store in China on May 1, 2010. The store, located in the Shanghai World Expo Performing Arts Center, is currently the largest NBA store outside the United States. "We pride ourselves on being the most popular sport in China," said Collins Qian, NBA China Chief Operating Officer. "We see an increased popularity of our brand." The NBA has about 150 people working in four NBA China offices, with the purpose of promoting the league and the game.[126]

Experts estimate that about 300 million Chinese play basketball in their country – a number approximately equal to the entire population of the United States. This revelation makes NBA executives and league officers ecstatic at the possibility of adding their league to the Chinese culture. NBA viewership in China has increased 31% from 2007-08 to 2009-10 to more than 2.1 billion viewers per season. Chinese viewership online has also increased 60% in those same years, proving an increased interest in that area of the world. At this time, more than half of the league's online traffic originates from outside the United States.

Reports also mention that the NBA is interested in expanding to Russia. With new New Jersey Nets owner Mikhail Prokhorov becoming the first Russian owner in NBA history in 2010, the league opened an office in Russia, naming a new executive as a managing director. "We see [Russia] as a strategic market," said NBA International President Heidi Ueberroth. "The Prokhorov deal only serves to accelerate our plans. We are focusing on growing the game and it's already been a key part of our strategy. It is really important for our partners…and we are looking at all kinds of events and additional media opportunities." The NBA also has offices in Italy, France, England, Spain and Turkey. A new office is planning to be opened in India in the next few years.[127]

The response from the fans and the media? "Bring on European expansion!" says Yahoo! Sports writer Kenny Smith. "Add approximately six new franchises at once. They would make up the new Euro Division… there is talent out there and it's creeping into the NBA instead of making a splash all at once.

"So, come on – expand your mind and be global," Smith concludes in his piece. "The commissioner is. And trust me, you will be wearing that Team Italia fitted [jersey] and the Greece throwback [jersey] one day. Count on it."[128]

Expansion in Major League Baseball

When Major League Baseball expanded in 1961, they added the New York Mets and Houston Colt .45s to the circuit. In the 1961 expansion draft, both teams paid $75,000 for each of 16 "average" players they selected, $50,000 for each of three "other" players and $125,000 for each of four "highly-skilled" players. However, the two franchises performed so poorly that just two years later, another expansion draft was held to help the struggling teams. The Mets and Colt .45s were allowed to select four players each from the existing teams in an attempt to shore up their organizations – ultimately to little avail (these were the "clown teams" Clarence Campbell referred to in his argument against expansion).

Over the next 47 years, MLB added numerous teams, but the league has remained at 32 since 1998. Teams have moved from the National League to the American League and vice versa, but expansion teams have not since been added, allowing baseball to have a long-term, steady business model, one that has been consistent for more than a hundred years.

Between 1961 and 1998, MLB added 14 teams to their leagues. No expansion team experienced a winning record in their first year of existence. All but the Colorado Rockies had fairly weak attendance numbers, yet the four most recent additions (Rockies and Florida Marlins in 1993 and Tampa Bay Devil Rays and Arizona Diamondbacks in 1998) showed consistent increased fan attendance at each home game.

This increase in home attendance is not unusual, based on a 2007 study performed by Kevin Quinn and Paul Bursik, entitled "Growing and Moving the Game: Effects of MLB Expansion and Team Relocation 1950-2004," which showed numerous effects of expansion. The number of MLB teams per 10 million U.S. inhabitants has decreased almost every decade since 1900, when it was at a high of over five teams per 10 million people. It reached a low in 1960 of just over one per 10 million based on the U.S. population increasing faster relative to the number of teams. After the rate increased in the 1970s, the number once again decreased to where it is today, between one and two teams per 10 million people.

The study goes on to show that out of each of the 14 aforementioned teams added to the league between 1961 to 1998, just one (Arizona Diamondbacks) had a winning record after the first three years of existence. The Diamondbacks even won the World Series in their fourth year, something none of the other 13 teams accomplished. Because the draft procedures remained generally the same each time the league expanded, it is easier to compare the early success of MLB expansion teams relative to other professional sports.

Baseball's attendance also increased as the league expanded. Although league attendance dropped to an average of about 11,000 per game in 1953, it continued to grow in subsequent years to a high of over 31,000 average attendance per game in 1992. After the player's strike in 1994-95, the sport's popularity sank, with attendance not far behind. Dropping to fewer than 25,000 average fans per game, the league struggled once again. But with a few more teams added, attendance numbers increased, reaching an average of about 30,000 fans per game in 2004.

Due to the competitive imbalance between expansion teams and existing teams, opposing fans had little interest in seeing these new teams, which were mostly comprised of less talented players. In response, attendance was negatively affected when a new expansion team played on the road.

But with over 12 years of league financial stability since the strike, numerous fans and media outlets believe that expansion is inevitable in the coming years – even if it occurs outside the borders of the United States. Tom Van Riper of *Forbes* cites the World Baseball Classic (an international baseball tournament played every four years) as a tool for attempting to grow the game overseas. "It's…about growing the reach of Major League Baseball to markets where the game is already big, namely Asia and Latin Americas," says Van Riper. "Sports business experts think that to extend its powerful arm overseas, the league may soon be ready to ramp up its initiatives in those markets."[129]

As Van Riper points out, although 34 nationalities are represented on Major League Baseball's rosters, over 80% of baseball's 241 foreign players come from either Latin America or Asia and 91 of those players come from the Dominican Republic. These foreign regions account for $13.5 billion of revenues for MLB in television and merchandise money.

With 17 players from either Korea or Japan on major league rosters, the game is becoming more popular in those Asian countries. It seems only a matter of time before the MLB expands the game overseas, possibly creating an MLB Japan or MLB Asia that can help generate even more revenues for the league. Baseball already earns over $100 million annually from foreign television deals, but that is still less than 5% of all revenue generated by Major League Baseball.

Revenues aside, many others do not like the idea of expansion and do not expect the idea to come to fruition anytime soon. Maury Brown of the website *Biz of Baseball* reminds fans that baseball's TV viewership is down. The 2007 World Series, which lasted just four games, was watched by an average of over 17 million people. However, the 1978 World Series, at a time in which the country's population was significantly less than today, was viewed by over 44 million people over six games, almost three times the aforementioned amount.

But MLB set another record for paid attendance in 2007; their revenues topped $6 billion and television ratings increased for over two-thirds of the teams in the league. "It's safe to say that America is back to having its love affair with MLB and in a big way," writes Brown.[130]

Expansion seems to be a continually sensitive issue in baseball. Numerous sports management students in schools across the United States write final term papers questioning why many large metropolitan cities lack an MLB team, despite baseball being one of America's most popular sports. For example, for over a decade, Portland, Oregon has desired to be considered for an MLB team. However, as of this date, their attempt has been to no avail.

Maury Brown also points out that the last two expansions in MLB (1993 and 1998) occurred after the league found itself in financial difficulty. In 1995, the league was emerging from the devastating players' strike, which pitted the owners and players against each other in a dragged out dispute. The owners wound up conceding $280 million to the players – money that could only be easily recovered through expansion fees.

"I don't think there's any doubt about it," said one analyst on the idea that baseball only expanded to make up their losses from the previous decade. "They did what most would business do, they sold stock, they sold interest in the clubs, in the expansion clubs…without it I think baseball would have had a very serious time." The analyst also explains that since baseball is currently performing exceedingly well financially, there is no need to use expansion fees as a generator of revenues.[131]

That's not to say that Major League Baseball – or the any other professional American sports league, for that matter – will stop expanding in the future. Based on current financial barriers to entry, just don't expect it to happen anytime soon. Simply remember what MLB Chief Operating Officer Bob DuPuy said regarding when expansion would happen: "When the moon and the stars and the planets and the money are aligned."

NHL Franchises, 1968-2010

1970 – Buffalo Sabres (expansion), still active

1970 – Vancouver Canucks (expansion), still active

1972 – Atlanta Flames (expansion) relocated in 1980

1972 – New York Islanders (expansion), still active

1974 – Kansas City Scouts (expansion), relocated in 1976

1974 – Washington Capitals (expansion), still active

1976 – Cleveland Barons (relocation from California), merged with North Stars in 1978

1976 – Colorado Rockies (relocation from Kansas City), relocated in 1981

1979 – Edmonton Oilers (expansion from WHA), still active

1979 – Hartford Whalers (expansion from WHA), relocated in 1997

1979 – Quebec Nordiques (expansion from WHA), relocated in 1995

1979 – Winnipeg Jets (expansion from WHA), relocated in 1996

1980 – Calgary Flames (relocated from Atlanta), still active

1981 – New Jersey Devils (relocated from Colorado), still active

1991 – San Jose Sharks (expansion), still active

1992 – Ottawa Senators (expansion), still active

1992 – Tampa Bay Lightning (expansion), still active

1993 – Mighty Ducks of Anaheim (expansion), still active as Anaheim Ducks

1993 – Florida Panthers (expansion), still active

1993 – Dallas Stars (relocated from Minnesota), still active

1995 – Colorado Avalanche (relocated from Quebec), still active

1996 – Phoenix Coyotes (relocation from Winnipeg), still active

1997 – Carolina Hurricanes (relocated from Hartford), still active

1998 – Nashville Predators (expansion), still active

1999 – Atlanta Thrashers (expansion), still active

2000 – Columbus Blue Jackets (expansion), still active

2000 – Minnesota Wild (expansion), still active

CHAPTER 15

Moving the NHL Forward The Future of Expansion

IN THE 34 YEARS since The Great Expansion, the NHL has added 19 teams to the league. Although some teams relocated and two merged, expansion has been the method of choice the NHL uses to add both funds and teams. Between 1970 and 1979, the league added nine teams – the last being four from the World Hockey Association. These four teams had to join in 1979 in order to continue operations after the WHA folded. But after this expansion, the NHL did not add new teams (other than relocation) until 1991, when the San Jose Sharks became the first expansion team in California since the Seals moved to Cleveland.

In the 1970s, the NHL continued to add teams as if it were a game, rather than a business. It may actually be the business aspect that convinced the league to expand, since each owner received millions of dollars as new teams were added. In 1969, when the NHL prepared for future expansion, Bill Jennings, head of the expansion committee, made the following announcement:

"After many months of Board and Committee meetings, we feel we have achieved a comprehensive blueprint for the long-range growth of the NHL. We are now ready to receive formal applications for two new franchises from any city of major league status in the United States or Canada. We are also considering further expansion, which could include all of the major hockey centers in the world.

"All of us in the NHL owe a debt of gratitude to our NHL Expansion

Committee of Mr. Wirtz, Jack Kent Cooke of the Los Angeles Kings, Gordon Ritz of the Minnesota North Stars and David Molson of the Montreal Canadiens. They did much of the work and planning to accomplish this present blueprint for growth."[132]

The league clearly enjoyed the brief popularity it was receiving from expansion in the 1970s. Additional teams were not added in the 1980s since four teams from the rival World Hockey Association had recently merged with the league. It was not until the 1990s that the NHL's desire to expand rose again. With new commissioner Gary B. Bettman on board, the belief was that if the NHL expanded operations to the West Coast, the Southwest and the Southeast, Americans' interest in ice hockey would rise due to increased visibility in most major cities in the United States. Most hockey fans had been surprised when, in the 1980s, the NHL declined to consider expansion after the high profile 1980 "Miracle on Ice" Olympic game won by the U.S. team over the Soviet Union. With this amount of exposure for the sport in the United States, fans believed that is was the perfect time for both expansion and a new national television contract in the United States.

"In the United States, we knew that we would not become a sport for the national networks," said John Ziegler in the '80s to an audience at the Empire Club in Toronto, Ontario. "The people in the south and southwest don't want to watch hockey and, as a business, it would be bad for the networks."

However, others believed that was a mistake. "Not having the games on TV was a detriment to growing our sport," said one league official to the *Toronto Globe and Mail*. "Unless your team was playing the Oilers, the sports fans didn't see Gretzky in the United States. It was a huge impediment and one that challenges us to this day."[133] In the early 1990s, the NHL expanded into five cities in just five years, adding the San Jose Sharks, Ottawa Senators, Tampa Bay Lightning, Florida Panthers and Anaheim Mighty Ducks. Business was expected to boom, but the league began having problems with SportsChannel America, which owned the TV rights to the NHL's games at the time. This infuriated fans, since ESPN was offering to renew the NHL's contract on what was becoming the country's most watched sports channel. Yet, Ziegler decided to take SportsChannel's deal because they offered double the money – apparently sacrificing popularity and exposure for quick profits.

The contract with SportsChannel ended in 1992, at about the same time as Ziegler's term as NHL President concluded. After a brief stint by Gil Stein as president, Bettman became the NHL commissioner (the "President" title was changed to "Commissioner" when Bettman was named). Bettman had worked with the NBA under commissioner David Stern, and jumped to the NHL at a critical time. The league recently experienced a boom in expansion, yet the business growth they desired was not forthcoming. Initially, Bettman declined to expand the league further in order to fix the unprofitable teams that currently existed. He permitted four teams to relocate in an attempt to firm up their financial situations. The North Stars relocated to Dallas, the Quebec Nordiques to Denver, the Winnipeg Jets to Phoenix and the Hartford Whalers to Raleigh, North Carolina.

Bettman would also sign numerous deals in the TV market, bringing ESPN back (even helping to create ESPN2, which was originally designed to carry NHL games to provide full league coverage), in addition to signing deals with FOX and ABC. After earning over $1 billion in TV deals for the NHL in less than a decade, Bettman and his staff decided it was now time to consider expanding the league again. "Expansion was intended to improve our footprint and make us a more prominent place on the national landscape in terms of media coverage and the like," Bettman explained after the 2005 lockout. "It made us truly competitive. In 1990, we were in 11 U.S. markets and we were perceived to be regional. Now we're in 22 U.S. markets.

"We have unprecedented exposure and, in fact, we have unprecedented revenues. In this Collective Bargaining Agreement in the last decade we have managed to grow revenues from a little over $400 million to $2 billion dollars. So in some respects, the business side, as it relates to revenues, has never been stronger."[134]

With that in mind, the league announced in 1996 that they were going to add four new teams over the next five years. To become a serious candidate for expansion, the league made prospective bidders fill out a long application for the NHL to review. Included in this application were questions regarding the market size, the estimated demand of hockey in the community, information about the corporate core of the community, any previous history of hockey in the city and most importantly, information about the building intended to house a potential new team.

Ultimately, bids were received from 11 different cities. Among them were Nashville, Atlanta, Columbus, Minneapolis/St. Paul, Houston, Oklahoma City and Hamilton, Ontario. The first franchise was awarded to Nashville. "We were ultimately rewarded an expansion franchise in '97, then we started playing in '98-99," said Ed Lang, the CFO of the Nashville Predators. "When the league decided they were going to go from 26 teams to 30, our owner back then, Craig Leipold, got involved and decided he was interested in trying to bring an expansion team to Nashville. We went through a fairly lengthy process."

Nashville had attempted to land an NHL team two years earlier in 1995 when the New Jersey Devils were in financial difficulty and experiencing problems with their lease and arena. Nashville offered a $20 million relocation bonus to the owners of the New Jersey Devils if the team would move to Tennessee. However, the Devils were unable to terminate their lease, and therefore remained in Northern New Jersey. After this failed attempt at relocating the Devils, Commissioner Bettman confirmed to Nashville that in the next wave of expansion, the city would be seriously considered as a candidate to join the NHL.

"In some cases like Columbus and Minnesota and Atlanta, they didn't even have buildings at that point in time, so they had to apply [to build an arena]," continued Lang. "At that time, we had already started building a building. It was well under construction, so all we had to do was supply how the building was being funded, the capacity, etc."

The people in charge of Nashville's bid went to New York City to make a formal presentation to the league – exactly as did the six expansion teams in 1965 for Clarence Campbell, Bill Jennings and their staff. Nashville's presentation included a video narrated by Amy Grant, a famous Christian rock singer. She helped make a comparison between the booming music industry and sports, ultimately making Nashville seem like a desired place to put a major league hockey team for the first time.

Shortly after the presentation, the Board of Governors visited Nashville to tour the city, meet the prospective corporate sponsors and inspect the building to ensure it was of the highest quality before formally awarding a franchise. When they arrived, the owners had gathered thousands of potential fans outside the building to welcome and cheer the Board of Governors. This show of appreciation and excitement, mixed with the incredible hospitality shown by the city of Nashville, convinced the NHL that Nashville was the next place to go.

The franchise was awarded to Nashville in June 1997. One of the criteria for the league was that the organization had to sell at least 12,000 season tickets by March of the following year. "If you were not able to do that, then they wouldn't award you the franchise," said Lang. As one would expect, the team was able to surpass that 12,000-ticket mark, thus the Nashville Predators were born.

Just south of Nashville, Ted Turner, former AOL Time Warner Vice Chairman and founder of Turner Broadcasting System, Inc., believed that Atlanta was also a perfect place for NHL hockey. Already the owner of the NBA's Atlanta Hawks and MLB's Atlanta Braves, Turner clearly had the financial depth to start and run an NHL organization. He created Atlanta Hockey Club, Inc. and applied to the league.

"They had NBA basketball in Atlanta and the old Omni [Coliseum] was becoming a great place to play," said Atlanta Thrashers President Don Waddell, who, as of 2011, has been in the organization since the franchise's founding. "They were talking about having two major tenants in the building – that was back in the 1996 and 1997 range. There was a group led by Ted Turner who wanted to apply for the franchise…The number one thing was that you had to have the resources to build an NHL team and the second was to have a building to play in," Waddell continued. "Those two things were pretty set."

The group continued pushing for a team and when they were finally awarded a franchise, wasted no time in putting together a management group that they believed could turn the new team into an immediate winner. Waddell was hired on June 23, 1998 to begin preparing for the league's expansion and entry drafts in 1999. By March 1999, the team had reached the 12,000 season ticket mark mandated by the league – and the Atlanta Thrashers were ready to establish themselves.

While the NHL believed that expanding to the South was the right move, both fans and media alike disagreed. "The NHL in markets like Nashville, Atlanta, Tampa, Miami…I could go on and on…doesn't make any sense," said Howard Bloom, the publisher of SportsBusinessNews. com. "When 'historians' look back at what happened to the National Hockey League they'll see a league in the 1990s that was driven by greed and utter lack of proper business acumen. The NHL expanded to 30 franchises and first and foremost believed expansion fees were a new form of revenue." In 2000, franchises were also awarded to both the Minnesota Wild and Columbus Blue Jackets, rounding out the last expansion of the NHL to date.

As previously discussed, the NHL has used expansion fees as a form of revenue since 1967. In fact, it was one of the reasons that the Original Six owners agreed to expand in the first place. "As long as they brought in new teams, it was an easy way to get money," said an unnamed former NHL owner. "But it is inevitable when you have that many teams you are going to have competition for players and player salaries are going to go up."

In addition to driving up league salaries, the league seemed only to be interested in doing what it could to sign a TV contract, which would put them on the same level as the NFL or MLB. "Chasing the pot of gold that was a national TV contract diluted the quality of the product," said a sports attorney as quoted in the *Washington Post*.

Others saw the game become diluted as well, including former Kings owner Bruce McNall – who acquired Wayne Gretzky from the Edmonton Oilers. "I love the game with its stars," he explained. "Unfortunately, what came with expansion is that teams need to win by taking away those stars. The 'star' becomes a defensive coaching system. Could a Wayne Gretzky do today what he did back then? He'd have to dump and chase today. Where does today's game allow the stars to shine?"[135]

Regardless of fan and media opinions on the future of NHL expansion, it is inevitable that the league will consider adding teams over the next few decades. The NHL has stated that it has no desire or need to expand anytime soon, nor are there any specific plans to do so in the future. Yet the NHL has identified specific cities that would be considered should the NHL decide to add more teams to the league at a later date.

Jason Kay, editor-in-chief of *The Hockey News*, believes that expansion could be imminent in the near future. He suggests five cities as the most likely recipients of NHL franchises: Winnipeg, Manitoba; Houston, Texas; Quebec City, Quebec; Seattle, Washington; and a second team in Toronto, Ontario.

Winnipeg once housed the WHA's and NHL's Winnipeg Jets, but the team was ultimately moved to Phoenix for a number of reasons, including increased operating costs, salaries and an inability to keep up with the rest of the league financially. It is the eighth largest market in Canada, featuring the MTS Centre with a capacity of just over 15,000. The arena was built in 2004 to house the AHL's Manitoba Moose and to perhaps convince the NHL to bring the Jets back to Winnipeg. The NHL declined, yet Commissioner Bettman stated that Winnipeg will definitely be considered for future league expansion. Nonetheless, if Winnipeg should be selected for expansion, their arena will most likely need to be enlarged and upgraded to meet NHL standards.

Houston is in the largest state in the continental United States and is its tenth largest market. Its Toyota Center has a capacity of 17,800 for the AHL's Houston Aeros. Originally considered for expansion in the 1990s, Houston has been lobbying for an NHL team for over a decade. They contend that if Dallas can support a team, Houston, a city with almost the same population, can also support one.

Quebec City was once home to the WHA's and NHL's Quebec Nordiques before moving to Denver to become the Colorado Avalanche, and subsequently winning a Stanley Cup in their first season. The Quebec City market is the seventh largest in Canada, although the arena, Le Colisee, can seat just 15,399. They currently are the home of the Quebec Major Junior League's Quebec Remparts. The city is the largest Canadian market without an NHL team.

Toronto, of course, is the home of the Maple Leafs. Their Air Canada Centre seats 18,819 and consistently sells out for a team that seems to consistently miss the playoffs. The city also support the Toronto Marlies, the Leafs' AHL farm team. Three Ontario Hockey League teams are also located near Toronto, proving that the largest market in Canada can successfully support multiple hockey teams. Adding another NHL team to the Toronto market runs the risk of usurping the territory of Maple Leaf Sports and Entertainment, one of the most influential sports team ownership groups in North America. But according to Bettman and his staff, the league will act in the best interest of the business of professional hockey.

Seattle has not had an NHL team in its history. The Pacific Coast Hockey Association's Seattle Metropolitans won the Stanley Cup in 1917 and were also a part of the famous Stanley Cup Final in 1919, which was cancelled due to the influenza epidemic. The city is currently home to the WHL's Seattle Thunderbirds. The Thunderbirds' home, the Key Arena, seats just 15,177 and is aging. It most likely would need renovations and an expanded seating capacity should Seattle acquire an NHL franchise.

Other cities suggested by Kay, and which have been mentioned by other members of the media in the past, are Cleveland, the 17th largest market in the United States; Hamilton, which has tremendous support from the city and from Research In Motion's Jim Balsillie, who has continuously attempted to place a team there; Las Vegas, since the NHL seems intent on placing a team in the city full of nightlife; and Kansas City, since the league is confident in its ability to support a major league team, after hosting numerous NHL exhibition games.

Bettman claims that all options are on the table in any discussion on future expansion. However, much of the media believes that that the league only plans to pursue future expansion in the United States. The game is already the most-watched sport in Canada and is the country's national pastime, but in the United States, hockey is the fourth among professional sports. It is therefore logical to expand the game in the United States, a market with room left to grow.

There also were numerous reports that the NHL is considering expansion to Europe at some point in the next ten years. This story surfaced after Deputy Commissioner Bill Daly announced in 2008 that he envisioned the NHL having a presence in Europe within a decade. This "presence," however, was never specified as expansion. It could also mean that European countries will develop an interest in watching and following NHL games and the Stanley Cup playoffs. Nonetheless, with about 30% of NHL players having nationalities in Europe, it is difficult to argue the possibility that the NHL could grow the game by locating teams overseas.

In actuality, the next logical choice for future expansion seems to be either Toronto or Hamilton. There is so much support for the game in Ontario that the market could likely support a second team. Critics claim this to be unfair to the Toronto Maple Leafs and that it would be detrimental to their business. Those who make this claim this should read the history of the expansion of the New York Islanders and New Jersey Devils, both of whom were required to pay fees to the New York Rangers for infringing on their market. Today, the demand for Rangers tickets is still just as high as it was prior to the two other New York area teams joining the league.

Although Toronto is not as large a metropolitan area as New York City, many more hockey fans live in that area than in any city in the United States. The Greater Toronto Area has a population of over 5 million, while the Toronto Maple Leafs have over 4,000 fans on the season ticket waiting list – a wait which could last 20 years.

"One of the surest investments right now, I think in the world, would be a second NHL franchise in Southern Ontario," said Oakville MPP Kevin Flynn. "Everyone I have talked to and any economist report, tell us it is a job creator and it's a profit maker." Flynn has been urging the Ontario government to pull for a second NHL team to be placed in the Greater Toronto Area. "It really is the center of the hockey world. This is what we are known for."[136]

In tough economic times in the United States, sports games are often one of the first luxuries to be deleted from the family budget. During the economic recession from 2008-2010, revenue of U.S. sports teams grew at a very slow rate and even declined in some markets. The NHL, surprisingly, saw overall revenues increase, not from attendance, rather from sponsorships. During difficult economic times in Canada, fans still attend hockey games – especially in Toronto where a ticket to a Maple Leaf game seems as valuable as a ticket to the Super Bowl. Fans tend to continue to support ice hockey in Canada, often regardless of the cost or their economic situation.

The general consensus among fans and the media is that expansion should not be considered for the foreseeable future. Many believe the NHL is large enough with 30 teams, while others believe the number is too high. "If the NHL needs anything, it's contraction," says one NHL fan. "I'm in favor of dumping four teams and dropping the league to 26. Or, while we're at it, dropping to 24 would make for even-sized divisions…The concentration of teams in stronger markets with more talent to choose from seems financially sound to me.

"But then again, I'm not an economist."[137]

Most fans are not economists and therefore are not in a position to analyze the NHL's financial situation and the prospects of success in the near future. But as Lyle Richardson of FOX Sports explains, if the NHL expands, "then it's based solely on a short-term cash grab for the 30 owners, rather than on doing what's best for the league. That's what fuelled the expansionist policy in the 1990s. It was done more based on who had the money to pay for a franchise, rather than placing one in a market that would sustain it and thus grow the game's excitement.

"The NHL doesn't need any more teams," Richardson concludes. "What it needs to do is nurture those clubs that are struggling to establish themselves in the current non-traditional hockey markets."[138]

On the contrary, Mike McAllister of *Sports Illustrated* suggests "there are certain voids in the geographical makeup of the four major sports, voids that could be filled with…expansion." Relocation, he explains, works just as well. But relocation increases the musical chairs game that is often played in professional sports leagues whenever a team is struggling. "Expansion is a much more humane approach to the problem," he says, "don't you think?"[139]

McAllister suggests four sports-starved cities that most deserve a professional sports team. Las Vegas is his number one choice – a city which has been seriously considered, though not publicly, by the NHL and NBA. The NHL Awards show has been held in Las Vegas the last few years and has received a warm reception, while the NBA has slowly considered the popular city as a location for a new team.

Portland, Oregon is another place McAllister says should get a team. The city is the largest metropolitan area in the United States without a Major League Baseball team. It is also the largest city with just one pro sports team (the NBA's Trailblazers). Portland has begun a campaign to build a new stadium in order to convince the other three leagues to gravitate toward the city. The Portland group bidding for an MLB team estimates that a franchise would bring about $433 million in state tax revenues over 25 years and another $53 million in income taxes from employees during that same time period.

What about Los Angeles, McAllister asks? The L.A. metropolitan area is home to two NBA teams, two MLB teams and two NHL teams. Yet McAllister suggests that the area could most likely support another NHL team. He also suggested Houston as another city, since it is the largest city in the United States without an NHL team. The last professional hockey team to play in the city was the Houston Aeros of the WHA, which folded in 1978. With a Greater Houston population of almost 6 million, expansion into the Houston area would seem a logical next choice.

Although it is believed that Commissioner Bettman is interested in further NHL expansion, he has never confirmed the idea. "As I sit here today, I'm not in a position to say that we're going to engage in a formal expansion process right now or at anytime," said Bettman in his 2008 State of the NHL address. "That could change at any point. That's not a headline. I just never say never to anything. But as we sit here today… we're not engaging in an expansion process."[140]

NHL Deputy Commissioner Bill Daly explained that the league is currently focused on making their current markets healthier and not spreading the game around for scraps of money. "I believe Daly when he says expansion is not a front burner issue for the NHL at this moment," said SportsNet columnist Mike Brophy. "However, I also believe sources that insist it is a front burner issue for some of the league's powerful movers and shakers. And if the owners want another one-time cash grab, well, all we have to do is look at the league's most recent expansions to understand it will happen no matter how slim the new team's chances of survival."[141]

However, Adam Proteau of *The Hockey News* also has problems with the NHL's philosophy of U.S. expansion, which he believes they will not follow. "When the Coyotes, Thrashers, Panthers, Islanders or other teams run out of new ownership options, Bettman will have little choice but to move some back to Canada," Proteau writes on his weekly column, "Screen Shots." "But when that happens, it is extremely likely Bettman will also introduce (a) a second NHL franchise for Southern Ontario; and (b) a $300-400 million expansion fee for that new organization, to be divvied up amongst owners unconcerned with a product that dilutes when the league increases its number of teams. And that old-school, craven money grab will nauseate observant hockey fans to no end, even after they see unmitigated joy in the eyes of old

Nordiques and Jets enthusiasts reveling in Bettman's forced atonement. One step up, one step back: that's the signature story of the Gary Bettman Era," he concludes.[142]

Regardless of media suggestions, the desires of the fans and their accusations directed toward the NHL, those on the Board of Governors seem to believe that future NHL expansion is necessary. And they know what will eventually need to be done.

"I think [expansion] is a good thing for the game," said Philadelphia Flyers founder Ed Snider. "We're no different than any other league. In fact, we have fewer teams in the United States than any other league. When I came into the league, there was one American player. Now we have all these American kids playing in the league, plus Russians, Czechs – which we couldn't have in the Cold War – Finns, Swedes. It's a worldwide pool of talent. These players are better, faster, more skilled than they've ever been."

Snider continued: "I'm in favor of expansion to cities that make sense and to communities that make sense. You know, the hockey people – and I'm a hockey person, I mean the GMs and coaches – often times are against expansion. But from a business and league point of view, it's a good thing, because it expands the sport. The naysayers say that hockey has a very small base of loyal fans. That's a bunch of bull. We have millions of fans in this *city*. So that's a great thing for the city.

"But more importantly, it's a great thing for [the league], because we have great fans."[143]

Epilogue: The Ultimate Decision – Success or Failure?

Earning degrees in both psychology and business, I believe there is only one way to draw conclusions regarding the success or failure of expansion in the NHL – statistics, numbers and more statistics. The first subject which comes to mind when considering expansion is the analysis of the expansion fees – which go directly into the pockets of existing NHL owners. As previously mentioned throughout the book, The Great Expansion cost each of the six new teams $2 million in franchise fees – a number equal to just over $13 million in 2010 dollars.[144]

Just three years later in 1970, the fee increased to $6 million, equal to over $33 million today. Expansion fees remained at that level until 1979, when World Hockey Association teams had to pay $6 million to the NHL, equal to about $18 million in today's dollars. When the NHL decided to expand again in 1991 and 1992, new teams were charged $45 million each to be accepted into the league, equal to around $70 million today. Not including the additional required indemnity fees, the entry fee increased one final time to $80 million in 1998, equal to over $100 million today.

Almost ten years after the most recent NHL expansion, the average franchise was worth just over $220 million in value, according to *Forbes*. The least valuable franchise, as of 2009, was Phoenix, valued at about $138 million. Therefore, if the league were to expand in the near future, this would suggest that the expansion fee should be close to $130 million. This ensures that the expansion fee paid would establish the baseline value for the new team.

In comparing the NHL with the NBA, NFL and MLB, as discussed in Chapter 14, the NHL has the lowest expansion fees, resulting in the lowest amount of money the league receives per new team. In 1995, each NBA team received $4.6 million of the $125 million paid each by Toronto and Vancouver. The MLB teams each received $4.8 million of the $130 million fee paid by Arizona and Tampa Bay in 1998 and 1999, respectively. In the NFL, existing teams received $15.9 million each in

1999 from Cleveland and a whopping $23.3 million each in 2001 when Houston Texans paid an astonishing $700 million to enter the league.

Considering that the NHL is the least popular of the four major sports and generates the least revenue, it is understandable why expansion is a high-risk proposition – success is not guaranteed. Critics have said hockey does not belong in the Sun Belt. But the NHL has an undeniably exciting product to sell, especially since the rule changes, which took place after 2005 lockout, created a faster paced game. The NHL is wisely attempting to spread professional ice hockey across the continent to prove it is not just a cold weather sport or a game that only belongs in Canada.

The NHL is to be commended for an outstanding job marketing the game in recent years. But fans and potential owners do not flock to hockey as they do to the NFL or MLB. Football can exist with the league as it is now without considering expansion due to their multi-billion dollar television contract. Similarly, MLB and to an extent, the NBA can do the same, despite their television deals not being at the same financial level as the NFL. Ice hockey stereotypically remains popular in cold weather locations. However, fans certainly exist in non-traditional markets such as Tampa Bay, Phoenix and Florida. But the attendance numbers and statistics for these teams show that unlike more traditional, northern markets, they only manage to sell out their stadiums when their teams perform well.

Toronto has not won the Stanley Cup since 1967 and is one of two teams as of 2010 to have missed the playoffs each year since the lockout. Yet, they have a waiting list of about 20 years for season tickets and they sell out every Maple Leafs home game. The Montreal Canadiens are in the midst of their longest Stanley Cup drought since their inception, yet they still manage to pack over 20,000 fans in the building each night. In Florida and Phoenix, however, fans generally stay away from the rink unless their team is performing well or the Stanley Cup playoffs are in town.

In the minds of most fans, the NHL should prevent expansion from continuing anytime soon and instead, as Bill Daly suggests, focus on keeping current franchises healthy. The NHL expanded under extreme business pressure in 1967, since every night was a sellout when the Original Six teams played. Therefore the NHL had only two possible additional revenue sources: a viable TV contract and expansion fees. It was therefore imperative to expand the league, not only to obtain the expansion fees, but also a more valuable TV contract.

Expansion places large amounts of cash in the owners' pockets and can be a windfall for the NHL. But entry fees paid can be gradually repaid to the expansion teams as needed through revenue sharing. Therefore, it is questionable to continue expanding the league rather than focusing on ensuring that the current 30 teams remain exciting, talented and profitable. Fans and sponsors would surely be more supportive of 30 talented and successful teams than a league of 40 where many teams might struggle. While NHL expansion has had successes and failures over the last few decades, any attempt at further expansion needs to be carefully calculated and considered in order to keep the NHL and its teams financially secure.

About the Author

Alan Bass is a freelance sports writer who has covered the 2010 Stanley Cup Final, the NHL Draft, and NHL rookie and training camps. He is the general manager of the Muhlenberg College Division II hockey team. He currently lives in Cherry Hill, New Jersey.

Bibliography

Fischler, Stan. Interview by author. Personal interview. Phone, May 16, 2010.

Olmstead, Bert. Interview by author. Personal interview. Phone, May 17, 2010.

Cooper, Bruce "Scoop". Interview by author. Personal interview. Phone, May 19, 2010.

Kurtzberg, Brad. Interview by author. Personal interview. Phone, May 20, 2010.

Torrey, Bill. Interview by author. Personal interview. Phone, May 26, 2010.

Ziegler, John. Interview by author. Personal interview. Phone, June 2, 2010.

Fletcher, Cliff. Interview by author. Personal interview. Phone, June 3, 2010.

McGregor, Jack. Interview by author. Personal interview. Phone, June 22, 2010.

Riley, Jack. Interview by author. Personal interview. Phone, June 24, 2010.

Bowman, Scotty. Interview by author. Personal interview. Phone, June 29, 2010.

Seiling, Rod. Interview by author. Personal interview. Phone, July 5, 2010.

Hadfield, Vic. Interview by author. Personal interview. Phone, July 5, 2010.

Lang, Ed. Interview by author. Personal interview. Phone, July 9, 2010.

Waddell, Don. Interview by author. Personal interview. Phone, August 7, 2010.

Snider, Ed. Interview by author. Personal interview. Phone, November 12, 2010

"1967 NHL Expansion Draft Picks at hockeydb.com." The Internet Hockey Database. http://www.hockeydb.com/ihdb/draft/nhl1967x.html.

"1967-68 Los Angeles Kings History." Los Angeles Kings. http://kings.nhl.com/club/page.htm?bcid=26245.

"1967-68 NHL Expansion." Pittsburgh's Online Hockey Museum. http://pittsburghhockey.net/PensPages/66-69ERA/67Expansion.html.

"1968-69 Los Angeles Kings History." Los Angeles Kings Home. http://kings.nhl.com/club/page.htm?bcid=26246.

"1969-70 Los Angeles Kings History." Los Angeles Kings Home. http://kings.nhl.com/club/page.htm?bcid=26247.

2009-10 Los Angeles Kings Media Guide. Los Angeles, CA: Chromatic, Inc., 2009.

A Day That Changed the Game. DVD. New York, NY: National Hockey League, 2009.

AP. "Hockey Next in Expansion Derby." *Associated Press (New York)*, February 7, 1966.

AP. "Hockey's Massive Expansion Big Surprise." *Associated Press (New York)*, February 13, 1966.

"Al Shaver's Last Call." Minnesota North Stars Memories. http://www.northstarshockey.com/lastcall.htm.

Allen, Kevin. "Intriguing expansion sites not in league's immediate future." USA Today. http://www.usatoday.com/sports/hockey/columnist/allen/2008-10-23-nhl-expansion_N.htm.

"Are you old school or new wave on these NHL issues?" Sports Illustrated. http://sportsillustrated.cnn.com/2007/hockey/nhl/01/18/values.debate/.

Baker, Chris. "A Look at Expansion in the NBA." Los Angeles Times. http://articles.latimes.com/1987-04-19/sports/sp-2064_1_expansion-team.

Beddoes, Richard, Stan Fischler, and Ira Gitler. *Hockey! The Story of the World's Fastest Sport*. Revised ed. New York: The Macmillan Company, 1971.

Bell, Jarrett. "From upstart to big time, how the AFL changed the NFL." USA Today. http://www.usatoday.com/sports/football/nfl/2009-06-14-sw-afl-cover_N.htm.

Broad Street Bullies. DVD. Los Angeles, CA: Home Box Office, 2010.

"Brodeur is a Fraud: Estimating 1970s Save Percentages." Brodeur is a Fraud. http://brodeurisafraud.blogspot.com/2009/04/estimating-1970s-save-percentages.html.

"Brodeur is a Fraud: Team Effects in the Original Six." Brodeur is a Fraud. http://brodeurisafraud.blogspot.com/2008/12/team-effects-in-original-six.html.

Brophy, Mike. "Brophy: Greed fueling NHL expansion." Sportsnet. ca. http://www.sportsnet.ca/hockey/2008/09/17/brophy_nhl_greed_expansion/.

Brown, Maury. "Why MLB Relocation/Expansion Won't Be Happening Soon." The Biz of Baseball. http://www.bizofbaseball.com/index.php?option=com_content&task=view&id=1703&Itemid=41.

Brown, Maury. "Expansion, not relocation, is Portland's ticket to MLB." Portland News. http://portland.bizjournals.com/portland/stories/2007/11/19/editorial3.html.

"CBA: The price of expansion." Dallas Stars Blog - ESPN Dallas. http://www.andrewsstarspage.com/CBA/8-17cba.htm.

Carroll, Dink. "Playing the Field." *Montreal Gazette*, February 10, 1966.

Carroll, Dink. "Playing the Field." *Montreal Gazette*, February 14, 1966.

Chevalier, Jack. *The Broad Street Bullies: The Incredible Story of the Philadelphia Flyers*. New York: Macmillan Publishing Company, 1974.

"Chronological History of the National Football League." Vaughan Tech. http://www.vaughantech.com/nfl.html.

"Commissioner's State of the NHL News Conference." New York Times. http://slapshot.blogs.nytimes.com/2008/05/25/commissioners-state-of-the-nhl-press-conference/.

Cooper, Bruce C. "The Philadelphia Flyers." *Professional Sports Teams Histories: Hockey.* (1993). Detroit, Michigan.

Cooper, Bruce C. "The Pittsburgh Penguins." *Professional Sports Teams Histories: Hockey.* (1993). Detroit, Michigan.

Cooper, Bruce C. "The Los Angeles Kings." *Professional Sports Teams Histories: Hockey.* (1993): Detroit, Michigan.

Cooper, Bruce C. "The History of the AHL in Philadelphia." HockeyScoop.net. http://www.hockeyscoop.net/ahlphl/.

Cruise, David. *Net worth: Exploding the myths of pro hockey.* New York: Viking, 1991.

Curran, Pat. "Maybe We're Wrong." *Montreal Gazette*, February 8, 1966.

Curran, Pat. "Great Boost Says Molson." *Montreal Gazette*, February 10, 1966.

Curran, Pat. "U.S. Playoff TV Deal in Jeopardy." *Montreal Gazette*, March 14, 1966.

Daley, Arthur. "Hockey's Expansion Step Was Late, but Momentous." *Milwaukee Journal*, February 24, 1966.

"Dear Lord Stanley: NHL Expansion: It Worked So Well The First Time." Dear Lord Stanley… http://dearlordstanley.blogspot.com/2007/06/nhl-expansion-it-worked-so-well-first.html.

Deford, Frank. "Hockey: Why Can't The NHL Just Keep It Canadian?" NPR: National Public Radio. http://www.npr.org/templates/story/story.php?storyId=113077058&ft=1&f=1055

Diamond, Dan. *Years of Glory 1942-1967: the National Hockey League's official book of the six-team era.* Toronto: McClelland & Stewart, 1994.

Dryden, Ken. *The Game.* 20 ed. New York, NY: Wiley, 2005.

Duplacey, James. *Hockey's Book of Firsts.* Pennsylvania: Jg Press, 2008.

"ESPN.com: Sports Business - Forbes Franchise Values." ESPN. http://espn.go.com/sportsbusiness/s/forbes.html.

Val D'Or Star, "Expansion's Good For Players," June 30, 1966.

Fahrenkrog, Jeff. "The Rise and Fall of the Salomons." St. Louis Game Time. http://www.stlouisgametime. com/2009/3/21/804454/the-rise-and-fall-of-the-s.

Fischler, Stan & Shirley. *Fischlers' Hockey Encyclopedia*. New York City: Crowell, 1983.

"Flyers Alumni - Snider." Philadelphia Flyers Alumni Association. http://www.flyersalumni.org/snider.htm.

"Flyers History - Philadelphia Quakers." Flyers History - Philadelphia Quakers. http://quakers.flyershistory.net/.

Frayne, Trent. *The mad men of hockey*. New York: Dodd, Mead, 1974.

"Future of the NHL: Expansion teams on the horizon!" NHL.com - NHL Fans. http://media.fans.nhl.com/_Future-of-the-NHL-Expansion-teams-on-the-horizon/blog/393871/111820.html.

Goold, Derrick. "Birth of the Blues." St. Louis Today. http://more. stltoday.com/stltoday/news/special/pd125.nsf/0/8562839b99ebb2 9186256e0700728192?OpenDocument.

Greenberg, Jay. *Full Spectrum: The Complete History of the Philadelphia Flyers*. New York, NY: Triumph Books, 2000.

Hart, Simon. "Olympics hold the key to the NBA's expansion ambitions." Telegraph.co.uk. http://www.telegraph.co.uk/sport/ othersports/basketball/ 5506489/Olympics-hold-the-key-to-the-NBAs-expansion-ambitions.htmls.html.

Havill, Adrian. *The Last Mogul: The Unauthorized Biography of Jack Kent Cooke*. 1st ed. New York: St Martins Pr, 1992.

Heufelder, Bill. "Big League Hockey Returning to City?" *Pittsburgh Press*, January 18, 1966.

Heufelder, Bill. "LA's Owner Gives Sports New Twist." *Pittsburgh Press*, June 15, 1966.

"History Of MLB Franchise Movement & Expansion." Fack Youk.

http://fackyouk.blogspot.com/2010/01/history-of-mlb-franchise-movement.html.

"History of NHL Expansion." The Puck Report. http://www.puckreport.com/2009/05/nhl-expansion.html.

"Hockeycentral | NHL | Movers and Sharpers | Expansion." Hockey Central. http://www.hockeycentral.co.uk.

"How Important are Playoff Wins for NHL Market Success?" Bird Watchers Anonymous. http://www.birdwatchersanonymous.com/2008/02/how-important-are-playoff-wins-for-nhl.html.

Hunter, Douglas. *Scotty Bowman: A Life in Hockey.* Chicago, IL: Triumph Books, 1999.

"In the Beginning." Minnesota North Stars Memories. http://www.northstarshockey.com/begin.htm.

Isaacs, Neil David. *Checking back: A history of the National Hockey League.* 1st ed. New York: Norton, 1977.

"John Ziegler (1977-1992)." The Sports E-Cyclopedia (Est. 2001)-The Ultimate Sports Resource. http://www.sportsecyclopedia.com/nhl/comish/ziegler.html.

Kay, Jason. "Winnipeg should be at top of new-team list." The Hockey News. http://www.thehockeynews.com/articles/19378-THNcom-Blog-Winnipeg-should-be-at-top-of-newteam-list.html.

Klayman, Ben. "NBA pushes China expansion with new league store." Reuters. http://www.reuters.com/article/idUSTRE64C04320100513.

Kurtzberg, Brad. *Shorthanded: The Untold Story of the Seals: Hockey's Most Colorful Team.* Authorhouse, 2006.

"Leafs go 43 years w/o Cup. Who coulda known?" Behind The Net. http://www.behindthenethockey.com/2010/4/26/1444756/leafs-go-43-years-w-o-cup-who.

"Letter." Minnesota North Stars Memories. http://www.northstarshockey.com/letter.htm.

Litsky, Frank. "N.F.L. Expansion Surprise - Jacksonville Jaguars." The

New York Times. http://www.nytimes.com/1993/12/01/sports/ pro-football-nfl-expansion-surprise-jacksonville-jaguars.html.

Lombardo, John. "NBA Continues Plans For Global Expansion, Will Open Office In Russia." Sporting News. http://www. sportingnews.com/blog/The_Baseline/ entry/view/56600/ nba_continues_plans_for_global_expansion,_will_open_office_ in_russia.

Luker, Rob. "A recent history of NHL revenue: An in-depth look at Forbes' data." From The Rink - SB Nation's NHL hockey blog. http://www.fromtherink.com/2008/ 10/30/649750/a-recent-history-of-nhl-re.

"Major League Baseball Expansion Drafts." Sports Mogul. http:// www.sportsmogul.com/content/ExpansionDrafts.html.

McAllister, Mike. "Topping the Expansion List." Sports Illustrated. http://sportsillustrated.cnn.com/2005/writers/mike_ mcallister/05/23/expansion.cities/index.html.

"Minnesota North Stars (1967-1993)." The Sports E-Cyclopedia (Est. 2001)-The Ultimate Sports Resource. http://www. sportsecyclopedia.com/nhl/minnystars/northstars.html.

"Minnesota North Stars Legends." North Stars Legends. http:// northstarslegends.blogspot.com/.

"Minnesota North Stars Memories." North Stars Hockey. http:// www.northstarshockey.com/.

Morreale, Mike G. "St Louis Blues History." St. Louis Blues. http:// blues.nhl.com/club/page.htm?id=39464.

"NBA Growth Timetable." Basketball.com. http://www.basketball. com/nba/ history.shtml.

"NHL Expands," *Evening Independent (New York)*, February 9, 1966.

"NHL Expansion." Sports Junkie. http://www.sportsjunkie.info/ NHL%20Expansion.htm.

"NHL Expansion and Relocation Since 1967." Dallas Stars Blog - ESPN Dallas. http://www.andrewsstarspage.com/ index.php/site/comments/nhl_expansion_and_relocation_ since_1967/1696-2008-09.

"NHL Expansion in the Early 1990s: Florida and California Welcome New Professional Hockey Teams." Suite101. http://national-hockey-league-nhl.suite101.com/article.cfm/nhl_expansion_of_the_early_1990s.

"NHL Expansion in the Late 1990s and Early 2000s: Hockey in Two New Cities and a Return to Two Former NHL Homes." Suite101. http://national-hockey-league-nhl.suite101.com/article.cfm/nhl_expansion_in_the_late_1990s_and_early_2000s.

NHL History of the Philadelphia Flyers. DVD. Directed by Robert Newman. Burbank: Warner Home Video, 2006.

"NHL Outlines Formula For 1970-71 Expansion and Future of League." *The Hockey News*, October 16, 1969.

"NHL's Expansion Follies Started in '66, Writer Says -- NHL FanHouse." NHL Fanhouse. http://nhl.fanhouse.com/2009/09/23/nhls-expansion-follies-started-in-66-writer-says/.

"NHL's future lies in Canada, reports say." National Post. http://www.nationalpost.com/ m/story.html?id=1526310.

"Chicago Blackhawks vs. Montreal Canadiens, Stanley Cup Final Game 5, 1965." *NHL: Greatest Games in Montreal Canadiens History.* DVD. New York, NY: Warner Home Video, 2008.

"Detroit Red Wings vs. Montreal Canadiens, April 16, 1954, Game 7 Stanley Cup Final." *NHL: Greatest Moments in Stanley Cup History.* DVD. New York, NY: Warner Home Video, 2007.

"Toronto Maple Leafs vs. Detroit Red Wings, April 25, 1964, Game 7 Stanley Cup Final." *NHL: Greatest Moments in Stanley Cup History.* DVD. New York, NY: Warner Home Video, 2007.

"Detroit Red Wings vs. Montreal Canadiens, April 14, 1955, Game 7 Stanley Cup Final." *NHL: Greatest Moments in Stanley Cup History.* DVD. New York, NY: Warner Home Video, 2007.

"National Hockey League (NHL) Expansion History." Rauzulu's Street. http://www.rauzulusstreet.com/hockey/nhlhistory/nhlhistory.html.

"New York Americans (1925-1942)." The Sports E-Cyclopedia

(Est. 2001)-The Ultimate Sports Resource. http://www.
sportsecyclopedia.com/nhl/ nya/nyamericans.html.

"North Star Green Preservation Society." North Star Preservation.
http://northstarpreservation.blogspot.com/.

O'Brien, Andy. "Here's How NHL Expansion Could Work." *Ottawa
Citizen*, May 1, 1965.

"Oakland-California Golden Seals History." YouTube. http://www.
youtube.com/watch?v =7ABkKt5_D1w.

"Objective NHL: Parity." Objective NHL. http://objectivenhl.
blogspot.com/2008/12/parity.html.

"Objective NHL: Worst post-67 Cup Winning Team?" Objective
NHL. http://objectivenhl.blogspot.com/2008/12/worst-post-67-
cup-winning-team.html.

"Pittsburgh Penguins (1967-Present)." The Sports E-Cyclopedia
(Est. 2001)-The Ultimate Sports Resource. http://www.
sportsecyclopedia.com/nhl/pittsburgh/ penguins.html.

"Pittsburgh Penguins History." CBS Sports. http://cookies.cbssports.
com/nhl/teams/history/PIT/pittsburgh-penguins.

"Pittsburgh Penguins History." LetsGoPens.com - A Pittsburgh
Penguins Site. http://www.letsgopens.com/pens_history.php.

"Players Lose Ground with NHL Expansion." New
York News. http://www.nypost.com/p/sports/item_
M8gbnl52gScVpT2Vr4vcWN/1.

Popelka, Greg. "1967 NHL Expansion Draft." *Spiritus-Temporis* 1
(2009). http://theclevelandfan.com/index.php?option=com_conte
nt&view=article&id=4233&catid=7:general-archive&Itemid=7.

"Possible MLB Expansion." FanNation - The Republic of Sport.
http://www.fannation.com/blogs/post/17470.

Povich, Shirley. "Move Over - Here Comes Hockey!" *St. Petersburg
Times*, February 12, 1966.

Proteau, Adam. "Screen Shots: The good and bad of Gary
Bettman." The Hockey News. http://www.thehockeynews.

com/articles/33930-Screen-Shots-The-good-and-bad-of-Gary-Bettman.html.

Quinn, Kevin G., and Paul B. Bursik. "Growing and Moving the Game: Effects of MLB Expansion and Team Relocation 1950-2004." *Journal of Quantitative Analysis in Sports* 3, no. 2 (2007).

"Quiz Answers." Minnesota North Stars Memories. http://www.northstarshockey.com/answers.htm.

Rappoport, Ken. "The AFL-NFL merger was almost booted... by a kicker." NFL.com. http://www.nfl.com/news/story?id=09000d5d81206b90&template=without-video-with-comments&confirm=true.

Richardson, Lyle. "Just Say NO to NHL Expansion." Fox Sports. http://community.foxsports.com/Spector/blog/2007/01/24/Just_Say_NO_to_NHL_Expansion.

Rostad, Knut A. "Coming Together: The Fiduciary Standard and the NFL - Practice Strategies." Wealth Manager Web. http://www.wealthmanagerweb.com/Exclusives/2010/7/Pages/Coming-Together-The-Fiduciary-Standard-and-the-NFL.aspx.

Rovell, Darren. "NHL franchise fees: Is price right?" ESPN: The Worldwide Leader In Sports. http://assets.espn.go.com/nhl/s/expansion4a.html.

Schlossberg, Dan. "MLB Expansion." The Baseball Guru - A World of Baseball!. http://baseballguru.com/dschlossberg/analysisdschlossberg10.html.

Showers, Bob. *Minnesota North Stars: History and Memories with Lou Nanne.* Beaver's Pond Press, 2007.

Slugger, SNB. "Cities That The NFL Could Expand To In Coming Years." FanIQ. http://www.faniq.com/blog/Cities-That-The-NFL-Could-Expand-To-In-Coming-Years-Blog-23090.

Smith, Kenny. "Bring on European expansion." Yahoo! Sports. http://sports.yahoo.com/ nba/news?slug=ks-europe101507.

"St. Louis Blues Home." St. Louis Blues. http://blues.nhl.com.

"St. Louis Blues (1967-Present)." The Sports E-Cyclopedia (Est. 2001)-

The Ultimate Sports Resource. http://www.sportsecyclopedia.com/nhl/stlouis/blues.html (accessed July 23, 2010).

"St. Louis Blues History." CBS Sports. http://www.cbssports.com/nhl/teams/history/STL/st-louis-blues.

Van Riper, Tom. "Major League Baseball Goes Global." Forbes.com. http://www.forbes.com/2005/12/20/baseball-gm-disney-cx_tvr_1220baseball.html.

Montreal Gazette, "Vancouver Remains Minor Hockey City." February 10, 1966.

Washburn, Gary. "NBA owners cool to expansion." Seattle Post-Intelligence. http://www.seattlepi.com/basketball/360047_expansion22x.html.

Wright, Ben. "History - Franchise Timeline." Atlanta Thrashers. http://thrashers.nhl.com/club/page.htm?bcid=e3d0ef7c1b024d88a3caa4b96fd42ae6.

"Year by Year Team Finishes." Minnesota North Stars Memories. http://www.northstars hockey.com/finish.htm.

Endnotes

1. *A Day That Changed the Game.* DVD. New York, NY: National Hockey League, 2009.
2. Frayne, Trent. *The mad men of hockey.* New York: Dodd, Mead, 1974, p.80, via
3. Beddoes, Richard, Stan Fischler, and Ira Gitler. *Hockey! The Story of the World's Fastest Sport.* Revised ed. New York: The Macmillan Company, 1971.
4. Beddoes, Richard, Stan Fischler, and Ira Gitler, p.24.
5. Beddoes, Richard, Stan Fischler, and Ira Gitler, p.24.
6. Beddoes, Richard, Stan Fischler, and Ira Gitler, p.25.
7. Beddoes, Richard, Stan Fischler, and Ira Gitler, p.44.
8. Beddoes, Richard, Stan Fischler, and Ira Gitler, p.44.
9. Beddoes, Richard, Stan Fischler, and Ira Gitler, p.12.
10. Cruise, David. *Net worth: Exploding the myths of pro hockey.* New York: Viking, 1991, p.133
11. "Hockeycentral | NHL | Movers and Sharpers | Expansion." Hockey Central. http://www.hockeycentral.co.uk.
12. Cruise, David, p.133
13. Cruise, David, pp.133-4
14. Cruise, David, p.131
15. Cruise, David, p.131
16. Povich, Shirley. "Move Over - Here Comes Hockey!" *St. Petersburg Times*, February 12, 1966.
17. Cruise, David, p.138
18. Cruise, David, p.139
19. Beddoes, Richard, Stan Fischler, and Ira Gitler, page 92.
20. Cruise, David, p.140
21. Beddoes, Richard, Stan Fischler, and Ira Gitler, page 93.
22. O'Brien, Andy. "Here's How NHL Expansion Could Work." *Ottawa Citizen*, May 1, 1965.
23. O'Brien, Andy.

24. Heufelder, Bill. "Big League Hockey Returning to City?" *Pittsburgh Press*, January 18, 1966.

25. Curran, Pat. "Maybe We're Wrong." *Montreal Gazette*, February 8, 1966.

26. Carroll, Dink. "Playing the Field." *Montreal Gazette*, February 10, 1966.

27. Curran, Pat. "Great Boost Says Molson." *Montreal Gazette*, February 10, 1966.

28. *Montreal Gazette*, "Vancouver Remains Minor Hockey City." February 10, 1966.

29. Povich, Shirley.

30. AP. "Hockey's Massive Expansion Big Surprise." *Associated Press (New York)*, February 13, 1966.

31. Carroll, Dink. "Playing the Field." *Montreal Gazette*, February 14, 1966.

32. Daley, Arthur. "Hockey's Expansion Step Was Late, but Momentous." *Milwaukee Journal*, February 24, 1966.

33. Curran, Pat. "U.S. Playoff TV Deal in Jeopardy." *Montreal Gazette*, March 14, 1966.

34. Heufelder, Bill. "LA's Owner Gives Sports New Twist." *Pittsburgh Press*, June 15, 1966.

35. *Val D'Or Star*, "Expansion's Good For Players." June 30, 1966.

36. *NHL History of the Philadelphia Flyers*. DVD. Directed by Robert Newman. Burbank: Warner Home Video, 2006.

37. Popelka, Greg. "1967 NHL Expansion Draft." *Spiritus-Temporis* 1 (2009). http://theclevelandfan.com/index.php?option=com_content&view=article&id=4233&catid=7:general-archive&Itemid=7.

38. Cruise, David, pp.148-9

39. *NHL History of the Philadelphia Flyers*.

40. Kurtzberg, Brad. *Shorthanded: The Untold Story of the Seals: Hockey's Most Colorful Team*. Authorhouse, 2006, p.4

41. Kurtzberg, Brad, p.5

42. Kurtzberg, Brad, p.6

43. Kurtzberg, Brad, p.6

44. Kurtzberg, Brad, p.6

45. Kurtzberg, Brad, p.7

46. Kurtzberg, Brad, p.10

47. Kurtzberg, Brad, p.11

48. Showers, Bob. *Minnesota North Stars: History and Memories with Lou Nanne.* Beaver's Pond Press, 2007, p.115

49. Cooper, Bruce C. "The Los Angeles Kings." *Professional Sports Teams Histories: Hockey* . (1993): Detroit, Michigan, p.3.

50. Cooper, Bruce C., p.3.

51. Havill, Adrian. *The Last Mogul: The Unauthorized Biography of Jack Kent Cooke.* 1st ed. New York: St Martins Pr, 1992, p.154.

52. Havill, Adrian, p.157.

53. *2009-10 Los Angeles Kings Media Guide.* Los Angeles, CA: Chromatic, Inc., 2009.

54. Havill, Adrian, p.157.

55. Beddoes, Richard, Stan Fischler, and Ira Gitler, p.98

56. Showers, Bob, p.115

57. Showers, Bob, p.116

58. Showers, Bob, pp.14-5

59. Showers, Bob, p.17

60. "Letter." Minnesota North Stars Memories. http://www. northstarshockey.com/letter. htm.

61. "Al Shaver's Last Call." Minnesota North Stars Memories. http://www.northstars hockey.com/lastcall.htm.

62. "In the Beginning." Minnesota North Stars Memories. http:// www.northstars-hockey.com/begin.htm.

63. "Flyers History - Philadelphia Quakers." Flyers History - Philadelphia Quakers. http://quakers.flyershistory.net/.

64. Greenberg, Jay. *Full Spectrum: The Complete History of the Philadelphia Flyers.* New York, NY: Triumph Books, 2000, p.1.

65. *A Day That Changed the Game.*

66. *A Day That Changed the Game.*

67. Greenberg, Jay, p.2

68. Greenberg, Jay, p.3

69. Greenberg, Jay, p.3

70. Greenberg, Jay, p.3

71. *Broad Street Bullies.*

72. *Broad Street Bullies.*

73. Greenberg, Jay, p.4

74. Greenberg, Jay, p.5

75. Greenberg, Jay, p.5

76. "Flyers Alumni - Snider." Philadelphia Flyers Alumni Association. http://www.flyers alumni.org/snider.htm.

77. Greenberg, Jay, p.13

78. Greenberg, Jay, p.13

79. Greenberg, Jay, p.14

80. Greenberg, Jay, p.14

81. *A Day That Changed the Game.*

82. Greenberg, Jay, p.12

83. Beddoes, Richard, Stan Fischler, and Ira Gitler, pp.120-1

84. *A Day That Changed the Game.*

85. *Broad Street Bullies.* DVD. Los Angeles, CA: Home Box Office, 2010.

86. *A Day That Changed the Game.*

87. Chevalier, Jack. *The Broad Street Bullies: The Incredible Story of the Philadelphia Flyers.* New York: Macmillan Publishing Company, 1974, p.7

88. Chevalier, Jack, p.7

89. *A Day That Changed the Game.*

90. Dryden, Ken. *The Game.* 20 ed. New York, NY: Wiley, 2005.

91. Chevalier, Jack, p.8

92. *A Day That Changed the Game.*

93. Cooper, Bruce C. "The Pittsburgh Penguins." *Professional Sports Teams Histories: Hockey* . (1993). Detroit, Michigan, p.4

94. "1967-68 NHL Expansion." Pittsburgh's Online Hockey Museum. http://pittsburghhockey.net/PensPages/66-69ERA/67Expansion.html.

95. "1967-68 NHL Expansion." Pittsburgh's Online Hockey Museum. http://pittsburghhockey.net/PensPages/66-69ERA/67Expansion.html.

96. Cruise, David, p.139

97. Fahrenkrog, Jeff. "The Rise and Fall of the Salomons." St. Louis Game Time. http://www.stlouisgametime.com/2009/3/21/804454/the-rise-and-fall-of-the-s.

98. Hunter, Douglas. *Scotty Bowman: A Life in Hockey.* Chicago, IL: Triumph Books, 1999, p.97

99. *A Day That Changed the Game.*

100. Hunter, Douglas, p.105

101. Hunter, Douglas, p.110

102. *A Day That Changed the Game.*

103. Hunter, Douglas, pp.114-5

104. *A Day That Changed the Game.*

105. Goold, Derrick. "Birth of the Blues." St. Louis Today. http://more.stltoday.com/stltoday/news/special/pd125.nsf/0/8562839b99ebb29186256e0700728192?OpenDocument.

106. *A Day That Changed the Game.*

107. Fahrenkrog, Jeff.

108. Fahrenkrog, Jeff.

109. Fahrenkrog, Jeff.

110. "St. Louis Blues Home." St. Louis Blues. http://blues.nhl.com.

111. Fahrenkrog, Jeff.

112. Fahrenkrog, Jeff.

113. Fahrenkrog, Jeff.

114. Fahrenkrog, Jeff.

115. Fahrenkrog, Jeff.

116. Fahrenkrog, Jeff.

117. Fahrenkrog, Jeff.

118. Fahrenkrog, Jeff.

119. Fahrenkrog, Jeff.

120. "How Important are Playoff Wins for NHL Market Success?" Bird Watchers Anonymous. http://www.birdwatchersanonymous.com/2008/02/how-important-are-playoff-wins-for-nhl.html.

121. "Are you old school or new wave on these NHL issues?" Sports Illustrated. http://sportsillustrated.cnn.com/2007/hockey/nhl/01/18/values.debate/.

122. Bell, Jarrett. "From upstart to big time, how the AFL changed the NFL." USA Today. http://www.usatoday.com/sports/football/nfl/2009-06-14-sw-afl-cover_N.htm.

123. Bell, Jarrett.

124. Rappoport, Ken. "The AFL-NFL merger was almost booted... by a kicker." NFL.com. http://www.nfl.com/news/story?

id=09000d5d81206b90&template=without-video-with-comments&confirm=true.

125. Baker, Chris. "A Look at Expansion in the NBA." Los Angeles Times. http://articles.latimes.com/1987-04-19/sports/sp-2064_1_expansion-team.

126. Washburn, Gary. "NBA owners cool to expansion." Seattle Post-Intelligence. http://www.seattlepi.com/basketball/360047_expansion22x.html.

127. Klayman, Ben. "NBA pushes China expansion with new league store." Reuters. http://www.reuters.com/article/idUSTRE64C04320100513.

128. Lombardo, John. "NBA Continues Plans For Global Expansion, Will Open Office In Russia." Sporting News. http://www.sportingnews.com/blog/The_Baseline/entry/view/ 56600/nba_continues_plans_for_global_expansion,_will_open_office_in_russia.

129. Smith, Kenny. "Bring on European expansion." Yahoo! Sports. http://sports.yahoo. com/nba/news?slug=ks-europe101507.

130. Van Riper, Tom. "Major League Baseball Goes Global." Forbes.com. http://www.forbes.com/2005/12/20/baseball-gm-disney-cx_tvr_1220baseball.html.

131. Brown, Maury. "Why MLB Relocation/Expansion Won't Be Happening Soon." The Biz of Baseball. http://www.bizofbaseball.com/index.php?option=com_content&task=view&id=1703&Itemid=41.

132. Brown, Maury.

133. "NHL Outlines Formula For 1970-71 Expansion and Future of League." *The Hockey News*, October 16, 1969.

134. "CBA: The price of expansion." Dallas Stars Blog - ESPN Dallas. http://www.andrewsstarspage.com/CBA/8-17cba.htm.

135. "CBA: The price of expansion."

136. "CBA: The price of expansion."

137. "NHL's future lies in Canada, reports say." National Post. http://www.nationalpost.com/m/story.html?id=1526310.

138. "Dear Lord Stanley: NHL Expansion: It Worked So Well The First Time." Dear Lord Stanley... http://dearlordstanley.blogspot.com/2007/06/nhl-expansion-it-worked-so-well-first.html.

139. Richardson, Lyle. "Just Say NO to NHL Expansion."
Fox Sports. http://community.foxsports.com/Spector/
blog/2007/01/24/Just_Say_NO_to_NHL_Expansion.
140. McAllister, Mike. "Topping the Expansion List." Sports
Illustrated. http://sportsillustrated.cnn.com/2005/writers/mike_
mcallister/05/23/expansion.cities/index.html.
141. "Commissioner's State of the NHL News Conference." New
York Times. http://slapshot.blogs.nytimes.com/2008/05/25/
commissioners-state-of-the-nhl-press-conference/.
142. Brophy, Mike. "Brophy: Greed fueling NHL expansion
- Sportsnet.ca." Sportsnet.ca. http://www.sportsnet.ca/
hockey/2008/09/17/brophy_nhl_greed_expansion/.
143. Proteau, Adam. "Screen Shots: The good and bad of Gary
Bettman." The Hockey News. http://www.thehockeynews.
com/articles/33930-Screen-Shots-The-good-and-bad-of-Gary-
Bettman.html.
144. *A Day That Changed the Game.*
145. "Consumer Price Index Calculator," www.bls.gov/data/
inflation_calculator.htm.

CPSIA information can be obtained at www.ICGtesting.com
Printed in the USA
BVOW040749201011

274128BV00001B/114/P